Hiking Canada's Great Divide Trail

D1082421

HIKING CANADA'S GREAT DIVIDE TRAIL

3rd edition

Dustin Lynx

RMB

Copyright © 2018 by Dustin Lynx
Third Edition

All rights reserved. No part of this publication may be reproduced, stored in a retrieval system, or transmitted in any form or by any means – electronic, mechanical, audio recording, or otherwise – without the written permission of the publisher or a photocopying licence from Access Copyright. Permissions and licensing contribute to a secure and vibrant book industry by helping to support writers and publishers through the purchase of authorized editions and excerpts. To obtain an official licence, please visit accesscopyright.ca or call 1-800-893-5777.

RMB | Rocky Mountain Books Ltd.
rmbooks.com
@rmbooks
facebook.com/rmbooks

Cataloguing data available from Library and Archives Canada
ISBN 9781771602624 (paperback)
ISBN 9781771602631 (electronic)

Cover photo: iStock.com/yvesgagnon1974

All photographs are by Dustin Lynx unless otherwise noted.

This book contains information licensed under the Open Government Licence – Canada.

Printed and bound in Canada by Friesens

Distributed in Canada by Heritage Group Distribution and in the U.S. by Publishers Group West

For information on purchasing bulk quantities of this book, or to obtain media excerpts or invite the author to speak at an event, please visit rmbooks.com and select the "Contact Us" tab.

We acknowledge the financial support of the Government of Canada through the Canada Book Fund and the Canada Council for the Arts, and of the province of British Columbia through the British Columbia Arts Council and the Book Publishing Tax Credit.

DISCLAIMER

The actions described in this book may be considered inherently dangerous activities. Individuals undertake these activities at their own risk. The information put forth in this guide has been collected from a variety of sources and is not guaranteed to be completely accurate or reliable. Many conditions and some information may change owing to weather and numerous other factors beyond the control of the authors and publishers. Individuals or groups must determine the risks, use their own judgment, and take full responsibility for their actions. Do not depend on any information found in this book for your own personal safety. Your safety depends on your own good judgment based on your skills, education, and experience.

It is up to the users of this guidebook to acquire the necessary skills for safe experiences and to exercise caution in potentially hazardous areas. The authors and publishers of this guide accept no responsibility for your actions or the results that occur from another's actions, choices, or judgments. If you have any doubt as to your safety or your ability to attempt anything described in this guidebook, do not attempt it.

For my family: Julia, Roche and Tenaya Lynx.
You are my true inspiration.

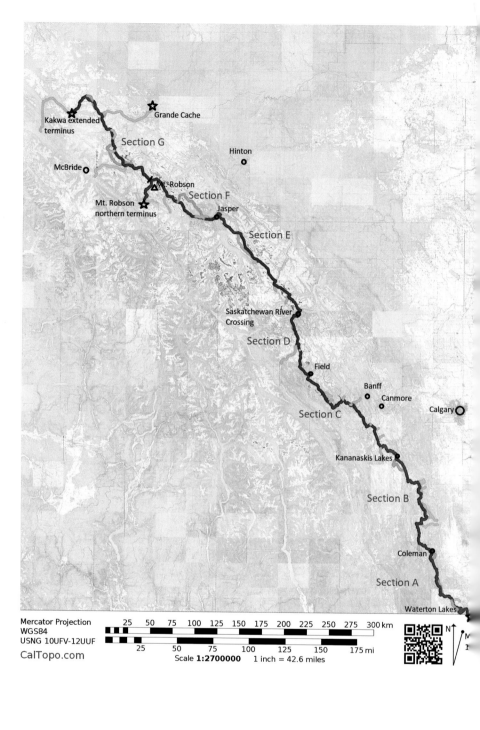

Kakwa extended
terminus

Grande Cache

Section G

Hinton

McBride

Mt. Robson

Mt. Robson
northern terminus

Section F

Jasper

Section E

Saskatchewan River
Crossing

Section D

Field

Banff

Canmore

Calgary

Section C

Kananaskis Lakes

Section B

Coleman

Section A

Waterton Lakes

Mercator Projection
WGS84
USNG 10UFV-12UUF

CalTopo.com

25   50   75   100 125 150 175 200 225 250 275 300 km

25   50   75   100   125   150   175 mi
Scale 1:2700000   1 inch = 42.6 miles

N

CONTENTS

ACKNOWLEDGEMENTS

I am extremely thankful to River Taig for his help with the third edition of this book. His app was as indispensable for me as I am sure it will be for future hikers. I also want to thank Alice Bodnar and Ryan Linn at Atlas Guides for granting me permission to use material from the app.

Many thanks to the Great Divide Trail Association for carrying the vision of a nationally recognized trail. I am thankful for the help and support of Brad Vaillancourt and Dave Hockey. Your contagious energy helped me to write this updated edition of the guidebook. And, I can't forget to thank the hard work and dedication of those volunteers who build and maintain the trail.

My gratitude goes out to others who have contributed to this edition. In no particular order, these folks are Ben Mayberry, Li Brannfors, Larry Tyler, Erin "Wired" Saver, Brian Tanzman, Ryan Silk, Liz Thomas, Naomi Hudetz, Wendy Bush, "Canadoug," SpiritEagle (Jim and Ginny Owen), Jordan Tamborine, Dan Albert, Rogier Gruys, and Rick Bombaci.

I would also like to thank family, friends, and all those who contributed to previous editions of this guidebook. I appreciate all your help and support over the years!

Julia, Roche and Tenaya Lynx, Barbara Dewhirst, David and Diane Simon, Agnes Bauer, Aaron Phoenix, Roy and Jill Howard, the Hodges family, Mateo Antonelli, Jerry Auld, Doug Mouser, Randy Kading, Chris Townsend, Royce and Sherrill Robertson, John Dunn, Rich Botto, Wayne Van Velzen, Hugo Mulyk, May Torgerson, Brian Patton, Jenny L. Feick, Dave Higgins, Marion Harrison, Edwin Knox, Gillean and Tony Daffern, The Whyte Museum of the Canadian Rockies, Paul Leech "The Trail Wizard," Paula Duncan, Miro Rak, Carl Potter, Chris Willett, Jean-Guy Bergeron, Jim Thorsell, Bart and Barbara Robinson, Karsten Heuer, "Marmot," "Lindy," Michael Kwek, John Barge, Chic Scott, and Donna and Roger Nelson of Gemtrek Maps.

INTRODUCTION TO THE 3RD EDITION

If I wanted to keep things fun and interesting and continue learning and challenging myself then I had to break this mold of being an 'on-trail' backpacker. I needed to expand my horizons to get outside of my comfort zone... and do something different.

—Andrew Skurka, from a 2011 *National Geographic Live* presentation, youtu.be/hMf7TypZwtc.

It is a long time since I first thru-hiked the Great Divide Trail, in 1996. Much of the route I mapped is still considered 'main route' and there are more protected areas such as Castle Wildland Provincial Park and Castle Provincial Park, north of Waterton Lakes National Park. There are more hikers now, and people are finding different ways to experience the GDT, such as trail running, epic equestrian trips or bringing their dog with them. GPS is omnipresent; so too is the use of smart phones and internet connectivity. As this book goes to print, there is a low-cost app available for the GDT. Most importantly, the Great Divide Trail Association has risen again.

What hasn't changed is the fact that once you commit yourself to the GDT you alter your journey in life, perhaps in a big way! You know you will experience a stark beauty and magnificence that perhaps no other long-distance hiking trail can offer in such abundance, but what you might not appreciate at the outset is how this route will push you out of your comfort zone.

In my own case, hiking the GDT led me to becoming an author, moving to Canmore, raising a family there and returning to the trail year after year for day hiking, backpacking, skiing, mountain biking, scrambling, climbing, packrafting, and trail running. Whenever it seemed I was growing complacent, my love of the route and for the Canadian Rockies would push me back outside of my comfort zone: getting certified as a hiking guide, becoming a board member of Bear Conflict Solutions Institute and even running my own businesses so that I could have more flexibility to enjoy where I live.

Where I suffered from a lack of information for the first edition of this book, I now have the opposite problem: there is so much information out there now. In truth, with all the online resources now available, including the app, I questioned the necessity of updating this guidebook. Amidst the praise were also harsh criticisms in reaction to the first and second editions of this book. In the spirit of stepping outside our comfort zone to invite learning and personal growth, I am listening to those who wanted this edition and giving voice to the critics.

In this edition, I am cleaning up the distances and aligning them with the Atlas Guides app and the GDTA's official track. Although this guidebook will remain a comprehensive resource, it needs to reflect the app and other resources now available, such as the GDTA website. Hikers have asked for and will receive here a better handling of elevations, including elevation profiles. I have altered the section distance outlines to better help with planning and booking campsites. The planning resources have ballooned by 50 per cent in this edition. Thru-hikers, please note: I have incorporated all the hiker notes passed down through the generations up to the 2018 season.

Since the second edition of this guidebook, there have been significant changes in the national parks in regards to planning your hike on the GDT. You can now reserve backcountry campsites online for Banff, Jasper, Yoho and Kootenay National Parks well in advance of your hike. Jasper National Park has rezoned its backcountry, meaning that much of the GDT route is now in 'wildland,' or decommissioned territory, and Banff National Park seems to be following this example. I've accounted for all these changes and I am happy to announce the addition of two major new alternate routes in Jasper National Park: Six Passes and Elysium Pass. These are my favourite hikes in Jasper and I hope you consider them when you plan your journey.

I wrote this edition of the guidebook nearly from the ground up for a wider audience. In summary, the third edition of *Hiking Canada's Great Divide Trail* is a better resource for planning your trip on the GDT.

Thank you.
Dustin Lynx

Quick glossary of terms

thru-hike: means hiking the entire GDT route

section hiker: a hiker who does a section or two each season

SOBO and **NOBO:** 'southbound' and 'northbound' hikes or hikers

zero-day: a rest day, when you hike 'o' kilometres

yo-yo: thru-hiking the whole route and then going the other way, back to the beginning

WHAT IS THE GREAT DIVIDE TRAIL?

The GDT surpassed all my expectations and I had built it up pretty big in my mind. It has set the bar for what I want in a thru-hike. It had just the right balance of community, challenge, clearly defined trail, alternate routes, cross country, and solo hiking. More improvements are being made each year, and I highly recommend getting out there before the rest of the world finds out about it!

—Erin "Wired" Saver, from a blog post after her 2015 thru-hike: walkingwithwired.com/2015/10/advice-to-future-gdters.html.

'Canada's Great Divide Trail' gives the impression that the route is a maintained trail and that it has some sort of official recognition as a unified entity. In fact, much of the 'trail' is a patchwork of old, unmaintained, unofficial, unsigned, unmarked, and/or unmapped paths, and significant portions involve route-finding, bushwhacking, scrambling, or cross country alpine travel. 'Great Divide Route' more accurately conveys the reality of the situation.

—Rick Bombaci, from a trip report documenting his 2008 thru-hike.

For now I'll say that the GDT was an amazing experience. Usually amazingly beautiful and inspiring, and sometimes amazingly frustrating and challenging, but always visceral, raw, and making me feel alive every single day of the trip. The Hayduke Tr in the US SW is the only other of the 16 long-distance hikes I've completed where I can say that every day the scenery is world-class at some point, no matter the classification/protection level of the land. Definitely in my top 2 for most scenic long-distance trails.

—Li Brannfors, from email correspondence documenting his 2012 GDT thru-hike.

The Great Divide Trail (GDT) is not a continuous, marked trail – not yet, at least. Perhaps you have heard of it from friends or read about it in *National Geographic* or *Backpacker* magazine, and in your mind the idea of the GDT is stored in the same place of your brain where you have placed mention of other long-distance hiking trails, like the Pacific Crest Trail (PCT) or the Appalachian Trail (AT). However, as you can tell by the opening quotations from past thru-hikers, the GDT is a challenging wilderness route and people react to the reality of it in different ways. This is not the PCT or the AT!

The GDT is a wilderness hiking route patched together through an array of protected areas and forestry districts using existing trail networks, roads, OHV (off-highway vehicle) tracks, and cross-country navigation (walking with no trail at all). Despite the history of the route dating back 50 years now, the GDT has suffered from a lack of interest until recently with the re-emergence of the Great Divide Trail Association (GDTA) and a cadre of volunteers determined to gain official recognition for the trail. They are actively working with relevant authorities to maintain, mark and build trail.

The main route of the GDT follows the spine of the Canadian Rockies (the hydrological Continental Divide) as closely as possible, from the Canada/USA border, in Waterton Lakes National Park, 980km to the original northern terminus, in Mount Robson Provincial Park and optionally another 150km to an extended northern terminus in Kakwa Provincial Park and Protected Area in BC. Most of the route is in the protected jurisdiction of national and provincial parks – about 60%. The core area of these parks is recognized as the Canadian Rocky Mountain Parks UNESCO World Heritage Site.

> *Renowned for their scenic splendor, the Canadian Rocky Mountain Parks are comprised of Banff, Jasper, Kootenay and Yoho national parks and Mount Robson, Mount Assiniboine and Hamber provincial parks. Together, they exemplify the outstanding physical features of the Rocky Mountain Biogeographical Province.*
>
> —UNESCO World Heritage List: whc.unesco.org/en/list/304.

Core to the GDT hiking community is the affectionately named 'original' GDT, south of Fording River Pass near Highwood House (in Section B), built by the original GDTA in the 1980s. This is a hundred kilometres long and currently being extended to the south, near Deadman Pass, close to Coleman, Alberta. The expected completion date of this additional 30km of trail is approximately 2022. But don't think for a moment that this is the only focus of the current GDTA organization – they are hard at work in all areas of the route, including the promotion of the GDT as a nationally recognized trail.

I assume you are reading this guidebook because you plan to hike a portion of the GDT or perhaps thru-hike the whole distance. Well, the effort of planning your adventure is worth it! Your journey will be what you make of it, but the GDT will ensure that it involves plenty of challenge. As you read this guidebook and gather information from other resources, you will start questioning yourself. What do I do if I encounter a grizzly bear? How does the permitting system work – wait, is it a system? How will I safely ford raging glacial torrents!? Which campsites are worth staying at?

The complexity of planning and then hiking the entire GDT, from end to end, is severe enough that if you are considering the GDT as your first thru-hike, you should look to another long-distance trail first, to build your experience. Consider joining a week-long guided hike such as the Alpine Club of Canada has started offering (alpineclubofcanada.ca). The GDTA at greatdividetrail.com/discover-the-gdt warns how challenging the route can be:

> ...hiking conditions are often strenuous and potentially hazardous, difficult mountain navigation, glacial stream crossings, deceptively short hiking season, harsh weather including potential summer snowstorms, grizzly bears, mosquitoes, and remote trail exit points for resupply or potential emergency access.

The GDT is a serious endeavour for even the veteran thru-hiker. If you have hiked other long-distance trails, don't be fooled by the comparatively short distance of the GDT (the PCT is 4300km, for example). The GDT has obstacles such as decommissioned trails and chilly creek fords that will slow your daily progress and a potentially confusing permitting system with less than optimal resupply options that could befuddle your planning process. To put it in perspective, your next trip after this one could easily happen in the untracked tundra and remote ranges of Alaska or the Yukon with the experience you gain from the GDT.

The GDT spans 979km from the international border in Waterton Lakes National Park to the info centre in Mount Robson Provincial Park. Mount Robson is the highest peak in the Canadian Rockies, at 3954m (12,972ft), and is the original northern terminus.

There is an excellent and wild route that follows the Divide perhaps more closely than any other part of the GDT. It continues north of the trail junction for Mount Robson, all the way to the trailhead for Kakwa Provincial Park and Protected Area on the Walker Creek forest service road. This is the extended northern terminus, and is 1133km from the international border at Waterton.

Both Mount Robson and Kakwa Lake are exceptionally beautiful and deserving end points for the GDT but Mount Robson is recognized worldwide and is far more convenient to access, so this is where most thru-hikers choose to start or end their hike. There are currently about 30 people thru-hiking the GDT each year, a number that is expected to keep rising at a modest rate.

- The GDT crosses the Great Divide at least 30 times.
- 60% of the extended route is in protected parks.
- 65% of the extended route is in Alberta, with the remainder in British Columbia.
- 4% of the route follows active roads and highways.
- The original (and signed) GDT is 9% of the extended route and growing!

The GDT route currently crosses:
- 2 UNESCO World Heritage Sites made up from 7 of the parks listed here.
- 5 national parks: Waterton Lakes, Banff, Kootenay, Yoho and Jasper.
- 9 provincial parks: Akamina–Kishinena, Castle, Elk Lakes, Peter Lougheed, Height of the Rockies, Mount Assiniboine, Kootenay-Cline, Mount Robson and Kakwa.
- 2 wildland provincial parks: Castle and High Rock.
- 2 wilderness areas: Beehive Natural Area and White Goat.
- 2 special management areas: Kananaskis Country and Willmore Wilderness Park.
- 5 forest districts: Castle, Bow/Crow, Rocky Mountain, Columbia and Robson Valley.

The highest point on the GDT is the 2585m (8481ft) unnamed 'Michele Lakes' Pass in the White Goat Wilderness Area in Section E, just north of David Thompson Highway 11.

The lowest point is at 1051m (3448ft) at Old Fort Point on the Athabasca River, in Jasper at the end of Section E. Including the extended northern terminus, the lowest point is the Kakwa Provincial Park trailhead at 950m.

The southern terminus of the GDT is also the junction with the Pacific Northwest Trail and the Continental Divide Trail. So, if you are a SOBO hiker, you have your choice to continue to Mexico on the CDT or to the West Coast, near Seattle. Some NOBO hikers have started their trip by first doing part of the PNWT. In fact, a group of hikers has gone from Jasper all the way to the southern terminus of the CDT on the Mexico–USA border recently.

On that point, the GDT is not the same as the 'Great Divide Mountain

Bike Route,' which runs 4455km from Banff, Alberta, to Antelope Wells, New Mexico, at the Mexican border. This route is popularized by an annual bike race called the Tour Divide (see tourdivide.org). While many sections of the GDT are accessible by mountain bike, a continuous journey isn't possible or even permitted. At the time of writing, the record for the Tour Divide race was 13 days, 22 hours, 51 minutes, set by Mike Hall of Yorkshire, England, in case you were wondering.

To dispel any possible confusion, the 'Great Trail,' formerly known as the Trans-Canada Trail, is not the GDT. The Great Trail is a multi-use trail that crosses Canada and goes from coast to coast to coast. Learn more about that route at thegreattrail.ca.

HISTORY OF THE GDT

The Great Divide Trail has a disproportionately long history compared to the amount of trail built in its name. Today it is largely an unmarked route despite public support and past government approval for an official trail. Lack of signage notwithstanding, the GDT is the grand path of the Canadian Rocky Mountains and inspires hikers to trace its heights each season.

We know that human history in the Canadian Rockies goes back at least 10,000 years. First Nations people have a long history of living, hunting, and travelling through these mountains. The first Europeans that came to this part of the world, such as David Thompson, a surveyor and mapmaker extraordinaire, depended on aboriginal guides. There is an interesting chapter of discovery documented by A.O. Wheeler, a commissioner appointed to survey and mark the interprovincial boundary between Alberta and British Columbia from 1913 to 1924. For the purposes of this essay, however, I will focus on the specific history – as far as I could determine it – of the named route, the 'Great Divide Trail.'

The GDT started as a youthful and courageous idea. The first record of a Great Divide Trail appears in the minutes of the national park's standing committee meetings in Banff and Jasper in 1966. The Girl Guides of Canada proposed the idea of a trail running the length of the British Columbia and Alberta boundary, along the Rocky Mountains.

In the two years following the Girl Guides proposal, other public support for the Great Divide Trail grew. The first formal proposal landed in the western regional office of Parks Canada in May 1967. A local architect and mountaineer named Philippe Delesalle saw the GDT as a route that would provide backcountry access for all park users. He focused on the Divide between Kananaskis Lakes and Yoho Valley, which he believed already had an excellent trail system. In his proposal to Parks Canada, Delesalle wrote: "This area... should be made more accessible to all the visitors who wish to walk away from the car parks and enter into closer contact with nature." He felt Parks Canada needed only to establish shelters every 10 miles along the route to encourage trail use. Delesalle felt the public would support the idea of the GDT at the time and offered his services to complete the project. (Note: Phillippe Delesalle won the Summit of Excellence Award for mountain architecture – specifically for his work designing lodges and huts – at the Banff Mountain Film and Book Festival in 2011.)

Despite Delesalle's proposal, the GDT would simply have remained an idea on a desk unless a Banff local named Jim Thorsell hadn't taken the first steps to get it established. Working as a research consultant for Parks Canada, Thorsell led a trail-use survey in 1967. After administering the survey, Thorsell believed the Great Divide Trail could become the trunk trail of the national parks, accessing the backcountry and linking many of the existing trail networks of the time. Thorsell reported in his 1968 memorandum to the National and Historic Parks Branch in Ottawa that "...The time is now right for this Department to show leadership in making the GDT a reality." He and his crew completed the first round of feasibility studies, noting trail conditions, taking photos, cataloguing natural features and detecting possible use conflicts within the national parks.

With no official response forthcoming from Parks Canada, Thorsell prepared a "Provisional Trail Guide and Map for the Proposed Great Divide Trail" in 1970. Produced for the National and Provincial Parks Association of Canada, this pamphlet was the first guide ever prepared for the GDT. In it, Thorsell clearly describes the route extending out of the national parks, south to the international boundary, to link with the proposed Continental Divide Trail in the USA. Brian Patton and Bart Robinson, authors of the first of many editions of the popular *Canadian Rockies Trail Guide*, supported Thorsell's vision of the GDT and included a description of the route in their guidebook published in 1971.

The GDT received some measure of federal approval shortly after the release of Thorsell's "Provisional Trail Guide and Map." Jean Chrétien, the Minister of Indian Affairs and Northern Development, issued a communiqué endorsing the proposed Great Divide Trail. Chrétien stated that Parks Canada would undertake the project with the objective of completing it by 1975.

In response to the minister's communiqué, Parks Canada formed the Great Divide Trail Committee to steer implementation of the trail. The committee consisted of the National and Provincial Parks Association of Canada (NPPAC), the Canadian Youth Hostel Association, the Bow Valley section of the Alpine Club of Canada, and Parks Canada planners. In 1971 and 1972 the committee contracted the Canadian Wildlife Service to study the feasibility of the GDT in Banff, Jasper and Yoho national parks. These studies generated several recommendations, most of which concerned re-routing the GDT away from high use areas such as Lake O'Hara.

In 1973 the committee issued a status report defining the criteria for development of the GDT. The report recommended unobtrusive campgrounds rather than shelters, a trail quota system, separation of horse and hiker trails, routing the GDT away from high-use areas and discouraging day use of the GDT. However, five years after Chrétien's directive to establish the GDT, the concept of the trail had not moved beyond the planning stage.

Outside the framework of Parks Canada, the GDT gained provincial support in Alberta. Based on support from the Alberta Wilderness Association and public interest in the GDT, the Alberta Environment Conservation Authority recommended developing a system of trails along the Great Divide as early as 1973. This opened the way for an advocacy group to establish the GDT south of Banff National Park.

In the summer of 1974, having received a federal Opportunities for Youth grant, six young and enthusiastic students set out to explore possible routes for the Great Divide Trail outside the national parks. They collectively covered an estimated 4800km on foot, taking inventory of existing trails and types of land use in the area between the USA border and Banff National Park. Barely pausing to catch their breath, the team went on to compile their notes and recommendations in a report called "Project: Great Divide Trails."

Following the completion of their report, this dedicated group founded the Great Divide Trail Association (GDTA). Several organizations demonstrated support by joining the association, including the Alpine Club of Canada, the Canadian Youth Hostel Association, the Alberta Wilderness Association, the Sierra Club and the Outdoor Recreation Council of British Columbia. Other clubs, consisting of skiers, naturalists, ranchers, hunters, anglers, equestrians and environmentalists, also joined the association, boosting its membership to over 150. The association aimed to implement the GDT as an equestrian and hiking trail based on the provisional route that arose out of the original group's efforts.

While momentum for the GDT grew outside the national parks, enthusiasm within the parks waned owing to concerns about overuse. To finalize the criteria for the development of the GDT, Parks Canada ran a special field study in Yoho National Park in 1974. In 1975 Parks Canada stalled in its planning process, citing a lack of adequate trail planning methodology. In 1976, in conjunction with the Great Divide Trail Committee, a graduate student at the University of Calgary completed a doctoral study of the GDT. Bart Deeg, a student in the faculty of environmental design, titled his work "A Proposal for a Trail Planning Methodology: A Case Study: The Great Divide Trail." The paper addressed the issue of overuse on backcountry trails in the national parks and strongly encouraged Parks Canada to complete the GDT by providing the very methodology that was lacking. However, the issues surrounding overuse remained unresolved and Parks has yet to endorse the route to this day.

The Great Divide Trail Association carried the vision of the route much further than Parks Canada. The GDTA began trail construction in summer 1976. Funded by both the private and the public sectors, the work continued for the next decade with the support of the Alberta government.

Each year, the GDTA hired up to three people for the trail crew and organized volunteers to help. According to Jenny Feick and Dave Higgins, two of the original six students to survey the GDT, provincial support for the trail waned when political tides shifted in the mid-1980s. Lacking provincial support, the GDTA had difficulty motivating a volunteer work force to invest their time and energy in a trail that might not exist the following year. By 1987 the association that had initiated, built and cared for the only segments of the Great Divide Trail ever established, disbanded.

After Parks Canada gave up on the idea and the GDTA faded from existence, the concept of the GDT sank into a low public profile. Although some had heard about the Great Divide Trail, few could say for certain whether it existed. However, the GDT was more than a myth to the few who hiked a substantial portion of the route. Decaying sheets from a trail register near the Baril Creek ford read: "Across the Roof of Canada. We started at USA and Canada border on 6-24-89. On to Grande Cache." Another message, written in 1996, read: "Rich Botto and Rick Heinrich from S.D., USA, started May 25th, Waterton Park—hiked over Castle River Divide, N. Kootenay Pass, Crowsnest Pass, N. Fork Pass and on way to Fording River Pass. Snowshoed nearly every day since. Rick Heinrich leaves at Lake Louise. I'm heading to the Yukon." A euphoric Botto writes in the trail register at Kakwa Lake, 900km farther north, that he is leaving the trail and dropping down to the Rocky Mountain Trench to buy a bicycle to continue to the Yukon.

Though the GDT languished in popularity compared to other long-distance hiking routes in North America, Dave Higgins and others continued to toil in the field, maintaining parts of the original GDT. They rebuilt bridges and cleared trail, largely funded from their own wallets and driven by a passion for the route.

My wife, Julia, and I moved to Calgary in 1995 with the dual purpose of completing our bachelor's degrees and hiking the GDT between semesters. The best route description we could find came from a combination of Thorsell's work published at the back of the *Canadian Rockies Trail Guide* and from a book called *High Summer*, written by Chris Townsend documenting his 1988 hike from Waterton to Liard River, in northern British Columbia. Partway through our research, we decided to keep all our notes to share with other long-distance hikers in the future, perhaps through a guidebook – we didn't know for sure at the time. We travelled to the American Long Distance Hiking Association – West's annual gathering, held in Oregon that year, to meet with Chris Townsend. He signed our copy of *High Summer* and gave us all the information he could. We hiked the route during the summer of 1996.

After we presented our hike to the public at the University of Calgary

Dustin Lynx assembling trail data post hike, 1996, in Calgary, Alberta.

in September 1996, Dave Higgins approached us and informed us that we had failed to hike the original GDT, the only stretch built and marked as the Great Divide Trail – coincidentally the very stretch he had toiled and spent money to keep alive! The three of us shared in a sentiment of disbelief. How could we have invested so much time in research and missed that trail? At the same slideshow, Tony and Gillean Daffern, the founders of Rocky Mountain Books, approached us and asked if we were interested in writing a guidebook.

Hiking Canada's Great Divide Trail appeared in 2000 after several rewrites and a lot more hiking. As an arts major, I had decided to write the entire description in the first person because I thought it would be gripping – my editors disagreed. With the book in hand, Julia and I accepted as many speaking engagements as possible, especially ones that involved free accommodations, food and a stipend such as Lizard Creek Lodge in Fernie, BC, had offered.

We moved to Canmore, Alberta, and started our family in 1998. We started hearing from thru-hikers each season. Their trip reports made us ache to be back on the trail for a whole summer. I kept their notes and suggestions and wrote the second edition of the guidebook in 2007.

Then a miraculous thing happened: a group of hikers and enthusiasts known as the Friends of the Great Divide Trail who had worked together maintaining the original GDT decided they needed to formalize their organization to better advocate for this amazing route. In 2013 they founded a new organization that would continue the 1970s name, the Great Divide Trail Association (GDTA). You can read more about their story and access invaluable resources at greatdividetrail.com.

At present the best thing you can do to ensure the future of the GDT is to join the GDTA and get involved. The shared vision is stated as:

Dustin and Julia Lynx on the 'original' Great Divide Trail, 1998.

The Great Divide Trail Association is dedicated to maintaining, protecting and promoting the Great Divide Trail, and with your support we can preserve the GDT and its wilderness experience for generations to come!

The history does not end there, of course. Thanks to the *Wild* effect spawned by Oprah's Book Club endorsing Cheryl Strayed's 2012 story about her adventures on the PCT, the GDT is garnering more attention than ever as hikers look for a less travelled and 'wilder' long-distance hiking route. I doubt the GDT will be as overwhelmed as the PCT in recent years, but it is benefiting from all the people who have rediscovered hiking.

In December 2016, River Taig released an app with Atlasguides.com tracing the whole trail with an intricate GPS track and written descriptions. Hikers will now be able to comment on sections of trail as they hike and share that information with other hikers as they pass in and out of wifi and cell phone coverage each season. Combined with a thriving Facebook group called Great Divide Trail Hikers, people now have a solid communications platform to connect with others, share information and recount their trip reports.

I sincerely hope the GDT will become an official trail, recognized by the provincial and federal governments. Ideally, this will lead to a continuous corridor of protected areas that outdoor enthusiasts, wildlife and locals can all benefit from in the scope of the wider Yellowstone to Yukon wildlife corridor. The GDT is unlike any other trail in North America, with its own significant history. Your decision to discover this trail for yourself will undoubtedly contribute to the future of this spectacular route.

PLANNING YOUR TRIP ON THE GDT

Despite the buzz surrounding long-distance 'thru-hiking,' you do not need to hike the whole GDT to appreciate this wilderness route. You can spend a week or just a few days to get a taste of the longer trail, depending on where you decide to go. In this edition, I'm organizing the planning part of the book around the questions 'when,' 'where' and 'how.' (I've already covered 'what' the GDT is, and you yourself are providing the 'why' and 'who.') This method of organizing topics will make sense when I demonstrate how to construct a sample itinerary.

Compared to most other long routes in North America, the GDT has a narrow window of optimal weather during which you can safely schedule your long-range plans. We will begin with this important factor.

When to hike

> Hi all! Made it to Blairmore/Coleman. Trail Report: There's still a lot of snow in the high country. Pretty much every north-facing slope was still full, but passable and not unsafe. I was definitely a wee bit early. The hunters camp at Jutland Creek was buried, but fortunately the ridges around La Coulotte were all good. The remaining snow there actually made it easier to travel!
>
> —Leslie Gerein, posted June 25, 2016, on the Great Divide Trail Hikers Facebook page.

Underestimating the weather and the potential effect of the remnant snow pack can severely affect your plans for hiking any portion of the GDT. If you start too early, you will face obstacles that you maybe haven't considered before: postholing up to your crotch in heavy, wet snow; collapsing snow bridges over stream crossings; difficult route-finding; slippery footing on icy hillsides; having to pitch your tent on snow; and even the potential for late-season snow avalanches. In short, imposing your schedule on the Canadian Rockies simply will not work.

Consider the following story from my 1996 thru-hike:

> Julia and I planned to start hiking in early June from the international border. I wanted to have as much time as possible that summer to explore the trail and the second

week of June seemed like a late start considering we had to leave our apartment at the end of May. The information centre in Waterton reported a higher than normal snow pack in the high country, so we decided to pack snowshoes at the last minute.

It started snowing the night before our departure. We drove south from Calgary on the Cowboy Trail in a white-out blizzard. By the end of that day, there was 25cm (almost a foot) of fresh snow covering the campground in Waterton. When we checked in at the information centre to arrange our wilderness passes [now called 'backcountry permits'], they simply told us not to go. The avalanche risk was too high, they explained. Avalanche risk? It's nearly summer, I thought!

We drove back to Calgary that evening and had to wait another two weeks before starting again. Even then there was still too much snow on the 2565m Tamarack Summit in Waterton Lakes National Park, so we began hiking from the Red Rock Canyon trailhead, in the northern part of the park. There was snow nearly from the start and no tracks from other hikers. I followed the pawprints of a grizzly sow and her cub up to the Twin Lakes campsite and pitched the tent on a 2m (6ft) snowpack that night. We had to wear all our clothing and jackets to bed and still shivered through the night.

The snowpack depth varies from year to year and region to region. During some years, the southern Rockies may have disproportionately more snow than anywhere else in the mountain range, for instance. It also depends on what elevation you will be hiking at: the Rockwall trail in Kootenay National Park, covered in Section C, is much higher than the Amiskwi River trail in Section D.

If you are starting your hike after mid-July, the snowpack won't be an issue. However, if you plan to start earlier, you should communicate with staff at the information centre closest to your point of departure – perhaps several times in the weeks and days leading up to your departure. Be warned: simply checking websites isn't enough. While websites have interesting stats, local knowledge will be the most helpful. You shouldn't plan to start your hike any earlier than mid-June, period – even during a reportedly 'warm' spring or 'low' snow year.

New snow can fall at any time during the year in the Canadian Rockies but generally melts within a few days during the summer. In terms of planning your trip, however, the snow can start accumulating in the high country (above 2000m) starting in mid-September. I wouldn't plan your trip on the GDT to go past the third week of September unless it is an exceptional year.

To summarize, the prime hiking window is generally mid-July to mid-September, only two months! Outside that period you should gather as much local information as you can before heading out or continuing on. Park information centres that maintain trail reports are the best places to contact. The trail reports themselves can be a little misleading and simply say "snow covered," and not indicate if people are hiking on that trail yet. Refer to the 'Contacts' section at the end of this book to find the appropriate information. Because the GDT isn't an official route, it is helpful to know the names of the trails from the route descriptions in this book when talking with staff at the information centres. For example, if you inquire about the state of the GDT in Section C in Kootenay National Park, you will want to ask about conditions on the 'Rockwall trail.'

Where to hike

This can be a difficult decision if you only have limited time and want to experience the best that the route can offer.

Refer to the 'Selected hikes' appendix on page 316 to get some ideas for day hikes, overnight trips and longer weekend backpacking forays. These are highlight areas of the GDT and generally have easy vehicle access. Some of these are little 'thru-hikes' where you start at one trailhead and finish at another so that you don't double back on the same trail.

If you have a week or more to spend on the GDT, refer to the main trail description and consider hiking a section or two. The descriptions in the introduction to each section should give you an idea if it is right for you and what highlights (or obstacles) you can expect. Section C is likely the most popular of the whole GDT, as it follows maintained, marked trails by such landmarks as Wonder Pass, Mount Assiniboine, Sunshine Meadows, and the Rockwall. Section E is the next most popular, with several convenient access points between segments of the route. If the cross-country hiking in the White Goat Wilderness at the southern end of Section E doesn't appeal to you, you can hop on the GDT at Nigel Pass, accessed farther north, near the Icefields Parkway.

When you start considering several sections or the entire route in a single hike, you enter the realm of long-distance hiking. It takes about eight weeks to hike the entire 1133km (extended) route, which, as you've already learned, is the duration of the optimal weather in the Rockies. If you plan to hike the 'whole' GDT, you will need to decide whether to start or finish at the original northern terminus at Mount Robson or to include the extended northern terminus at Kakwa Lake, 150km farther. It doesn't sound far, but the most northern section (G) has difficult access and resupply options and is largely cross-country travel in remote wilderness.

Lastly, in our discussion of 'where,' there is the possibility of incorporating alternate routes into your journey. As you read the trail description or scroll through the Google Earth map on the GDTA website, you will see parallel trails that depart and rejoin the main route. In general, these alternates are at a higher elevation, a little longer and more scenic, as they avoid road walking or swampy valleys. Some alternate routes such as Wonder Pass in Section C have become main route over time. Others, like the Mount Rowe and Barnaby Ridge routes in Section A, are only suitable for very experienced backpackers with a tolerance for scrambling (using feet *and* hands to climb or descend). While there is some talk of installing via ferrata hardware (ladders) on Barnaby Ridge, even then it would still be too precipitous for many hikers.

In summary, where you go on the GDT has a lot to do with the time you have available and that optimal window for hiking. When it comes time to make your itinerary and put your plan in writing, consider incorporating the alternate routes. Refer to the 'Alternate routes' appendix on page 324. Each alternate is also listed in the flow of trail description. Before you're ready to work on your itinerary, however, we need to discuss access. Where you choose to begin and end your GDT journey will dictate the limits of your itinerary.

Access and transportation – Where to start and finish along the GDT

This topic affects thru-hikers planning to cover a significant portion of the route. Specific information on access trails and trailheads is covered in the introduction to each segment. The map on the GDTA website and the commercially available GDT app also show access trails.

Your journey on the GDT will be what you make of it. Over the years, hikers have used alternate termini based on their preferences (for instance, to only hike in the parks) and on the limitations of available transport to and from the route (like the remote Kakwa Lake). Here, I describe three popular southern termini and four northern ones, as well as how to access them, along with prices current at the time of writing.

East Glacier, Montana

Although I don't describe any of the trails in Glacier NP in this guidebook, some thru-hikers opt to extend their journey farther south. It makes sense; this is a highlight of the Continental Divide Trail. The CDT links East Glacier, Montana, with the official southern terminus of the GDT at monument 276 on the international border in Waterton Lakes NP. Keep in mind that while you don't need to present your passport NOBO (where you are instead encouraged to check in at the RCMP detachment in the town of Waterton), you will need it SOBO to present at the Goat Haunt ranger station.

- **Air:** Glacier Park International Airport in Kalispell, Montana, is 1.5 hours' drive away. There are at least two shuttle services: Kalispell Taxi & Airport Shuttle, 406-752-4022, and Glacier Taxi, glaciertaxi.com, 406-250-3603 or 406-206-6022.
- **Bus:** Greyhound.com serves Kalispell, Montana. 1-800-231-2222 within USA. 214-849-8100 outside USA.
- **Rail:** Amtrak.com will take you directly to East Glacier! 1-800-USA-RAIL within USA. 215-856-7952 outside USA.
- **Hiker shuttle:** Glacier National Park offers daily shuttles to the Chief Mountain Border Crossing (nps.gov/glac/planyourvisit/shuttles.htm). From there, the Waterton Outdoor Adventure Company offers daily hiker shuttles from Chief Mountain crossing to Waterton. hikewaterton.com. 403-859-2378.

Waterton Lakes, Alberta

This is the official southern terminus of the GDT. Monument 276 on the international border is another 6.4km south of the Lakeshore Trail trail-head, or you can pay to take a boat to the Goat Haunt ranger station on the south shore of the lake and hike north to reach the terminus.

- **Air:** Calgary International Airport or Glacier Park International Airport in Kalispell, Montana. Airport Shuttle Express, Calgary, airportshuttleexpress.com. From Kalispell: Kalispell Taxi & Airport Shuttle, 406-752-4022, and Glacier Taxi, glaciertaxi.com, 406-250-3603 or 406-206-6022.
- **Bus:** Greyhound.ca has bus stations in Pincher Creek and Lethbridge, Alberta, but you would have to take a taxi from either of those locations to Waterton. Pincher Creek is the closer of the two, at 45 minutes' drive away. Contact Greyhound Canada at 1-800-661-TRIP (8747). Pincher Creek Taxis: 403-632-9738.
- **Rail:** Viarail.ca doesn't serve this area. The closest train station is Edmonton. However, amtrak.com serves East Glacier, Montana. 1-800-USA-RAIL within USA. 215-856-7952 outside USA.
- **Boat:** The Waterton Shoreline Cruise Company offers a ferry to Goat Haunt in Glacier NP, watertoncruise.com, 403-859-2362. The price is $32 per person one way, including taxes. It is a 7.4km hike to get to

the border and the southern terminus of the GDT (see the 'Alternate routes' appendix, page 324).

- **Hiker shuttle:** Waterton Outdoor Adventures offers daily hiker shuttles from Waterton to the Chief Mountain Border Crossing, where hikers can connect with a Glacier National Park shuttle. hikewaterton.com, 403-859-2378.

Kananaskis Lakes, Alberta

From Peter Lougheed Provincial Park at the start of Section C, km 345.0, it is possible to hike almost entirely in the protected areas of national and provincial parks to any of the northern termini and skip the roads and OHV trails which the GDT relies on in both of its southernmost sections.

- **Air:** Calgary International Airport. For custom shuttle service from the airport to the Upper Kananaskis Lake trailhead, contact airportshuttleexpress.com for rates and schedules. The banffairporter.com shuttle service can take you to Canmore for $66, including taxes, and from there you can hire a taxi. The trailhead is an hour away from Canmore. Canmore Taxi serves Kananaskis, 403-679-0076.
- **Bus:** Sundog Transportation and Tours offers transport to trailheads upon request, sundogtours.com, 888-786-3641. They also offer an airport shuttle from Calgary and Edmonton airports to the Banff and Jasper areas respectively.

Jasper, Alberta

Immediately after completing the stunning Skyline Trail, some choose to end their trip in the town of Jasper, simply for the convenience. There is also a sign at the northern Skyline trailhead – below Signal Mountain at km 838.2 – that declares "Northern Terminus of the Great Divide Trail." It's the only such sign I know of at the time of writing.

- **Air:** Edmonton International Airport is over five hours away but there are several transportation services linking the airport with Jasper, including the airport shuttle offered by Sundog, sundogtours.com, 888-786-3641, for $105, including taxes, one way.
- **Bus:** Contact Greyhound Canada at 1-800-661-TRIP (8747), greyhound.ca. One-way tickets are $70 at the time of writing. The buses stop in every small town on the way, which adds two hours to the trip, compared to the shuttle service.
- **Rail:** Viarail.ca offers service here. Contact 888-VIA-RAIL (1-888-842-7245). The cost is $95, including taxes, and the trip takes over five

hours to the Edmonton station, where you would have to arrange for a taxi to the airport if needed. Edmonton Transit Service (ETS) offers a direct route, #747, to the airport for just $5.

Mount Robson Provincial Park Visitor Centre, British Columbia

This is the original northern terminus and likely where most thru-hikers on the GDT start or end their journeys. The busy visitor centre is on the Yellowhead Highway 16, one hour's drive from Jasper. Public telephones and wifi are available here. If the visitor centre is closed, there is a public telephone at the nearby gas station.

- **Air:** See Jasper access description above.
- **Bus:** Contact Greyhound Canada at 1-800-661-TRIP (8747), greyhound.ca. This isn't a regular stop for the company; it is called a "flag-down stop" and has daily departures east to Jasper (and Edmonton) and west ultimately to Vancouver that both leave very early. The one-way cost to Jasper is less than $30. You must phone ahead to arrange this service (or they won't stop for you).
- **Hitchhiking:** This is a legal and well-used form of transportation by many hikers in the parks. However, the more people there are in your group, the more stuff you have and the possible presence of dogs may affect how 'attractive' you look to the drivers roaring by. A sign helps, like "Jasper – Please."

Kakwa Provincial Park trailhead at Bastille Creek

This is the extended northern terminus and it isn't straightforward to access, unfortunately. The trailhead is 74km from the Yellowhead Highway 16, on the Walker Creek forest service road – a gravel track that is unsuitable for cars without high clearance.

- **Air:** The Prince George airport is serviced by Air Canada, Westjet and others. It is 1.5 hours' drive to the Walker Creek FSR junction on Highway 16, in the direction of McBride, BC. There are several taxi companies in Prince George, including PG Taxi at 250-564-4444, pgtaxi.ca.
  - » You can charter a helicopter out of McBride. See the Transportation section of the 'Contacts' appendix at page 341 for Yellowhead Helicopters.
- **Bus:** Contact Greyhound Canada at 1-800-661-TRIP (8747), greyhound.ca, to arrange a flag-down stop. The closest towns on

the map to the Walker Creek FSR intersection are Dome Creek and Crescent Spur.

- **Rail:** Via Rail lists Dome Creek as a 'stop on request' station that is five hours away from Jasper and costs $77.70, including taxes, for a one-way ticket. It is $22.05 for a 2.5-hour trip to Prince George. Dome Creek is 20km north of the Walker Creek FSR intersection.

Grande Cache, Alberta

In recent years, some hikers have opted to finish at Grande Cache, leaving the main route at km 1065.7 and hiking over 63km to a trailhead near town. (See the 'Alternate routes' appendix, page 324.)

- **Air:** Grande Prairie Airport, grandeprairieairport.com, is much closer than Edmonton – only two hours driving. Consider this airport when looking for flights if you choose the Grande Cache alternate terminus.
- **Bus:** Greyhound doesn't provide service to Grande Cache. The Grande Cache Community Bus Service does, however, at a cost of $30, including tax, one way. Contact the recreation centre at 780-827-2446 for rates and to make a reservation. You must book 48 hours in advance as per their brochure. Buses run each day to Grande Prairie and Hinton (near Jasper). Greyhound does provide service to both of those towns. As mentioned above, there is an airport at Grande Prairie (grandeprairieairport.com).

Dogs

The GDT is dog-friendly: they can walk over 90% of the route with you! Furthermore, the environment is more conducive to your dog's well-being than other long-distance trails in North America, according to River Taig, author of the Atlas Guides GDT app:

> Most trail-worthy dogs such as Labrador retrievers suffer far more in heat than in cool and wet conditions. Relative to its southern cousins, the GDT is relatively cool and offers considerably more water. Another important factor that favours the GDT relative to, say, the more volcanic Pacific Crest Trail is that the soils and rock that dominate in the Canadian Rockies tend to be less abrasive underfoot. On my 2016 thru-hike with my Labrador retriever, Opus, she never had serious problems with her pads.

In regards to wildlife on the GDT, it is important to keep your dog leashed or in the tent with you at night. The leash should be less than 3m (10ft) long, and I would add that for convenience sake it should be able to

Opus with her human, River Taig, on the Wallbridge Glacier alternate route (Section G).

attach securely to your backpack shoulder or waist straps so that you can hike hands-free. A harness that attaches around the canine's chest seems appropriate if you are looking at doing some of the alternate routes that include a bit of scrambling, so that you can assist with steep obstacles, even lowering or raising your dog. If they carry their own food in a doggie backpack, make sure it isn't their only harness, because it must be stored at night with your food, away from bears.

Parks regulations insist on using leashes with dogs because of the potential hazard to the dog, wildlife and you. A dog that is running free is likely to come running back to its owner if in trouble and if that 'trouble' happens to be a 250kg (550lb) bear, you could be thrown into a dangerous situation. Other wildlife can be sensitive to dogs too, like moose, elk, caribou and deer. An ungulate defends itself with its hooves and can cause grievous injuries to your canine friend.

Consider the long-term effect on wildlife before you let your pooch off leash. The parks were created to give the remaining wildlife a refuge where they can carry out their lives undisturbed by people and their domesticated dogs. An Alberta Parks ecologist, John Paczkowski, recently completed a year-long study of wildlife corridors in the Canmore area (cbc.ca/news/canada/calgary/canmore-wildlife-corridor-human-1.4021290) and determined:

> We have almost 100,000 people who are having their dogs out there in the wildlife corridors and we have 60,000 separate events of dogs being off-leash in and around wildlife corridors. ... It's not only [the law] that you keep your dog on a leash, if you

want to have wildlife on the landscape and using these corridors, it's something you have to do.

Ideally you have put in some mileage with your dog before starting the GDT and know how they will react in most situations. It is your responsibility to make sure that whatever leash and harness system you adopt will work for the duration of your hike on the GDT. It's simply not fair to wildlife to do otherwise. It's also not fair to other dog owners if you decide it's okay for *your* dog to be off leash, because in the end it will only result in tighter regulations, as in the US national parks where dogs aren't permitted. There are exceptions, however.

For the northern sections, D, E, F and G, you should know in advance that several river crossings are unbridged, which means that your dog should be a good swimmer. Care should be taken to let them swim across under their own power. A leash could drown them in this situation, so it makes sense to take it off for this purpose. The current will carry them downstream while they swim, so choose a suitable crossing well above any hazards. You don't want to see them washed into a confluence with a stronger river or over a waterfall. Don't assume that you can go after them or carry them, as you will have your hands full with your own efforts crossing.

When you plan your itinerary, account for the 100km prohibited zone in Jasper National Park from the Nigel Pass trailhead (segment 26) north to the end of the Skyline trail, on the edge of the town of Jasper. The only alternate route for walking around this sensitive caribou habitat is the South Boundary Trail, which ends on the Miette Hot Springs road, 61km east from the town of Jasper. Your options include skipping this part of the trail or finding a kennel service in Jasper or Hinton. The Hinton SPCA offers a dog boarding service for $20/night. See hintonspca.blogspot.ca for more details. Keep in mind that Hinton is 45 minutes' drive east from the town of Jasper. There doesn't appear to be an advertised dog boarding service in Jasper itself at the time of writing. Other closed areas are smaller in scope such as picnic spots, public beaches and public buildings. Look for posted signs in these areas.

When you pack your first aid kit, be sure to include any items for your dog. If your dog uses booties, pack some extra ones. You can buy some things in the towns close to the GDT such as Waterton, Blairmore, Banff and Jasper. Keep your dog in mind if you arrange for accommodation or a taxi, shuttle, train or bus ride and ask in advance if dogs are allowed. You might not be aware that Garmin makes a GPS tracking collar for dogs – this might be handy if your dog slips away.

There are no specific permits you need to arrange in advance of your trip for hiking with your dog. It is always best to check park websites and with info centres before you leave, though. There are temporary restrictions issued on occasion. If you choose a Greyhound bus for transport, be aware that dogs aren't permitted unless they are registered service dogs. Ask in advance with any transporter to ensure your pooch will get a seat too.

Dogs are permitted to stay with you at car campgrounds in the national and provincial parks as long as they remain on leash. You must pick up after your dog in the campgrounds, of course, and be considerate of others.

Horses

You are permitted to bring your horse(s) on much of the GDT. You must obtain permits from the national parks and each of the BC provincial parks in advance of your trip. While I have heard back from riders who have taken their horses over considerable distances in the Canadian Rockies, such as Wendy Bush, I don't know of anyone who has attempted the entire GDT or even a full section, as described in this guidebook. This is likely because some of the route is difficult enough for passage on foot – I'm thinking of Conway Creek in Section D, on the north side of Howse Pass (7km of criss-crossing blowdowns)! Alternate routes such as Barnaby Ridge wouldn't work because they have too many short sections of scrambling. I have included Wendy Bush's 12-day itinerary and gear list from her 2009 trip that included the original GDT in southern Kananaskis Country – see page 330 in the 'Sample itineraries' appendix.

In this edition of the guidebook, I do reference horse access in terms of any restrictions or restrictive terrain. For example, I mention in Section C that horse travel isn't permitted in the Sunshine Meadows area of Banff National Park. The good news for equestrians is that a continuous route is on the way.

The GDTA is developing the Great Divide Alternate Horse Route that follows some of the present GDT and parallel trails where horse travel is more feasible and permitted. If you contact the GDTA they will send you a link to a Google Earth kmz file that shows the route. Details such as horse-friendly campsites and grazing areas are still being worked out and I'm sure the GDTA would love to hear from you if you would like to help develop and maintain this route.

Many of the trails described in this book wouldn't exist without horse travel. Section G follows a lot of horse trail. Horse teams are the only way for trail crews to access some of these remote and beautiful areas. Park wardens used to patrol on horseback until recently. While I do mention some of the horse campsites and horse-only trails, in this guidebook I didn't initially research the route for equestrians. The national parks have many resources for equestrians, including guides to the trails and campsites.

To find out more, visit each of the national park websites and search for 'horseback riding.' Banff National Park has an excellent resource page that includes all the information you would need for that park: pc.gc.ca/en/pn-np/ab/banff/activ/cheval-horse.

While BC Parks has a blog page for horseback riding, you still need to contact each of the parks individually to arrange a permit. The blog is here: engage.gov.bc.ca/bcparksblog/2016/05/12/horseback-riding-in-bc-parks.

Alberta Parks has a portal page for equestrians here: albertaparks.ca/albertaparksca/visit-our-parks/activities/equestrian, and while it doesn't appear that you require any special permits for horses in the provincial parks, I encourage you to contact the relevant info centres before going.

Horses are the only pack animal allowed in the national parks. Llamas and goats aren't permitted, for instance. You could, however, use these other pack animals in provincial parks with a permit. Outside the parks you can use any pack animal you would like.

Mountain bikes

The GDT route isn't navigable by mountain bike, due to terrain, park restrictions, or both. There are some exceptions and I do indicate bike access in this guidebook. If you are looking for a long biking route, however, check out the Great Divide Mountain Biking Route and the Tour Divide race: tourdivide.org.

Mountain biking is a convenient way to get to the GDT on access trails and roads. The national and provincial parks have designated bike trails. There are no special permits for bikes but you do need to check bike access and closures before you go. The information centre contact info is in the 'Contacts' appendix, page 338.

Trail running and fastpacking

The sports of trail running and fastpacking have been around for at least 25 years now. They are nothing new. What has changed in recent years is these sports' popularity. It seems like everyone is training for an 'ultra' now. I must admit, with a young family and a demanding day job, it became an essential way for me to access the GDT over the past decade. I enjoy backpacking but it's a special thrill to go light at a fast pace and cover 100km in a day of running – a distance that could take five or more days hiking.

For my 40th birthday in summer 2011, my wife, Julia, bought me a return helicopter trip to Mount Assiniboine so I could use the campsite there as a running basecamp. Over 33 hours, I ran two large loops, including a circumnavigation of Mount Assiniboine itself. It was a birthday I'll never forget!

The entire GDT route is open to trail running at this point. I can't see it being regulated, but no one ever thought mountain bike access up the Bryant Creek trail to Mount Assiniboine would ever be closed either. I think if runners and fastpackers abide by the same trail etiquette and park rules as hikers do, there won't be any issues.

I've tried to put together the logistics of running the entire GDT, but it is daunting. I've also supported others on their bid to run the whole route. The trick is to get a vehicle and support crew to enough places to be effective. Runners can carry a shelter and food enough for a few days, but anything beyond that is too heavy to run with. See the 'Sample itineraries' appendix on page 330 if you are interested in running the GDT. I think it's a worthy challenge that I know someone will figure out. Let me know if you do. In any event, be safe and carry bear spray – you can't outrun bears!

Passes, permits and campsite reservations

Unlike the Pacific Crest Trail in the USA, the GDT doesn't have a single pass you can purchase which is valid for the whole way. With that said, the process is straightforward if you look at it in a certain way: there are national park entry passes, national park backcountry permits, and backcountry campsite reservation and booking fees.

The national parks (and some provincial ones) have a quota system that regulates the number of people staying in the backcountry on any given day. This depends of course on people booking official and random campsites for each night of their trip. There are few spaces available at the established campsites, which constrains the number of people that are in each area and their impact on the environment.

The penalty for failing to secure a permit in advance of your trip could lead to fines which themselves aren't that expensive – under $1,000. However, the cost of potentially having to return to the provincial court in the area would be much more of an inconvenience and costly. Instead of looking at the potential outcome of avoiding permits, I suggest you use the system to your benefit. You need to know where you're going to camp each night for your itinerary anyway. The wider benefit is for the GDT itself: the various park managers are more likely to recognize the trail if they know it is supported by an enthusiastic community that supports their park's regulations.

National park passes (as of 2018)

Just as in other national parks worldwide, there is a fee for every person entering the park for each day they plan to stay. In most cases, you will purchase either a group or adult 'annual discovery pass' if you plan to spend more than a week in the national parks. The passes are valid in all national parks across Canada. Buy your pass online at commandesparcs -parksorders.ca or in person at a park gate or visitor centre during your trip. These are sometimes referred to as vehicle passes because you put them on your dash or hang the tag from the rear-view mirror. I recommend just picking up a pass as you enter one of the national parks. I understand there is currently a delay of four to six weeks for passes ordered online and delivered by mail. There are no entry or vehicle passes required for any provincial park or other area outside the national parks. Waterton Lakes NP has a 'Single Location' annual pass available online and at the gate. Although it is much cheaper than the Discovery Pass, it is only valid in that park.

DAILY NATIONAL PARK ENTRY PASS

Adult	$9.80
Senior	$8.30
Youth (0–17)	Free
Family/Group	$19.60
Commercial Group, per person	$8.30
School Groups, per student	$3.90

ANNUAL NATIONAL PARK PASS – 'DISCOVERY PASS'

Adult	$67.70
Senior	$57.90
Youth (0–17)	Free
Family/Group	$136.40

National park backcountry permits

To stay overnight in the backcountry of any of the five national parks along the GDT, whether you are random camping or staying in a campsite or a shelter, you are required to obtain a backcountry permit.

There is no reservation fee if you are leaving on your trip within 24 hours, but in most cases you must pay the non-refundable reservation fee. The online reservations system is available year round. Visit pc.gc.ca/en/voyage-travel/reserve or call 1-877-RESERVE (1-877-737-3783). At the time of writing, Waterton Lakes NP backcountry campsite reservations aren't available online; you still have to contact the visitor centre there directly, within three months of your trip Accordingly, there is still a three-month limit if you make reservations directly with any of the visitor centres by phone, email or in person, as illustrated in the following example.

Take the time to plan your hike on the GDT and make an itinerary so you know exactly where you will camp each night. Let's assume for this example that you are planning to hike the entire GDT northbound from the USA border to Mt. Robson. As soon as you have a workable itinerary – or on January 1, whichever comes first – visit the Parks Canada reservations website. Reserve each of the backcountry campsites you have included in your itinerary for Banff, Kootenay, Yoho and Jasper national parks. Expect to pay online for at least one reservation fee and $9.80 per night per person in your group. These permits will be mailed to you. Reserve the remaining campsites in Waterton Lakes over the phone. Call the Waterton Lakes info centre three months in advance of the start of your journey and mention you are hiking the GDT and that you have already reserved campsites in the other national parks. They might waive your reservation fee. They will ask you to pay with a credit card. You have the option to either have the pass mailed to you or pick it up when you arrive.

You have the choice to communicate with visitor centre staff by email. In that case, send your itinerary and indicate when would be a good time for an attendant to call you back. They won't process any credit card information sent by email – they will need to call you back to make the transaction and to adjust your itinerary if any of the sites you indicated will already be full on that day.

The GDTA has developed a cheat sheet that lists all the campsites in the parks as well as their amenities and whether you need a backcountry permit to stay there. See greatdividetrail.com/trip-planning-resources/campgrounds.

Backcountry campsite reservations – provincial parks

Backcountry permits and park entry passes aren't required for provincial parks. However, you will need receipts showing you have reserved and prepaid for a backcountry campsite in Peter Lougheed (Section C) and Mount Robson (Section F) provincial parks. You can reserve a backcountry campsite on the Berg Lake trail in Mount Robson park at discovercamping.ca.

While it is possible to make an online reservation in Peter Lougheed Provincial Park, it isn't recommended – the website just emails a form to staff who still have to process the order, leading to delays and missed bookings. This will change as the system improves; for now, call the Kananaskis backcountry mailbox at 403-678-3136.

BC provincial parks like Mount Assiniboine and Akamina–Kishinena, require that you pay a self-registration fee, in cash, when you arrive at the campsite. If you prefer not to carry cash, you can reserve up to two weeks in advance for Akamina–Kishinena, Mount Assiniboine and Elk Lakes at discovercamping.ca/Backcountry. Remember to carry the proof of payment with you when you go. The online payment doesn't ensure a reservation or booking of any kind – it's just another way of paying for a campsite that is officially 'first come, first served.' The fee is between $5 and $12 per night per person in BC parks and these fees do change.

Other parks not mentioned here did not require any such reservations, fees, permits or passes at the time of writing.

Other passes and permits for national and provincial parks

For equestrians in the national parks, you must purchase the appropriate passes and permits for each member of your party. For example, each person needs a park entry permit and a backcountry permit. Horses are permitted on most trails but you will require a grazing permit at $1.90 per horse per day. A monthly grazing permit is $24.50 per horse. Equestrians can also obtain a 'chainsaw' permit for select trails, on demand. See pc.gc.ca/en/pn-np/ab/banff/activ/cheval-horse. (The GDTA would love to hear an update if you do clear a section of trail!)

Outside the national parks, equestrians in BC parks must contact the park authority and obtain a permit for your horses at least one week in advance. This is on a park-by-park basis and in BC only – Alberta parks allow horses on designated trails, sans permit. Refer to the 'Contacts' list, beginning at page 338. I do my best to indicate horse access for each of the segments of the main route of the GDT. Equestrians should be aware that an alternate horse route is being developed by the GDTA. Currently you must email the association (greatdividetrail@gmail.com) and ask permission for access to this map and check greatdividetrail.com.

Anglers wishing to catch a fish anywhere in the national parks must have a valid national parks fishing licence, which is $9.80 per day or $34.30 for the annual pass. Outside the national parks, you must hold a provincial fishing licence, which you can obtain online for BC at fishing.gov.bc.ca or for Alberta at albertaelm.com/licensing.page.

Banff National Park has two shelters that are available for reservations: Bryant Creek and Egypt Lake. These are basic accommodations that provide wooden bunk bed platforms (you need a mattress) and a wood-burning stove with a supply of firewood. There are no amenities like you would expect to find at an Alpine Club of Canada hut, such as at Elk Lakes. The cost is $6.80 per night per person and currently the shelters can be reserved online or through the Banff or Lake Louise visitor centre up to three months in advance.

The only ACC hut en route is Elk Lakes Cabin near the trailhead for Elk Lakes Provincial Park (BC), at the end of the Elk Lakes forest service road in segment 13. It costs $25 per night and can be reserved through the ACC by calling 403-678-3200, extension 0. The office is open from 8:30 am to 9:30 pm daily. Dogs aren't permitted at ACC huts.

Dogs: No permit required. However, you do need to check closures and regulations for each park to find out more about handling and areas where dogs aren't allowed. For example, although equestrians in groups of two or more can travel over Allenby Pass during the restricted period of August 1 to September 30, dogs aren't permitted during that time. (Since dogs are required to be on leash, I'm not sure how equestrians would travel with dogs in the national parks anyhow...)

Mountain bikes: No special permit required but you must be aware of closures and regulations in each of the parks. In this edition of the guidebook, I do my best to list bike access in the introduction for each segment.

Resupply strategies

The last step before you can put together an effective itinerary is to figure out how you will arrange for resupply. There are several strategies for doing this, from mailing yourself boxes of food you packed before the trip, to buying food in towns as you hike. Not unlike reserving campsites, an effective resupply strategy depends on figuring out where you're going to be and when you'll be there.

For this reason the GDTA campsite cheat sheet lists resupply points – places where you can send your parcels of food to pick up later. There are more resupply options available. For a full list, see under 'Resupply stations' at page 342. You will need to know the round-trip distance back to the main route so you can properly account for total distance when you construct your itinerary.

In theory the faster you hike, the fewer resupplies you need. For example, if I can hike all of Section C in six days and have no problem moving at that pace with six days of provisions in my backpack, then I wouldn't need to stop at intermediate resupply points like Assiniboine Lodge or Sunshine Village. However, I have prior experience hiking this section. I know how fast I can do it. Without that experience, you should use whatever previous trail experience you have, and in most cases plan for longer than you think it would normally take you to cover the same amount of distance on a maintained trail.

Generally you will prepack food and either send it by post before you leave, or drive the boxes around to the places that will hold them for you. If you have spare food and supplies at a planned resupply stop, you can send them ahead in a 'bounce-box.' Unlike other long-distance trails, though, the GDT doesn't normally have 'hiker boxes' – where you can leave excess food – or as many 'trail angels' for that matter. A trail angel is usually a past hiker or someone who is sympathetic who lives near the route and helps thru-hikers each season.

Buying your supplies in stores on the way takes time and usually more money, since grocery stores, if they exist along the GDT, cater to tourists passing through in droves but only for the day. With that said, you can buy enough good food in Waterton, Blairmore, Field and Jasper. Camping fuel, by the way, is available in those towns and at Kananaskis Lakes and Saskatchewan River Crossing. There are limits to what you can mail in boxes. Check with Canada Post, canadapost.ca/tools/pg/manual/PGnonmail-e.asp, or whichever courier you use.

For a sample resupply strategy, refer to the sample itinerary in Appendix 3 at page 331. Personally, on my hike, we used a 'trail manager,' a friend we could trust who would send out boxes on a prearranged schedule. This strategy worked for us because we could call him and ask to add or remove items from boxes he hadn't sent yet. We could also ask him to delay sending boxes or send them elsewhere. He even drove out one of the boxes along with a birthday cake that my partner, Julia, had secretly ordered. As a side note, our friend kept tabs on where we were and functioned as our emergency contact – if we didn't call in when he expected, he would have alerted authorities after an agreed amount of time.

Based on personal experience, I would advise contacting potential resupply points such as postal outlets, hotels, and resorts to confirm that they will hold a package for you and for how long. Ask in advance about holding fees. You may have to bring some cash to pay a nominal holding fee at some of the resorts. Keep in mind that you must have some form of picture ID and a second form of identification to pick up your parcel from postal outlets, and that they are only open during business hours, during the week.

Mailing supplies to yourself isn't as straightforward as you would think. When you put your resupply box or boxes together, you should start with a sturdy cardboard carton that has few markings on it. Use filler to deaden empty areas of the packed box or cut it down so items such as zip-locks full of juice crystals are not tossed around and punctured. Use a large label that clearly shows your name for general delivery and includes a return address.

You should consider packing a rolling supply parcel (bounce-box) that contains bulk items you may or may not need at the resupply point. Consider packing batteries, tape, memory cards, first-aid supplies, labelling material, bulk stamps, extra non-perishable food, and clothing like socks and underwear into that parcel. If you don't need the parcel you can send it to the next resupply station and add any items you no longer need to carry.

It is unlawful to mail any pressurized or combustible agent. For example, you cannot mail bear spray, shaving cream, matches or lighters. Fuel also cannot travel by mail. (As mentioned, you can purchase white gas (naphthalene), propane, and butane at every resupply point between sections on the GDT.)

If you are coming to Canada from anywhere but the USA, you should bring all your equipment with you and purchase food and other supplies (like bear spray) in Canada. Once in Canada, you can assemble the resupply parcels and then mail them out. Mailing parcels from overseas is very unreliable. Even parcels sent from the USA can stall interminably at the border at Canadian Customs.

The more preparation you put into mailing supplies to yourself, the better. Preparing your first resupply parcel and sending it off into the cogs of the postal system is an anxiety-inducing experience, especially if you live across the country. Canada Post allows you to insure your resupply parcels for a small charge. I highly recommend buying insurance, since this is the only way you can track your box if it fails to arrive. Regular air or ground mail is untraceable as well as unpredictable. Luckily, postal insurance is cheap.

On a final note about resupply, account for seasonal closures when mailing your package. Postal outlets will hold an item for up to two weeks, or longer if notified in time. Resorts have different policies. In cases where you may have to send your parcel to a resort, telephone in advance to ensure they can hold your supplies, and even record the name of the person you spoke with. Try to deal with someone who will be working through the entire season. Remember to ask in advance about holding fees.

Making your Itinerary

Your itinerary is your recipe for success on the GDT. Refer to the appendix 'Sample itineraries' on page 330 for real-life examples, including trail running and a horse trip.

There is no right way to plan for a hike. Everyone has their own method of approaching something like this. Ideally you will want eight weeks for hiking the extended length of the GDT, starting mid-July and ending by mid-September. So let's work with that time window and assume you want to hike NOBO to Mount Robson from Waterton Lakes NP. That gives you a maximum of 56 days to cover 979.0km at an overall average of 17.4km per day. "Whoa!" you might say. "I don't know if I can hike that far in a day." Too fast? Well, adjust the total time you have available or select different termini.

Covering 17.4km/day is an average pace, but remember, you must account for the extra distance to access the trail, resupply, and do any alternate routes. And unless you plan to hike every day, you will want to consider rest days, or '0' days (as in okm).

Accessing the termini: 6.4km in Waterton to get to the border, 0km in Robson because you finish at the road.

The extra distance to a resupply location: 0km for Coleman, staying on the main route; 17.4km for Kananaskis Lakes info centre (unless you hitchhike); 2km for Saskatchewan River Crossing; and 8km for Jasper (for walking into town and then back out of town to Whistlers campground, as an example).

Alternate routes: After reading through the list of alternate routes in Appendix 2, and the trail description, you decide to hike the Barnaby Ridge alternate in Section A. This subtracts 2.4km. (**Note:** although it is shorter, it will take more time to hike than the main route. This is generally the case with any of the alternate routes.)

Rest days: You decide to have an extra day in Waterton so you can ease into starting the GDT, and a rest day at each of the resupply points. Subtract six days from your total number of days available.

Okay, let's recalculate. You now have 1004.4km to cover in 50 days of hiking. That is an average pace of 20.1km/day. Now you can work with the list of campsites at the start of each section in this book, or download and print it as a single list from the GDTA, greatdividetrail.com/trip-planning -resources/campgrounds.

Start with the date of your first night camping. In this example you are spending July 15 and 16 at the main campground in the town of Waterton and planning to hike the lakeshore trail to monument 276 and back on the 16th without a big backpack. For the night of July 17, look for a campsite that's around 8km from the town campground (because you've already covered the first 12.8km of total distance, to the border and back). You see that the next-closest one on the list is Alderson Lake, at 13.3km. That's good; you read that it's all uphill and your pack will be heavy. For July 18 you see that your only choice is Akamina Creek campsite, which is off trail by 2.5km. July 19, Lone Lake. July 20, Jutland Creek. July 21, Southfork Lakes (on the Barnaby Ridge alternate). July 22, Lynx Creek campground. July 23, Coleman. This means you will arrive in Coleman after hiking about 23km that day and that you'll likely arrive in the late afternoon and require accommodation in town. Looking at the 'Accommodations' contacts on page 340, you see you should stay at A Safe Haven B&B because you read that the hosts are trail angels. You make a note on your itinerary to call them and book not only the 23rd but the 24th as well. When you call, you discover it is okay to send your resupply parcel to them, which makes things even easier!

Using the section outlines and trail descriptions in this guidebook or the cheat sheet provided by the GDTA at greatdividetrail.com/trip -planning-resources/campgrounds, work your way through the list, plotting where you will be staying each night. Consider characteristics of the campsite such as its proximity to the GDT and whether or not you need a backcountry permit for it. It can be well worth the fee to stay in a national parks campsite if it has a food storage locker, for instance.

Mount Robson and Peter Lougheed provincial parks will require reservations too. The nights you aren't at reserved sites are a bit more flexible, but you will want to arrive at a reserved site on the evening you booked it for. While it's certainly possible to adjust your reservations during your trip, the change will cost you another reservation fee and the time on the phone or in the visitor centre with parks staff. Most importantly, you might not be able to find available campsites like you could when you initially reserved months in advance.

Building out the details of your itinerary, you can start to visualize what time of day you will arrive in town and whether the place where you plan to pick up your resupply parcel will be open. You can tell where you need to reserve accommodations. You will see gaps in your planning, like the extra 5km round trip to Akamina Creek campsite you will have to hike to keep your average pace. You may decide to skip a rest day at Saskatchewan River Crossing, for example, because it is too costly, and plan to spend a rest day at the highest point on the GDT, near Michele Lakes, or fishing at Pinto Lake. Be creative. Register with the Great Divide Trail Hikers Facebook group page (Facebook.com/groups/GDThikers) and get advice from others who have done the route. The more detailed your itinerary, the better.

Important tips for hiking the GDT

Outdoor gear is so specialized now that you can find companies devoted to making equipment solely for long-distance hiking and even ultra trail running. There are websites, books, and weekend seminars on these subjects. In my experience on the GDT, lightest is not always best. For example, I know I need a tent to get away from the mosquitos in the evening – it's my 'sanity' dome and I'll carry the extra weight to afford that luxury, even if I'm hiking alone.

In this section I focus on some of the specific challenges you might encounter on the GDT that should influence your planning and preparation for any trip length. Let's start with the most obvious, your safety.

Safety

Refer to the very back of this book, page 350, for emergency contacts and the procedure for using your inReach device or satellite transponder to initiate a rescue. Don't be afraid of who is going to pay for rescue. Just call.

To start with, let someone reliable know where you are going and when they can expect to hear from you. Give them a copy of your itinerary. Work out in advance whether that person will call for help on your behalf – it's a huge responsibility and shouldn't be taken lightly. There should be no confusion in your instructions. With that said, be realistic. If you are hiking for a week, chances are high that you could get behind by a day, perhaps two.

For this and many other reasons, I encourage you to either buy or borrow an emergency transponder. In fact, you can combine several gadgets in one with devices such as the Garmin 'inReach Explorer+' (see garmin.com). It is a robust GPS, emergency transponder, weather radio, and satellite communications device, all in one. You do not necessarily even need to contact family and friends to let them know where you are; they can track you with a web link which you give them before your trip, using a feature called MapShare. It also plays nicely with your smart phone with a free app. Keep in mind that you do need to activate a 'satellite plan' and in some cases a GEOS membership. If you rent, or borrow one from a friend, make sure you set up the emergency contact features beforehand and that the plans are paid up and active – take nothing for granted.

If you are loosely hiking with a partner and think you have different schedules or route options, consider each of you taking a transponder so you can stay in touch. By adding your hiking partner as an emergency contact, they may be able to locate and assist you in an emergency. The

...in inReach Explorer+ is a two-way communications device, allowing you to message from one device to another.

Emergency transponders currently rely on sending an emergency signal to GEOS when you press your SOS button (learn more at geosalliance.com). GEOS contacts local authorities around your location, and if your device is so equipped, they will stay in contact with you by text to update you on the progress of the rescuers. Most of the search and rescue (SAR) covering the GDT is professionally operated by the federal and provincial governments, the exception being outside the parks (in BC) in sections A, B, D, and G, where local SAR volunteers would come to your assistance.

Rescuers will expect to find a car parked at a trailhead indicating that the people needing rescue are still out there. It is exceptionally rare for them to deal with thru-hikers who normally do not have a car parked anywhere along the route. This means your emergency contact (listed with your one-way beacon device) should have a copy of your itinerary so that rescuers can get all the information they can – otherwise, they could go to the nearest trailhead and call the rescue off when they do not find a car parked there. These rescue professionals field a lot of distress calls each summer with limited resources, and they need to move on to the next case, based on evidence they find or don't find.

In any event, Parks Canada states: "While satellite phones and personal locator beacon devices such as SPOT can be useful, they cannot be relied upon absolutely. All backcountry travellers should be familiar with the abilities and limitations of the devices they chose to carry. They should also be prepared to carry out self-rescue and to keep themselves and their partners warm and sheltered during the time it takes for a rescue team to reach them." (pc.gc.ca/eng/pn-np/mtn/securiteenmontagne -mountainsafety/programme-program/res-sar)

Access to a cell phone signal is essentially non-existent for 99% of the GDT. Likewise, satellite positioning is accurate up to 5m on perfect terrain, with a fully powered device, with no obstructions or bad weather. If you trigger your beacon from the north side of a tall mountain on a snowy/ rainy day, though, your reported position could be quite far from your actual one.

This guidebook, the GDTA official map online and the Atlas Guides app provide information on trails that lead away from the GDT to the nearest road or vehicle access point if you need to leave the route or alternate route in an emergency. Keep in mind that nearby roads likely aren't very busy. In any case, you should be self-sufficient and able to survive long enough to await rescue. If you are hiking solo and are nervous about doing a certain section alone, get in contact with other hikers on the Facebook forum and find a partner. Hiking with someone else or with a group is safer than going alone.

If you are bringing a dog with you, its safety is also up to you. Parks Canada advises:

> Pets are welcome in the backcountry but must be leashed at all times. To a wild animal, your dog is a canine – a predator. Wildlife may flee, endangering themselves or their young. Alternatively, they may respond aggressively, endangering you and your pet. The best way to care for wildlife and your pet is to leash your animal companions.

I know more than one climber or backcountry skier who has not called for a rescue and painfully dragged themselves out with terrible injuries because they heard that Parks Canada would make them pay for rescue if they didn't have a valid pass or backcountry permit. This simply is not true. According to Parks Canada: "Rescue costs are normally recovered from the park user fees paid by visitors upon entry to the park" (pc.gc.ca/eng/pn-np/mtn/securiteenmontagne-mountainsafety/ete -summer.aspx#rescue).

Be extra cautious on any roadways shared with vehicles. The GDT crosses and follows three highways for a short distance of no more than 5km. In Jasper, however, there is a 22km road walk for thru-hikers listed as the main route. Yellowhead Highway 16 is an extremely busy road, full of distracted drivers during the summer months. It only takes a second of inattention while gawking at the scenery for a driver to swerve slightly onto the shoulder and injure or kill a pedestrian or cyclist. In fact, your presence on the side of the road is another distraction. For this reason, there are three alternate routes listed in particular for the GDT out of Jasper, at the start of Section F. I strongly urge you to arrange for a shuttle out of Jasper if you aren't interested in hiking one of the alternate routes. As for the other highway walking, stay well off the road and be vigilant. Equestrians should arrange for transportation rather than follow a highway shoulder.

I have scattered other safety tips throughout this book. In all cases, the more research you do about the GDT and hiking in the Canadian Rockies, the better. If you want to read about rescue stories through the GEOS centre, go to geosresponse.com/rescues-in-the-news.html.

Bears and safety around wildlife

Whenever I do presentations about the GDT, one of the first questions is inevitably: "Did you see any bears?" The answer, of course, is 'yes.' I have had many bear encounters on the GDT, with grizzly and black bears. I've only been charged once. That was in 2009 when exploring the Muskwa–Kechika Management Area for a possible northern extension to the GDT. In that case, I only carried a bear 'banger' as a means of deterrence (a noisemaker, essentially). The bear was unfazed by the first bang and I had to reload the finicky device while the bear charged at me. From that moment on, I have advocated for bear spray and will even carry it trail running, when I count my equipment weight by the gram.

The thing about bear spray is that it works better than any other deterrent, including firearms. It is relatively cheap and easy to use. If you don't have it, and the bear doesn't retreat when you stand your ground and talk firmly to it, you may either have to fight back or lay down in what I call the wrestler's pose (it definitely isn't playing dead): "Drop to the ground face down, interlace your fingers over the back of your neck and spread your legs to make it more difficult for the bear to turn you over" (wildsmart.ca/bearsmart.htm).

How does that sound? However, with bear spray in hand, you will likely be more confident when you encounter a bear, more able to stand your ground and avoid conflict. If you must use the spray, the bear will forever associate that burning sensation with humans and will likely avoid people in the future. This is called adverse conditioning (for the bear, not you).

While I hike, I practise drawing my bear spray canister and popping the safety off with a flick of my thumb (carefully). That way, when I do have a bear encounter, I almost unconsciously have the bear spray ready to use at a moment's notice. I have several different holsters for different activities and I know how to use each of them. My favorite is the SCAT belt (scatbelt.com) because it's easy to draw and doesn't flop around while I hike or run. If I take my backpack off, the SCAT belt comes with me. Avoid using the bear spray except when you need it. A canister only offers about eight seconds of continuous spray, and once you use it the plastic nozzle may deteriorate after a while and stop working.

Avoid bear encounters with these guidelines from Wildsmart.ca, which I've adapted for the GDT:

- Do not approach or feed bears. This could elicit an unsafe response that could lead to human injury and/or the destruction of the bear.
- To avoid surprise encounters (in areas of limited visibility or loud streamflows), make lots of noise by using your voice and calling out "hey bear" until you move out of that area. Trail runners and riders should call out more often the faster they are travelling.
- Watch for fresh evidence of bear activity, e.g., tracks, scat, diggings, or overturned rocks and logs. If you see these signs, be sure to call out or

be prepared to leave the area or hike around it. Have your bear spray in your hand and ready to use.

- Travel in groups. This includes equestrians and cyclists as well as hikers and runners.
- Cyclists, trail runners and equestrians need to slow down in areas of limited visibility, and call out, like hikers, to warn unseen bears of your presence around blind corners and in bushy areas.
- Keep your dog on leash. Don't let it get away if surprised. Ideally, your dog will sit quietly beside you in the event of an encounter, under control.
- Carry bear spray and know how to use it. Have it handy and don't pack it away. Keep it within reach at night. Check the expiry date on the container and replace as necessary. Dispose of old bear spray with your community's toxics roundup or give it away at the end of your trip to another hiker if you are flying and can't bring it on the plane with you.
- If you see or smell a dead animal and know there is a bear around, leave the area. Bears will defend their kills or scavenged carcasses.
- Respect all trail closures and information signs. They are there for your safety. Check in with info centres, monitor the GDTA website for alerts, and watch for notices posted at trailheads.
- Store your food and smelly items like toothpaste in a bear locker or hang it from poles provided for that purpose at campsites. If no facilities exist at your campsite, improvise a food hang 4m off the ground and at least 2m away from the tree, or use an approved bear canister or bag such as the Ursack (ursack.com).
- Don't eat food in your tent. Keep your tent scent-free if possible. Don't dispose of food around your tent. Never sleep with your food!
- Be aware of your surroundings. Don't wear headphones while you're hiking, riding, or running.
- Do not attempt to climb a tree, swim, or run away (trail runners). All bears in the Canadian Rockies can climb whatever you can and run faster than you can run or ride. Forget swimming. Stand your ground and talk evenly and forcefully to the bear.
- Don't stare in the bear's eyes. This can elicit aggression. Easier said than done...

Other wildlife encounters can be potentially dangerous as well, not just bears. All animals, including us humans, have an automatic response to a surprise encounter: fight, flight or freeze. Wildsmart.ca has information on what to do if you encounter a cougar, elk, moose, etc. In general, avoid being near any mother and its young – leave the area. Moose and ungulates in general can be deadly defending their calves.

Parks Canada has good information on this topic, at pc.gc.ca/en/pn-np/mtn/ours-bears/securite-safety/ours-humains-bears-people. Bear spray is available in every outdoor store in the Rockies and at a discounted price at the Banff town hall while supplies last. Although you can bring bear spray overland into Canada if the label is intact, you can't take it back into the USA if you declare it – and it's up to you whether to declare it or not. Airplanes don't allow bear spray at all, whether in carry-on or checked luggage.

> We arrived in Coleman today at the Safe Haven B&B (roast beef for dinner, yummmmm!). Two of us ended up taking a shortcut down from Willoughby Ridge (A40); about 400m down we turned a corner near a creek and came across a mama grizzly and her two cubs. They were about 20m away and seemed fine with ignoring us, but we were both glad we had bear bangers and spray handy. We ended up doing a couple km of bushwacking to avoid them. It was a good reminder to try to make noise whenever you approach flowing water so you don't scare the bears.
>
> —Ben Martin, July 7, 2016, on the Great Divide Trail Hikers Facebook group page.

Remember, the desired outcome of any encounter is for you and the bear to peacefully go in your respective directions. Sometimes bears will run off and other times they will just wait for you to clear the area. Each bear is an individual having a good day or a bad day, just like you. You will likely encounter a bear if you are hiking a significant portion of the GDT, which is great. Bears put the wild in 'wilderness.' Just be prepared and carry bear spray. Don't include books on 'bear attacks' as your nightly reading material on the trail.

Weather

The warmest month in the Canadian Rockies is July, which averages 23°C (73°F) in towns near the GDT. During the summer solstice, the Rockies experience an average of 16.5 hours of daylight. Considering the long, relatively warm days, it surprises visitors to learn that the snow pack persists on high passes and the northern aspects of mountains until late July. Overnight lows in the valley bottoms usually remain above freezing. However, keep in mind that the air cools 0.7°C for every 100m of elevation gain, so plan for lows of −5°C (23°F) in selecting your gear.

The highest temperatures at valley bottom rarely go above 30°C (86°F). Violent thunderstorms typically accompany these hot spells in July and August. In the mountains, these storms appear from nowhere and advance very quickly, with precipitation that can fall as rain, hail, or snow (or a mixture of all three if you're unlucky). There is no such thing as a 'warm' rain in the Rockies, and hypothermia is a real concern in such conditions if you are caught out with insufficient gear. If you are on a ridge crest or summit, get to lower ground if you hear a thunderstorm approaching! Better yet, avoid ridge crests if an electrical storm is looming. Either wait for the storm to pass before venturing up or divert to a lower alternate route.

Mosquitos, ticks and flies

The valley bottoms in the Canadian Rockies have a blessedly short mosquito season, in late June or early July. At higher elevations – where the GDT is located – mosquito season may last through July and toward the end of August, especially in areas with stagnant water such as a shallow lake or boggy meadow. A few hard frosts in August usually clear the air. The wetter the season, the more mosquitos there are. Mosquito-borne illnesses include the West Nile virus (canada.ca/en/public-health/services/diseases/west-nile-virus.html). So far, mosquitos aren't spreading Zika virus in Canada. There are rare cases of dog heartworm, though.

The most annoying biting insect in the Canadian Rockies is likely the horsefly, prevalent from June through August at all elevations of the GDT. Hordes of these flies may follow you at times, keeping you in sight through their brightly striped eyes until they get a chance to bite hard with their scissor-like jaws. You'll find that deer flies and blackflies join in the seasonal fun. However, their bites are slightly less painful. Though annoying, they aren't known to spread disease like mosquitos.

Tick season arrives before the snow clears from the high passes of the GDT in April, and lasts until the middle of June. You'll find ticks all summer and fall where sheep gather. I have only encountered ticks in the lower elevations of the first two sections, where cattle graze in the Castle and Bow/Crow forest districts of Alberta. Keep your guard up for the Rocky Mountain wood tick in subalpine meadows and other grassy areas. This tick can transmit Rocky Mountain spotted fever. This is a very serious and potentially lethal disease that develops within 12 days after an infected tick burrows into your skin. Early symptoms include chills, headaches and muscle pains, which later develop into a fever before turning into a sickly rash covering much of the body. Medical clinics in the area are aware of this disease and should be consulted if you suspect such an infection. *Keep the tick in a zip lock bag with a bit of moistened toilet paper in it, so that you can bring it with you to the clinic*! If you don't keep the tick, most doctors will advise you to take a six-week course of antibiotics as soon as possible to avoid future complications.

There is an active tick surveillance program in Alberta to track the spread of the blacklegged ticks that can spread Lyme disease. (The Rocky Mountain wood tick is a different species and isn't known to spread the disease.) Here are the findings by Alberta Health (visithealth.alberta.ca/health-info/lyme-disease.html and click the subhead "Tick submissions and Lyme disease cases):

> From 2013 and 2015, there was approximately a three-fold increase in the number of ticks submitted by Albertans. The proportion of blacklegged ticks positive for *B. burgdorferi* has not increased.
>
> Based on the current evidence, blacklegged ticks are not reproducing in Alberta.
>
> In Alberta, the risk of being bitten by a blacklegged tick is low. The risk of being bitten by a blacklegged tick infected with *B. burgdorferi*, the bacteria that can cause Lyme disease in humans, is even lower.

Europeans should be aware that the North American strain of Lyme disease is different and potentially debilitating, not to be taken lightly. Whereas Lyme disease may be treated like a common cold in Scandinavian countries, it is potentially more serious in Canada.

With any tick bite, there is the potential for you or your dog to display symptoms of 'tick paralysis,' caused by a little-understood neurotoxin. I've witnessed this myself when my daughter had partial paralysis in her face which passed as soon as we removed the tick. If you or a companion, whether animal or human, is bitten, keep the tick (as already mentioned) and submit it to Alberta Health for free testing as part of their tick monitoring program. The testing happens within a week normally and you will know for sure if the tick had the bacteria that can cause Lyme disease.

Your best defence on the GDT is awareness of ticks and your gear choices. Wear light-coloured, long clothing. Tuck pants into socks or gaiters and your shirt at your waist line. If you see ticks on your clothing while hiking, do a tick check alone or with your partner when you stop for breaks. Ticks will crawl around for hours and days once they get on you. Keep this in mind when you bring gear into your tent at night, especially your backpack! If you use a fully enclosed tent, it's a simple matter to scan for ticks before going to sleep and rest assured that no more are crawling into the tent to join you during the night. Consider doing a scalp check with your hiking partner. Though ticks prefer the hairline, they will bite anywhere, in my experience. It is a much more involved matter to do a tick check of horses and dogs but they'll love the attention.

If you find a tick embedded in your skin, resist the urge to panic.

Instead, pull out your first aid kit, get your tweezers and lightly grasp the tick as close to the skin as possible. Start gently pulling at it. Use small, repeated tugs. The tick will complain and kick at the air, and the repeated pressure will convince the tick to let go on its own. If you use the tweezers in a panic, too tightly, you will end up leaving the tick's mouthparts behind, under the skin, which could lead to infection, especially if you try to cut them out yourself, causing more harm to the area.

Gear

There are many books and online resources devoted to this subject. I recommend *Trail Life*, Ray Jardine's guide to lightweight backpacking, rayjardine.com/ray-way/Books/Trail-Life/index.htm. Although written for a spectrum of wilderness enthusiasts, this book thoughtfully discusses the challenges that face all thru-hikers. Jardine's backpacking methods aren't for everyone, but the topics he presents will stimulate your own ideas and more mindful planning of your thru-hike. Andrew Skurka's *The Ultimate Hiker's Gear Guide: Tools & Techniques to Hit the Trail* (2nd ed., 2017) is another good resource. Visit andrewskurka.com for more information. Check out backpackinglight.com while you are at it. Remember to use the Great Divide Trail Hiker's Facebook forum (Facebook.com/groups/GDThikers) and the resources offered by the GDTA at greatdividetrail.com.

Here are some concerns specific to hiking on the GDT that you may want to consider:

Your feet will be wet nearly every day. Waterproof footwear, Gore-Tex socks or anything else claiming to keep your feet dry won't work. They'll probably make it worse. Use footwear that you've tested on the trail before and that is quick-drying. If you use runners, maybe pack an extra pair in your bounce-box, in case they wear out too soon. Some hikers swear by Crocs as a camp shoe and even for hiking in all day. Sandals don't work off-trail in my experience – you need a barrier to keep pine needles and other debris from getting stuck under your feet and you don't want to keep stopping to shake them out. Trail runners (and hikers) should consider mini-gaiters, that are super light and keep stuff out of running shoes. Full-sized gaiters are overkill unless you insist on hiking in shorts.

I recommend light-coloured long pants that you can roll above the knee for most stream crossings. Supplex nylon and like materials are quick-drying *and* mosquito-proof. Be warned, though, that if you wear shorts through any segment described as 'bushy,' you had best be a masochist with an ample first aid kit! If the pants are light-coloured and you tuck them into your socks or gaiters, you can easily flick ticks off before they find a place to burrow under your skin.

Whatever shelter you use, make sure it can withstand a generous coating of wet summertime snow. A hammock will limit your sleeping choices because so much of the trail is in the alpine, where you won't find trees large enough to suspend it. Hammocks aren't permitted on the Skyline trail. Use a good sleeping pad and pack a repair kit if you use an inflatable mattress. I use red Tuck tape as my repair kit. As mentioned, a mosquito-proof shelter is gold on the GDT – or perhaps a collar of netting at the base of your tarp that you can tuck under your sleeping pad at night.

Hiking poles are very helpful for cross-country travel and fording streams. I use light, sectioned, carbon-fibre poles from Black Diamond for trail running and hiking.

Solar panels sound like a good idea, but in my experience they usually end up just being extra weight. Instead, consider bringing a battery pack that can recharge your devices. Remember to save energy on your smart phone by turning off its cell and Bluetooth functionality. My iPhone can last four days with cell reception disabled. Also turn down the screen brightness and turn the device off during the night. Sleep with your devices to keep them warm through cold nights. Cold batteries are inefficient. Disable features like 'raise to wake' on the iPhone.

Have good rain gear and dry clothing for the tent in the evening. I prefer a merino wool top and bottom, and keep it in a waterproof bag during the day. Resist the urge to wear it during the day; put on your damp clothes instead – you'll be thankful in the evening.

Consider a large, ultra-lightweight dry bag such as the 65-litre SealLine ILBE Dry Bag with a purge valve. This model is designed to fit inside your backpack and accommodate all your gear. After you seal it up, you can open the purge valve and expel excess air. I gave up on backpack covers and supposedly waterproof backpacks; I just needed to know my gear would stay dry no matter what.

I've already mentioned the Garmin inReach device and Garmin Astro dog beacon but want to clarify something with your electronic devices and gizmos: they won't work if they run out of battery power, so make sure you have at least large-scale maps for your area and a compass (and know how to use those). My other suggestion is to minimize your gizmos to hopefully just one device, like your smart phone with the GDT app that has all the maps pre-downloaded.

Telus and Rogers are the main cell phone providers around the GDT. I recommend Telus, since they own most of the towers and seem to have the best reception. Visit telus.com. There are Telus mobility providers in many towns near the GDT. Instead of buying a SIM card for local service, it might just be easier to see if your current provider can affordably extend your existing plan to western Canada. All the towns along the GDT have cell

GDT Thru-Hiker Special

Trails   Updated 2016-11-28

Waypoints Updated 2016-11-29

Photos: Downloaded: 5.7 MB ⬤

🔘 NR Canada Toporama ⬤
   Displayed on Map 641.5 MB

⭘ OpenStreetMap ⬤
   Downloaded 107.9 MB

⭘ Online Maps Only

service except Saskatchewan River Crossing, where you can find wireless internet access at The Crossing for a fee.

Remember to download the photos and maps into the GDT app before taking it on the trail!

Regulations and trail etiquette

The GDT passes through several distinct administrative districts: national parks, provincial recreation areas, provincial parks, wildland parks, wilderness areas and forest districts (or public land use zones). It is your responsibility to be aware of the regulations and abide by them. Permits and passes generally have the regulations stated on them. You can get more information from the appropriate info centre or website – this list only covers the main points that will affect your planning.

Provincial recreation areas and parks

- Camping in designated campsites only. Backcountry permit required. No random camping (making an impromptu campsite outside of designated campsites).
- Fires only permitted in provided facilities. Use of deadfall not permitted. Check current fire restrictions.
- Mountain biking on designated trails only.
- Dogs must be leashed.
- The use of horses and pack animals is limited to designated areas and trails.
- Consumption of alcohol is restricted to registered front country campgrounds. It is prohibited on trails, beaches, roads, washrooms, cook shelters, day use areas and picnic areas.

Wildlands and public land use zones

- Random camping permitted. You must be at least 1km from any backcountry facility, recreation area or roadway. Special conditions and permits may apply to some areas.
- Dogs must be leashed in wildland parks.
- It is recommended that dogs be leashed in public land use zones but not mandatory.
- Mountain bikes permitted EXCEPT in sensitive wildlife areas such as designated wildlife corridors. Check with visitor centres for more info.
- The use of horses and pack animals is limited to designated areas and trails.

National parks

- You require an entry pass to be anywhere in the park.

- You require a backcountry permit to stay anywhere overnight other than roadside accommodation and car campgrounds.
- In most areas, you must camp in designated campsites using the prepared tent pads.
- You may stay no longer than three nights in any campsite.
- In random camping areas, you must camp more than 5km from trailheads, at least 50m off trail and 70m from the nearest water source.

JASPER NATIONAL PARK ADDITIONAL BACKCOUNTRY REGULATIONS

- Hammocks aren't permitted at any Skyline Trail campsites nor at Jonas Cutoff.
- Two nights is the maximum length of stay at Snowbowl, Curator and Tekarra campsites (Skyline Trail), Jonas Cutoff and Four Point campsites (Brazeau Loop) and all wildland areas.
- Maximum group size is ten people in semi-primitive and primitive areas.
- Maximum group size is six people in wildland areas.
- Three nights is the maximum length of stay at most semi-primitive and primitive areas.
- Fires are only permitted in the metal grates provided in semi-primitive and primitive areas.
- Fires are not permitted in wildland areas.
- Due to lack of wood, fires are not permitted on the Skyline Trail, nor at Jonas Cutoff and Four Point campgrounds on the Brazeau Loop, nor in any wildland areas.
- To reduce your campsite's attractiveness to bears and other wildlife, all food, garbage, toiletries and cooking equipment must be hung from the food storage cables or in the food lockers provided at designated campsites. In wildland camping areas, bear-resistant containers are mandatory for storing food. Please clean food lockers after use.
- Use the pit toilets provided. When there are no facilities nearby, select a spot away from trails or campsites and at least 70m from water sources. Dig a hole 12 to 16cm. to the dark-coloured, biologically active soil layer. Loosely fill the hole with soil afterward. Use as little toilet paper as possible and carry it out or burn it.
- In regards to the mountain caribou habitat zones, including the Maligne River trail and alternate route:
  » Stay on designated trails; if you see caribou, give them space.
  » Dogs are not allowed in caribou habitat (segments 26, 27 and 28).

» Avoid hiking in caribou habitat during calving season (June to early July) and rut season (late September to early October).

All areas

It is illegal to remove, deface, injure or destroy plants, fossils and rocks.

Trail etiquette

From LeaveNoTrace.ca/principles: plan ahead and prepare, travel and camp on durable surfaces, dispose of waste properly (or pack it out), leave what you find, minimize campfire impacts, respect wildlife, and be considerate of other visitors.

Units of measurement and conversion tables

Welcome to Canada! If you are more familiar with the imperial units of measurement, use the following tables to help you convert from metric:

Temperature

0 °F	-17.78 °C	
10 °F	-12.22 °C	
20 °F	-6.67 °C	your sleeping bag rating for the Rockies in summer
30 °F	-1.11 °C	
32 °F	0 °C	freezing/melting point of water
40 °F	4.44 °C	
50 °F	10.00 °C	
60 °F	15.56 °C	
70 °F	21.11 °C	average high temperature for Jasper in July
80 °F	26.67 °C	
90 °F	32.22 °C	highest recorded temperature for Banff in August
98.6 °F	37 °C	human body temperature
100 °F	37.78 °C	

Distance / length

1 inch	2.54 cm
1 foot, or 12 inches	30.48 cm
1 yard	91.44 cm, or 0.91 m
1 mile	1.609 km

How to use this book

Intended audience

While I've written this book primarily for hikers and backpackers, I've increased the scope of this edition to include trail running, horse travel, mountain bike access and canine companions where possible. The trail descriptions are for those planning to travel any length of the GDT, whether NOBO or SOBO.

Sections and segments

You will notice that I've broken the main route into seven sections and labelled them with letters, A to G. Section F finishes at the original northern terminus, Mount Robson. I've divided each section into segments, which mostly coincide with access points where you can get on and off the route. Each segment has several waypoints that are numbered sequentially south to north in each section: for example, 'a1' to 'a48' in Section A and 'b1' to 'b40' in Section B. The waypoints were originally plotted with orienteering in mind: they are 'legs' that allow you to plot a course using a compass bearing. I do indicate intermediate distances within the longer legs, such as water sources, bridges, fords, highpoints and campsites.

Distance outline

Each section begins with a table that outlines the distances between campsites, resupply locations, and highpoints en route. This can be helpful in the planning stage and on the trail. The outline includes cumulative NOBO and SOBO distances. If a location is off-route I note it with an asterisk (*), and if you need a national parks backcountry permit to stay there, it will say (NP). If it is in a provincial park and requires a fee, it will be listed as (AB Parks) or (BC Parks). I also make special notes on some of the distance outlines. Not all waypoints are listed in the outline. For a full list of waypoints and exact coordinates, refer to the Waypoint list at the back of the book, page 345.

Elevation profiles

Every segment has a graphic from the Atlas Guides GDT app showing the elevation profile. The graphic shows the total NOBO ascent and descent as well as the average grade and distance. The graph shows the elevation in metres and the distance in kilometres. The colourful pin icons show campsites, parking areas, trailheads, junctions, summits, water sources, and other useful information, but are only practicable while using the app. The waypoint codes aren't displayed on this profile, however; they are mostly included as an alternate header in the app itself.

Difficulty rating and restrictions

This is a subjective rating for each segment. If I were to chart the difficulty of all 34 segments of the GDT, they would fall into a certain order. So, 'easy' means the segment is comparatively easy! I note if horses or bikes are permitted. Assume that dogs are allowed unless I state 'no dogs.' (Only segments 26, 27, and 28 in Jasper National Park were closed to dogs at the time of writing.) I thought about including a green, blue, black, and double-black rating, but compared to other trails in the parks, the GDT would mostly be black and double-black.

Maps

I list the National Topographic System (NTS) 1:50 000 scale maps and the applicable Gemtrek maps if available. The Gemtrek maps have the GDT route labelled on them as well as all the other trails. Gemtrek has ground-truthed all the trails on each of their maps with a GPS track. Keep in mind that the GDTA offers a track for download to your GPS. Tracks are available as Google Earth files, and you can open several of them at once and toggle map overlays, such as alternates and campsites. The Atlas Guides GDT app includes detailed maps which must be downloaded to your phone before your departure so that they will work when offline. The hiker's forum has links to printable map sets based on the NTS ones. To see a complete list of maps, see page 344.

Jurisdiction

Each segment lists the land manager(s) having jurisdiction over the area, such as national parks or forest districts. Refer to the 'Contacts' appendix for the specifics, including emergency contact info. It is a good idea to consult the national park websites or info centres before going, to learn of any trail restrictions or closures. The GDTA website tries to centralize these alerts and keep them up to date, especially during the hiking season.

Access

This is a description of where you can access the main route. Some segments have intermediate access points. Not all of them are practical and are only listed for emergency use. Segments are accessible at both ends.

Camping

I list the front country car campgrounds and backcountry campsites as well as any cabins. The distance outline at the start of each section shows this information in point form. The GDTA has an excellent list on their website, with distances, amenities, and permit requirements. If you plan to stay at a hotel, car campground, hostel, or B&B, I highly recommend making a reservation well in advance of your trip. See page 340 for a list of accommodations en route.

Information sources

At the beginning of each segment, I refer to other pertinent sources of information. For example, for segment 1, I list the Waterton Lakes National Park Information Centre. If you need to contact them, refer to the 'Contacts' appendix starting on page 338 for that information. I may also list other references here such as other guidebooks.

Remember, when you have wifi or cell coverage, to sync your GDT app. This will upload your comments and download others'. Check the GDTA website and any park websites for last-minute closures. You may learn an area is closed due to an aggressive bear or that an essential bridge is washed out. Don't rely solely on the information in this guidebook, as it is meant primarily as a planning resource and route description.

Resupply

This is a list of postal outlets, hotels, and resorts to which you can send a resupply parcel in advance. The GDTA has an excellent resource online which they keep updated by adding new contacts and removing ones that don't accept packages anymore.

Special notes

Information about a segment that doesn't fit under one of the previously mentioned headings is included here.

Route descriptions

The route descriptions focus on navigation and route-finding and include distances, waypoints, elevations, alternate routes, maps, and photographs. Terms like spring, seasonal spring, seep, seismic line, or hand cutline provide useful information about the characteristics of the trail, reaffirming some obvious but important aids to navigation. Waypoint data is indicated in brackets immediately following the location keyword stated in the text. For example:

> A steep ascent leads the route away from Blakiston Creek and after a gentle section the climb becomes steep again before attaining a saddle (2240, 1.6, a13) north of Festubert Mountain. A moderate descent on long switchbacks brings the trail down

to the Lone Lake outflow (2015, 1.0, a14). Lone Lake campsite is 200m farther, on the north side of the lake, and the warden cabin is not far beyond it.

The Festubert Mountain saddle waypoint information immediately follows the keyword, "saddle." Similarly, the Lone Lake waypoint follows the keyword "outflow." The first number is the approximate elevation in metres. The second number is the distance in kilometres from the previous waypoint. Therefore, Lone Lake outflow is 1.0km from Festubert Saddle. These values are now accurate within 100m increments based on actual GPS tracks. The third piece of data refers to a coordinate in the Waypoints index at the back of the book. The order of information within the brackets is always the same except at the beginning of a section, where the waypoint may be repeated from the end of the previous section of trail description. In that case, the distance is listed as '0.' Except for the Coral Pass alternate, waypoints only appear in the main route description.

I break the route description in each segment into blocks of text. Each block has a header such as

Lineham Ridge (Tamarack Summit) to Lone Lake campsite (7.9km, 334m up, 819m down)

This block of text describes the entire trail between the highest point on Lineham Ridge (also known as Tamarack Summit) and the Lone Lake campsite to the north. The distance, 7.9km, describes the length of this portion of the trail. In this case, Lineham Ridge has a waypoint but the campsite does not. The waypoint, a14, occurs 200m before the campsite, at the Lone Lake outflow. Therefore, this distance in the header is equal to the difference between waypoints a11 and a14, plus 200m to the campsite. If you find this confusing, don't read the headers and just go by the distances listed in each waypoint. The headers are used to describe useful landmarks for planning your day – you want to know where the main campsites are, for instance.

In this edition of the guidebook, I've added intermediate distances between waypoints. For example, by stating that the campsite is 200m farther, hikers will know where to expect it. These are cumulative distances. Where they occur several times between waypoints, they add up to the distance stated in the following waypoint. The only exception is the Six Passes alternate route, where I state absolute distances, which better fit the nature of that trail description.

New for this edition is the total elevation gain and loss stated in the header for each block of route description. Those elevations add up to the total elevation gain and loss expressed in the elevation profile graphic at the start of each segment. Hikers had commented that my simply stating the elevation with the waypoint data wasn't user-friendly. Hopefully, this change rectifies that issue.

You generally won't have any problem with water sources on the GDT. I've included notices to NOBO and SOBO hikers in the route descriptions where they should pick up water and the distance to the next water source, where it is important.

If you are using the Atlas Guides GDT app, you should know that it doesn't have all the waypoints listed in this guidebook. Where they do align, the waypoint number will appear as a subtitle, such as 'Lynx d1.'

Map graphics

Within the route descriptions, there are topographical 1:80 000 scale maps that graphically display summits, mountain ranges, water bodies, towns, trails and structures. In addition, these maps display campsites and waypoints mentioned in the description and are really only intended to give you a general idea of where to find the trail. Get the appropriate topo maps for your trip, as well as the GDT app from atlasguides.com. There is a map key beginning on page 344.

Alternate routes

I have placed alternate route descriptions in the flow of the route description for NOBO hikers. I refer to the alternate route name where it rejoins the main GDT route in the north, for the benefit of SOBO hikers. The only exception to this pattern occurs in segment 29, where there are three alternate routes at the start the segment. There is a list of all the alternate routes starting on page 324. I include ratings and other info that can aid in planning.

Selected hikes

This appendix, starting on page 316, will save you some time if you are looking for a day, overnight, or weekend trip. I recommend route variations between convenient access points, alternate routes, and access trails. These descriptions summarize details such as the length of the route, elevations and highlights, and then refer you to the main route description for further details.

Resources and contact information

This is a list of other resources and contacts that will help you prepare for your journey. Rather than repeat these contacts throughout the book, I've decided to group them together at the end, starting on page 338. Emergency contacts and procedures are at the back of the book for quick access. I've also included a list of waypoints in degrees to easily enter into Google Earth or your GPS device. Where I use coordinates in the route description, they are in UTM, which is the standard on NTS maps and more common for orienteering.

THE
Great
Divide
TRAIL

Section A: *International Boundary to Coleman*

Segments 1–6, 145.9 km

Location	Near waypoint	NOBO km	SOBO km
Boundary Bay campsite (Waterton NP)	a1	0.0	1133.2
Bertha Bay campsite (Waterton NP)	a2	4.0	1129.4
Waterton townsite car campground*	a2	6.4	1126.8
RESUPPLY: Waterton Lakes townsite*	a2	6.4	1126.8
Alderson Lake campsite (Waterton NP)	a4	13.3	1119.9
Carthew Summit	a6	17.2	1116.0
Akamina Creek (BC Parks)*	a8	28.2	1105.0
Lineham Ridge (Tamarack Summit)	a11	38.2	1095.0
Lone Lake campsite (Waterton NP)	a14	46.1	1087.1
Twin Lakes campsite (Waterton NP)	a16	52.7	1080.5
Sage Pass campsite	a17	54.9	1078.6
Font Creek campsite	a19	61.0	1072.2
Jutland Creek campsite	a22	66.7	1066.5
La Coulotte Peak	a26	73.3	1059.9
West Castle Road campsite	a28	81.4	1051.8
West Castle River campsite	a29	86.8	1046.4
Castle Mountain campground	a30	93.9	1039.3
RESUPPLY: Castle Ski Resort	a30	94.1	1039.1
Lynx Creek car campground	a36	114.2	1019.0
Lynx Creek campsite	a36	116.1	1017.1
Willoughby Ridge campsite*	a38	123.1	1010.1
York Creek campsite	a45	135.4	997.8
RESUPPLY: Coleman	a48	145.9	987.3

Introduction

Undeniably, the main attraction of the first section of the GDT is Waterton Lakes National Park. To say that this wilderness bends the imagination and moves the soul is no exaggeration. In combination with Glacier National Park to the south, this magnificent area has the honour of being the first International Peace Park ever declared. More recently, the park has gained the distinction of being designated as a Biosphere Reserve and World Heritage Site by the United Nations. The high, castellated peaks of Waterton stand right on the perimeter of the prairies, creating this area's special allure. For those entering the park from the flatlands, there are few foothills to warn of the impending magnitude of the peaks to come.

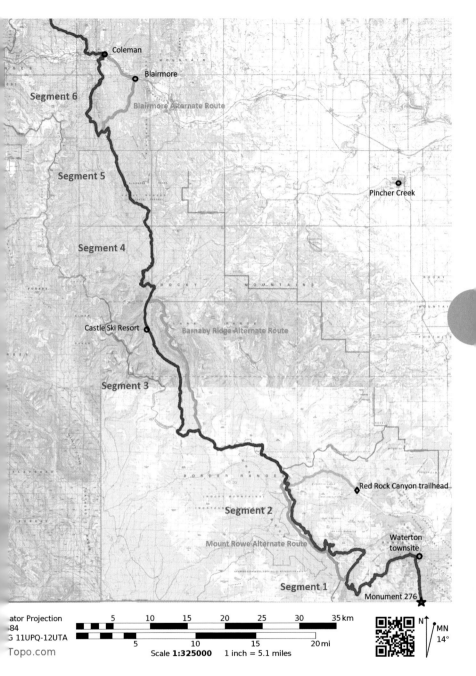

Coleman

Blairmore

Segment 6

Blairmore Alternate Route

Segment 5

Pincher Creek

Segment 4

Castle Ski Resort

Barnaby Ridge Alternate Route

Segment 3

Red Rock Canyon trailhead

Segment 2

Waterton townsite

Mount Rowe Alternate Route

Segment 1

Monument 276

ator Projection
84
G 11UPQ-12UTA
Topo.com

5 10 15 20 25 30 35 km

5 10 15 20 mi

Scale **1:325000** 1 inch = 5.1 miles

N
MN
14°

The GDT takes full advantage of the well-maintained trails in the national park. On the Tamarack trail, the route is adjacent to the Divide for over 20km. From high passes you can see over the glaciated peaks to the smooth prairie plateau, a magical vista during the golden hours of a sunrise or sunset. Encounters with Rocky Mountain sheep are probable. Just remember to give the rams the right-of-way on narrow mountain shoulders! Mule deer, grizzly bears and cougars are also common throughout the park.

Each backcountry campsite in the national park is within 7km of the next, with one exception: between Alderson Lake campsite and Lone Lake campsite the only camp in a 36.8km stretch is 2.5km off-route. Further complications may obstruct your itinerary, such as trail or campsite closures. In all cases, you should contact the Waterton Lakes National Park Information Centre when planning your trip and again just before you go.

To the north of Waterton Lakes National Park is an equally astonishing wilderness with a visible record of its neglect. Once considered part of the national park, the Castle forest district lost much of its protected status in 1921. Subjected to forestry, mining and oil industry pressures for the last half century, the district carries many visible scars. Despite the decline of these industries, access roads and seismic lines that should have been reclaimed by now are being kept open and even lengthened by off-highway vehicle (OHV) use. As of 2016 this area is now included in Castle Wildland Provincial Park or Castle Provincial Park, with a plan to phase out industrial and OHV access over several years. Find out more at albertaparks.ca.

Entering the Rocky Mountain forest district via Sage Pass from Waterton Lakes National Park, a path follows the Continental Divide for 25 spectacular kilometres over broad ridges and peaks. Normally a strong wind scours the relatively low crest of this part of the Rocky Mountains. What trees there are huddle together and only grow into short tangles on the exposed shale slopes. The rough trail through here is arduous but worth all the effort.

A final cross-country climb over a few pyramidal peaks delivers the route to a crossroads on the summit of La Coulotte Peak. Though the route-finding is easy, hikers report that this peak is one of the toughest climbs on the entire GDT. The main route follows an OHV trail into the West Castle River valley, which can be bushy and wet. The higher, alternate route continues cross-country, tracing the crest line of Barnaby Ridge for a breathtaking, and at times harrowing, 26km. After the long descent to Suicide Creek, past Barnaby Lakes, the main route becomes dependent on nearly 50km of OHV trails and roads to Coleman, Alberta.

A surprising highlight appears along the route. A pleasant trail climbs out of the Lynx Creek valley near the end of the section and follows the grassy crest of Willoughby Ridge for a dozen kilometres. The views of the Flathead Range on the Divide to the west and of Hastings Ridge to the east are substantial enough to justify following the GDT from Waterton through to Coleman. Attempts at finding or establishing a main route closer to the Divide have so far proved fruitless.

For equestrians, you will be happy to know that the main route described here is permitted for horses, with the following caveats:

> Backcountry camping with horses is permitted only at Lone Lake and Snowshoe Cabin, where corrals are provided. Prior permission from the Warden Service is required for the use of the Snowshoe corral, as it may be in use by park staff. An adequate supply of pelletized horse feed must be packed in and out, as horse grazing in the park is not permitted. Horses must be kept in corrals overnight and are not permitted within the campground. As with other backcountry users, horse users intending to overnight in the backcountry require a wilderness use permit. (pc.gc.ca/en/pn-np/ab/waterton/activ/experiences/equitation-horseriding)

Parks staff advise that horses aren't permitted at any of the vehicle-accessible campgrounds in the park. However, there is a commercial stable in the park called Alpine Stables – 403-859-2462, alpinestables.com – which offers trail rides and day and overnight trips. They are likely a good source of information on trail conditions in the park for equestrians, since they are out there every day.

During the summer of 2017, Waterton Lakes National Park had a severe forest fire event known as the Kenow Fire. Trails, roads and other infrastructure, such as the visitor centre were damaged or destroyed and may take years to rebuild. Check the park and GDTA websites for updates on which trails, campsites and roads are open. As of 2018, all trails that comprise the GDT route through the park are closed, as are the Akamina Parkway and the upper Red Rock Parkway.

SEGMENT 1 – International Boundary–Cameron Lake (24.7km)

A straightforward hike with a moderate ascent on excellent trail. Horses permitted. No bikes.

There are two ways to reach the southern terminus of the Great Divide Trail. Either follow the Lakeshore trail from Waterton 6.4km to the international boundary or, with passport in hand, take a boat to the Goat Haunt ranger station in Glacier National Park, at the southern tip of Upper Waterton Lake. After disembarking, follow the Lakeshore trail north 7.4km to the international boundary. Read more under 'Access and

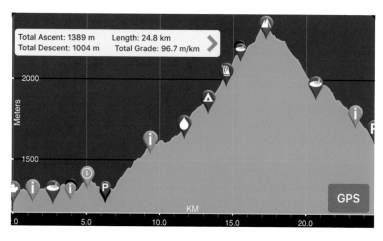

| Total Ascent: 1389 m | Length: 24.8 km |
| Total Descent: 1004 m | Total Grade: 96.7 m/km |

Waterton townsite from the Lakeshore trail, segment 1. Waterton Lakes National Park is where the mountains meet the prairies.

transportation' in the 'Planning your trip' section of the book. The remainder of this segment follows the Carthew–Alderson trail. It is a fabulous beginning for the GDT.

Maps: 82 H/4 Waterton Lakes and 82 G/1 Sage Creek; Gemtrek #16 Waterton Lakes NP.

Jurisdictions: Waterton Lakes National Park, Glacier National Park (USA), and Akamina–Kishinena Provincial Park (BC Parks).

South access: The gate to Waterton Lakes National Park is at the intersection between Highway 5, 40km west of Cardston, Alberta, and Highway 6, 50km south of Pincher Creek, Alberta. Highway 6, the Chief Mountain Highway, continues south from this major intersection to a seasonal USA border crossing, becoming Highway 17 in Glacier National Park. This port of entry is open from mid-May to mid-September. The nearest year-round

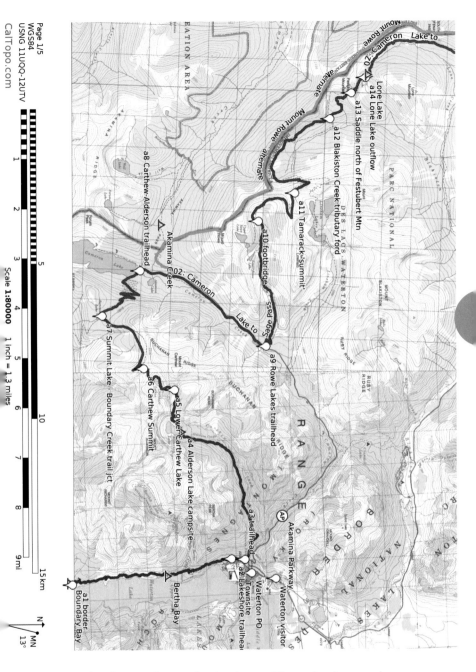

Scale **1:80000**   1 inch = 1.3 miles

N↑ MN
13°

international port of entry is the Carway/Piegan border crossing on Highway 2 south of Cardston.

Once in the park, follow Highway 5 into the town of Waterton, where it becomes Evergreen Avenue. Follow Evergreen Avenue over the Carthew

Creek bridge and park at the Cameron Falls trailhead parking area if you intend on hiking the Carthew–Alderson trail north. Drive 500m farther to the Lakeshore trailhead parking area if you plan to hike south to the international boundary. To find the marina, turn left off Evergreen Avenue onto Mount View Road as soon as you enter the town. Continue past Tamarack Village Square (Waterton's mall) to the T-intersection with Waterton Avenue and turn left.

North access: I suggest starting your hike at Cameron Lake if you are interested in hiking only the Carthew–Alderson trail. Turn right onto Akamina Parkway from Highway 5 across from the Emerald Bay picnic area, just west of the information centre. Follow the parkway 16km to the Cameron Lake parking area. The trailhead is beyond the pavilion, next to the lakeshore.

Car campgrounds and accommodations: The park-operated townsite campground has hundreds of sites for car campers and a tenting area if you are on foot. The walk-in portion of the campground has a $22.50 fee per night, which includes washrooms, hot showers, camp kitchens and food lockers in need of repair, but permits no open fires. The campground is open from mid-May to mid-October. The other two campgrounds in the park, Crandell and Belly River, are distant from the access points mentioned in this segment. There are 10 hotels and lodges in Waterton, all with expensive price tags during the summer months. Contact the park visitor centre for information and to make reservations well in advance of your stay. See the 'Contacts' section beginning on page 338. Contact Alpine Stables if you need to board a horse overnight in Waterton, as horses aren't allowed at any of the car campgrounds in the park.

Camping: Boundary Bay, Bertha Bay, and Alderson Lake require national park backcountry permits. The provincial park campsite at Akamina Creek is first come, first serve, with a $5 self-registration fee. Equestrians can only stay at the Akamina Creek campsite. Pay online in advance for Akamina Creek at discovercamping.ca/Backcountry.

Information sources: Waterton Lakes National Park information centre and the BC Parks webpage for Akamina–Kishinena Provincial Park, www.env .gov.bc.ca/bcparks/explore/parkpgs/akamina.

Resupply station: Waterton Lakes post office.

Trailhead services: Waterton Shoreline Cruises boat ride to the border and beyond. Sign up for a hiker shuttle at Tamarack Outdoor Outfitters in Waterton. They offer daily shuttle service to Cameron Lake, Red Rock Canyon, and to Chief Mountain Customs, where hikers can connect with a Glacier National Park shuttle.

Special notes: The natural beauty of Waterton Lakes National Park ensures

The international boundary marker, monument 276, Waterton Lakes National Park.

a high volume of visitors during the peak season of July and August. The wilderness here can lose its wild flavour amongst all the entrance fees, reservations, backcountry camping costs, and the throng of visitors. For section hikers and SOBOS, I recommend hiking in early fall when the crowds are confined to the town and the mountain slopes are resplendent with fall hues. The town largely shuts down by mid-October. If you started your hike in Glacier, south of the US border, contact Canadian Customs when you reach Waterton and have your passport number on hand. Phone 403-653-3535 for the Chief Mountain border crossing, which is open 7am–11pm each day from June 1 to Labour Day.

Additional reading: While at the information centre, make sure you get a copy of *Waterton Lakes National Park Visitor's Guide*. This free 44-page publication has a town map with a description of all the services in the park. You can also download it from waterton.ca/wp-content/uploads/2015/03/43253-Visitors-Guide-for-Web.pdf.

International Boundary to Bertha Bay campsite
(4.0km, 138m up, 133m down)

The southern terminus of the Canadian Rockies Great Divide Trail is at monument 276 on the Canadian border (1265, a1) with the United States. This is also the site of the Boundary Bay campsite and dock. While there is no trail register here, you can still initiate your journey with a note on a large message board. Refer to 'Access and transportation' at page 26 for the best way to get to this point. From the international boundary the main route follows the well-maintained Lakeshore trail north, climbing over a low ridge and descending to a spring in an exposed bank on the left side of the trail. The route continues parallel to the lakeshore on an undulating track 4.0km to the Bertha Bay campsite.

Bertha Bay campsite to Alderson Lake campsite
(9.3km, 709m up, 164m down)

One kilometre north, past the Bertha Bay campsite, you pass a signed trail junction for Bertha Lake before ascending 200m to a prominent lookout over Waterton Lake. A contouring descent on the Lakeshore trail brings the route to the Lakeshore trailhead (1305, 6.4, a2) at the end of Evergreen Avenue, not far from the south end of the Waterton Townsite campground.

From the gravel parking lot, a faint trail goes northwest through a grassy clearing. Follow this connector trail that traverses above Evergreen Avenue (or follow the road itself) to the Carthew–Alderson trail junction (1335, 0.5, a3), at a flight of stairs above the Cameron Falls trailhead parking area. If you were to keep following Evergreen Avenue, it would lead you past the small town to the national park visitor centre in 1km. If arriving from the USA, remember to call Canadian customs, 403-653-3535, to report your arrival and give them your passport number.

From the junction, follow the Carthew–Alderson trail as it begins a moderate ascent under tree cover to the west and climbs the Carthew Creek valley. The trail stays to the south and well above Cameron Creek. The moderate ascent persists and you will encounter a few seasonal tributary crossings that are usually dry by the late summer. The only reliable one, if you need water, is at 4.8km. The trail curves to the south, bringing you to the signed trail junction for the Alderson Lake campsite (1860, 6.4, a4). If staying here, turn left at the junction and the campsite is 200m away.

Lower Carthew Lake framed by Mount Alderson. Sublime views like this one make the Carthew–Alderson trail one of the most popular day hikes in Waterton Lakes National Park.

The descent from Carthew Summit toward Summit Lake. The snowy peak is Mount Custer in Glacier National Park in the USA.

Alderson Lake campsite to Carthew Summit
(3.9km, 504m up, 17m down)

Continue straight ahead on the Carthew–Alderson trail through thinning subalpine forest and begin a steep climb. Switchbacks bring the trail to the Carthew Creek ford and then continue up a cliff band to lower Carthew Lake (2165, 2.2, a5). The trail passes along the west side of the two lakes and ascends steeply up shale-covered slopes to Carthew Summit (2330, 1.7, a6), which lies on a long ridge of the 2630-m Mount Carthew. The pass deserves its lofty title of "Carthew Summit" because it is such a magnificent viewpoint.

Carthew Summit to Cameron Lake
(7.5km, 38m up, 690m down)

Long, sweeping switchbacks bring the trail off Carthew Summit to the southwest. The moderate descent becomes gentle as the trail contours west across open scree. Follow the route below timberline to the Boundary

Creek trail junction beside Summit Lake (1935, 3.4, a7). Continue following the Carthew–Alderson trail to the right, and in 1.1km you start descending several very long switchbacks to reach the Carthew–Alderson trailhead (1665, 4.1, a8) at Cameron Lake. There is a large parking lot and outhouses, but of more importance to hikers there is a small concession that sells overpriced snacks and drinks near the boat-rental shop. This can be a very busy place during the summer. Follow either the road shoulder or a trail paralleling it on the right to the next waypoint. Equestrians are allowed on the road shoulder only and should be mindful of traffic.

SEGMENT 2 – Cameron Lake to Sage Pass (29.7km)

*A strenuous but rewarding hike on excellent trail. No horses or bikes. *see special notes*

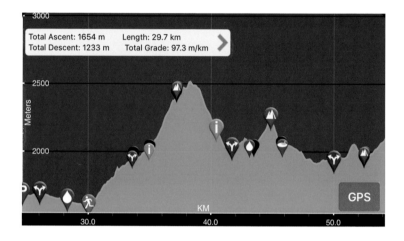

This high-level hike, adjacent to the Continental Divide, offers an almost continuous panorama. This segment known as the Tamarack trail is my favourite hike in Waterton Lakes National Park, owing to its proximity to remote alpine lakes and the Divide. This trail allows you to see a network of high-country routes arranged along shale-strewn ridges and summits. Travel in any direction seems possible.

Maps: 82 G/1 Sage Creek; Gemtrek #16 Waterton Lakes NP.

Jurisdictions: Waterton Lakes National Park and Akamina–Kishinena Provincial Park (BC Parks).

South access: The Tamarack trail starts from the Rowe Lakes trailhead parking area on Akamina Parkway, 10km west of its intersection with Highway 5, the park entrance road. This intersection is across from the

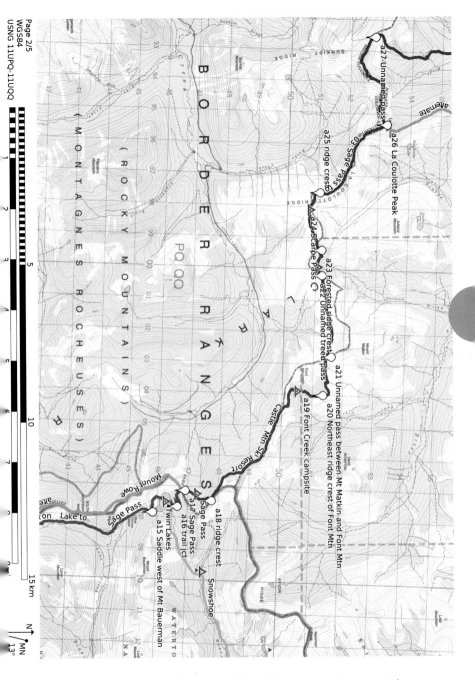

Emerald Bay picnic area, just west of the visitor centre. Cameron Lake
parking lot is another 6km west, past the Rowe Lakes trailhead, at the end

of Akamina Parkway. Only NOBO thru-hikers would begin this segment at Cameron Lake, though.

North access: Turn north off Highway 5 (aka the Park Entrance Road), 4.5km west of the park gate onto Red Rock Canyon Parkway. Follow the parkway for 14km to the end of the road at the Red Rock Canyon trailhead. Walk the Snowshoe trail 8.2km to the Snowshoe campsite and warden patrol cabin. Turn left to avoid the Lost Lake trail, cross a small bridge, and ascend another 2.9km to the signed Sage Pass trail junction, which is at kilometre 52.8 of the GDT. Keep left for the Tamarack trail and in 300m you will arrive at the Twin Lakes campsite.

Car campgrounds and accommodations: The park-operated Townsite campground has hundreds of sites for car campers and a tenting area for those on foot. The walk-in portion of the campground has a $22.50 fee per night, which includes washrooms, hot showers, camp kitchens and food lockers in need of repair, but does not permit open fires. The campground is open from mid-May to mid-October. The Crandell campground is on Red Rock Parkway about 7km from Highway 5, the park entrance highway. This park-operated campground has over 100 sites with washrooms and camp kitchens but no showers. The fee is $21.50 per night. This campground is open from mid-May to early September. Contact Alpine Stables if you need to board a horse overnight in Waterton, as horses aren't allowed at any of the car campgrounds in the park. There are several hotels in Waterton, for which you should make reservations well in advance if you plan to stay there. Consult the park info centre for a full listing.

Camping: The provincial park campsite at Akamina Creek is first come, first served, with a $5 self-registration fee. Pay online in advance for Akamina Creek at discovercamping.ca/Backcountry. The national park campsites are: Lone Lake, Twin Lakes and Snowshoe. Equestrians can stay at Akamina Creek but require a BC Parks permit in advance. Horses are also allowed at Lone Lake and Snowshoe. Equestrians may only use the corral at Snowshoe with prior permission from the Waterton Lakes National Park wardens.

Information sources: Waterton Lakes National Park visitor centre and the BC Parks webpage for the Akamina–Kishinena Provincial Park: www.env .gov.bc.ca/bcparks/explore/parkpgs/akamina.

Resupply station: Waterton Lakes post office.

Trailhead services: Sign up for a hiker shuttle at Tamarack Outdoor Outfitters in Waterton. They offer daily shuttle services to Cameron Lake and Red Rock Canyon, and to Chief Mountain Customs, where hikers can connect with a Glacier National Park shuttle.

Special notes: The Red Rock Canyon trailhead offers an easier start to the Tamarack trail and conveniently placed campsites compared to the Rowe Lakes trailhead mentioned as the south access. If you intend to thru-hike the GDT in Waterton Lakes National Park, account for the 32.6km distance between the Alderson Lake campsite on the Carthew–Alderson trail and the Lone Lake campsite on the Tamarack trail. You could arrange transportation to eliminate the 6-km walk along the Akamina Parkway to shorten this distance between designated campsites. A better solution is to hike 2.2km on the alternate route mentioned in this section to stay at the Akamina Creek campsite in British Columbia. You cannot reserve the campsite, however, and it costs $5 per person each night through self-registration. The BC Parks rangers stationed nearby keep the campsite in excellent shape and provide free firewood and good advice (if they are in). *Horses and bikes are allowed along Akamina Parkway (but be careful!) and up to the Akamina Creek campsite. Bikes aren't forbidden from Akamina–Kishinena park but it would be extremely difficult to lug a bike over the Mount Rowe alternate route. You could take the Snowshoe trail from Red Rock Canyon instead and push your bike over Sage Pass but I'm not sure where you would go from there except down the Castle River OHV roads. The GDT beyond Sage Pass isn't suitable for bikes.

Additional reading: Read *Mountain Footsteps* (4th ed., 2018), by Janice Strong, for additional information about Akamina–Kishinena Provincial Park. While at the Waterton Lakes National Park Information Centre, make sure you get a copy of the Visitor's Guide for the park. This free publication has a town map and a hiker's map along with a description of all the services in the park. You can also download it from waterton.ca/wp-content/uploads/2015/03/43253-Visitors-Guide-for-Web.pdf.

Cameron Lake to Lineham Ridge (Tamarack Summit) (13.5km, 947m up, 135m down)

Akamina Parkway is to the north of the long parking area at Cameron Lake, and from this point Waterton is 16km east by road. Follow the parkway (or parallel trail) 1.3km to the Akamina Pass trailhead parking area. If you wish to camp, take the Akamina Pass trail 2.2km over the Divide to the Akamina Creek campsite at the Forum Lake trail junction, in Akamina–Kishinena Provincial Park.

MOUNT ROWE ALTERNATE ROUTE—18.7KM INSTEAD OF 28.4KM. NO HORSES OR BIKES. *SEE SPECIAL NOTES.

You should consider hiking this alternate route through Akamina–Kishinena Provincial Park to Sage Pass, because it follows the Divide and avoids the Tamarack trail, which can be busy during high season. Don't even attempt it in bad weather! Reservations aren't necessary for the Akamina Creek campsite and you can random camp in the park, which means you can avoid the red tape of reserving campsites in Waterton Lakes National Park. The route is generally cross-country and devoid of water unless there is remnant snow. This way also presents some 'micro' navigational challenges where you must do some mild scrambling or walk around cliff bands on the ridges. Plan for at least a full day for a strong hiker to accomplish this route. River Taig adds: "Though nearly 10km shorter, taking this alternate will certainly cost hikers time, as they will be slowed by the very arduous ascent to Mount Rowe, challenging terrain, and water-heavy packs."

Follow the Akamina Pass trail from the signed trailhead and parking area on Akamina Parkway. This trail is an old roadbed, so it is wide and well graded. The easy ascent is mostly under forest cover but you do get an occasional view of Cameron Lake and the Summit Lake basin across the valley. In 1.5km you reach Akamina Pass and transect the all too obvious cutline that demarcates the provincial boundary. The campsite is about 700m farther along the trail and slightly downhill. On the way to the campsite, you will pass a self-registration kiosk at the Forum Lake trail junction—the cost is $5 per adult each night. The Akamina Creek campsite is still a couple hundred metres straight past the junction, farther downhill. If you turned left on the Forum Lake trail, you would come to the seasonally staffed Akamina–Kishinena ranger station. The rangers have a radio for emergencies. Owing to its proximity to the rangers, the Akamina Creek campsite is in excellent condition, with all the amenities, including chopped wood for the central cooking and eating area. The campsite has food lockers and abundant tent pads. Hikers report that the water pump has been removed, but there are springs nearby, up the cutline. I would expect the cabin would have a pump nearby.

From the registration box in Akamina Pass, turn north and follow the narrow trail past the provincial marker "4H" and embark on the steepening ascent toward Mount Rowe. The trail disappears after 500m, just past a weather station (which you don't need to go to – stay on the cutline). After a hearty bushwhack the cutline improves, allowing you to pick your own way to the col just west of Mount Rowe (you don't need to go right to the summit unless you want to). The col is about 2km from the Akamina Pass trail. Follow the crest for another 1.6km to the north, over a minor peak to the 2510m summit directly south of Tamarack Summit, on the main route. A narrow, shale-covered crest bridges the two summits. The proximity to Tamarack Summit makes this a tempting route to rejoin the main trail, but it is too difficult to attempt save for experienced climbers on rope.

From the unnamed peak the route can be deceptive. Look for frequent game trails on the east and north side of the ridge to avoid the dense brush on the ridge itself – stay far right, in other words, nearly at the cliff's edge, to find the most open route. Expect heavy bush, confusing game trails and large rocks to slow you down before reaching Festubert Mountain. Follow the Divide to ascend this peak, up three small cliff bands that present light to moderate scrambling. From the peak, it is easy going to South Kootenay Pass – the lowest point on the traverse – where you will find a horse trail following the park boundary cutline. It is 1km to the main route from here. Before you reach the top of Kishinena Peak, veer west from the cutline to regain the ridge. The next unnamed peak has an impassable cliff band 500m before the peak. Contour west toward the base of the cliff and look for an obvious trail. Decent trails ensue. Hike over the next peak and follow the ridge down to Sage Pass, watching for a well-used trail from the pass to a lookout over Twin Lakes.

End Mount Rowe alternate route – 18.7km instead of 28.4km

From the Akamina Pass trailhead, follow Akamina Parkway to the Rowe Lakes trailhead (1605, 5.3, a9). There is no shoulder along this already narrow and winding road, so I advise walking against traffic during daylight hours. (If the parallel trail on the south side of the road has been restored since road work and a fire in 2017, take the trail instead. Gemtrek calls this the Dipper trail.) Horses are allowed on the shoulder, but be cautious. From the Rowe Lakes trailhead, climb a section of switchbacks and ascend to the west through forest. The well-maintained trail, known as the Tamarack, stays high above the north bank of Rowe Creek and reaches the signed Lower Rowe Lake trail junction in a long meadow at the base of a debris chute. Continue straight ahead through forest. The Tamarack trail comes to a footbridge (2005, 5.0, a10) in Rowe Meadow, near a closed and reclaimed campsite. The footbridge spans the last water source for the next 9km to the north. For the next 20km the trail stays within an aerial kilometre of the Continental Divide. After crossing the bridge, avoid the Upper Rowe Lake trail by turning right at the trail junction. The Tamarack trail gradually climbs above timberline as it proceeds west and then north. The long traverse across scree changes direction once it reaches the Mount Lineham ridge crest and goes west. After a moderate climb, the precarious trail continues up steep, reinforced switchbacks to Tamarack Summit on Lineham Ridge (2565, 3.2, a11). This happens to be the second-highest point on the entire GDT and poses a formidable obstacle to hikers during the early season (before the third week of June).

A lone Rocky Mountain ram stands on Lineham Ridge.

Lineham Ridge (Tamarack Summit) to Lone Lake campsite (7.9km, 334m up, 819m down)

The trail, in good condition, angles down across scree to the northwest and then leaves the ridge crest for a moderate traverse across open slopes toward the south. Look for orange markers pegged to the ground to show the way. After a brief moderate ascent, you descend along the west bank of Blakiston Creek and encounter some faint switchbacks down to a tributary ford (1880, 5.1, a12). By late summer this is the last water source for the next 9km for southbound hikers. A steep ascent leads the route away from Blakiston Creek, and after a gentle section the climb becomes steep again before attaining a saddle (2240, 1.6, a13) north of Festubert Mountain. A moderate descent on long switchbacks brings the trail down to the Lone Lake outflow (2015, 1.0, a14). Lone Lake campsite is 200m farther, on the north side of the lake and the warden cabin is not far beyond it.

Beargrass glowing in the fading light south of Lineham Ridge in segment 2.

Lone Lake campsite to Twin Lakes campsite (6.6km, 209m up, 275m down)

A gentle, undulating descent brings you to the South Kootenay Pass trail junction in another 4.1km, followed by the Blakiston Creek trail junction 20m farther; walk straight past both, staying on the Tamarack trail. After a creek ford in Blue Grouse Basin the trail climbs moderately up to the saddle (2040, 5.9, a15) west of Mount Bauerman. Descend across scree to a signed junction for Lower Twin Lake on the right. Continue on the Tamarack trail to get to the Twin Lakes campsite in 0.9km from the saddle.

Twin Lakes campsite to Sage Pass (1.7km, 164m up, 4m down)

Still following the Tamarack trail, pass the lake outflow to the signed Sage Pass trail junction (1930, 1.3, a16), 400m past the Twin Lakes campsite. If you continued straight ahead on the Tamarack trail, you would pass the Snowshoe campsite in 2.9km and arrive at the Red Rock Canyon trailhead parking area in another 8.2km. At the junction turn left onto the Sage Pass trail and ascend steep switchbacks up to Sage Pass (2131, 1.3, a17). Here you stand on the Continental Divide and the Waterton Lakes National Park boundary with the Rocky Mountain Forest District in British Columbia. This is the northern terminus of a lengthy alternate route that is of greater interest to southbound hikers who are already acquainted with the dry and windswept crest of the Divide. Refer to the 'Mount Rowe alternate route' covered earlier in this segment for more details.

Twin Lakes campsite at dusk.

SEGMENT 3 – Sage Pass to Castle Ski Resort (39.7km)

Extremely strenuous ascents and descents cross-country, with sparse water sources on a high traverse. Possibly the hardest segment of the entire GDT. Horses and bikes permitted.

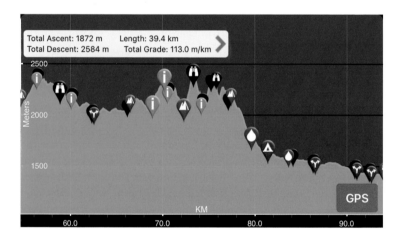

Total Ascent: 1872 m   Length: 39.4 km
Total Descent: 2584 m   Total Grade: 113.0 m/km

This bold segment of the GDT follows the Continental Divide along crests and over several prominent summits. The route starts as a faint trail before relying on cross-country travel. If you are an experienced hiker, accustomed to some scrambling and route-finding, you will want to take the Barnaby Ridge alternate route for the spectacular views. The main route eventually leaves the crest of the Continental Divide and descends the

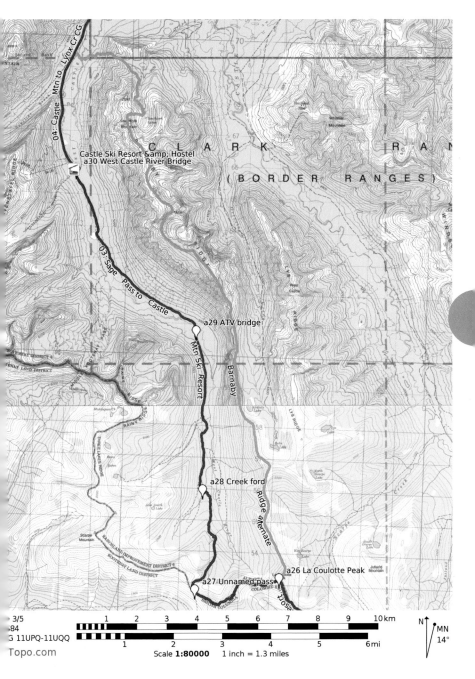

West Castle River valley to the Castle Ski Resort and the T-Bar Pub. The substantial alternate route doesn't meet up with the main route until 4km past the pub.

Maps: 82 G/1 Sage Creek and 82 G/8 Beaver Mines.

Jurisdictions: Waterton Lakes National Park, Castle Forest District (Alberta), and Rocky Mountain Forest District (BC).

South access: Turn north off Highway 5 (aka the Park Entrance Road), 4.5km west of the park gate onto Red Rock Canyon Parkway. Follow the parkway for 14km to the end of the road at the Red Rock Canyon trailhead. From the trailhead parking area, walk the Snowshoe trail 8.2km to the Snowshoe campsite and warden patrol cabin. Turn left to avoid the Lost Lake trail, cross a small bridge, and ascend another 2.9km to the signed Sage Pass trail junction, which is at kilometre 53.1 of the GDT. If you go left at the Sage Pass trail junction on the Tamarack trail, you would arrive at the Twin Lakes campsite in 300m.

North access: Castle Ski Resort is at the western end of the 30km-long Secondary Highway 774, most of which is paved. Highway 774 intersects with Highway 507 just east of the small village of Beaver Mines. Castle Ski Resort is 30km west of this intersection. If you are approaching the area from BC or from north of the Crowsnest Pass, turn south onto Highway 507 at Burmis, on Crowsnest Highway 3. If you're coming from the east or from the US, turn west onto 507 from Pincher Creek. Starting from either Burmis or Pincher Creek it is approximately 50km to the ski resort.

Car campgrounds and accommodations: There is a forestry recreation campground on the periphery of the Castle Ski Resort at the western extremity of Highway 774. After passing the resort you will see the campground on the left, before crossing a log bridge over the West Castle River. There is no fee and there is little restriction on where to camp. Many of the spur roads that emanate from Highway 774 seem to end at campsites on the bank of the West Castle River. This informal car camping will likely change in the near future, since this area was designated as a provincial park in 2016. Accommodations include the Castle Ski Resort and an Air B&B in Beaver Mines at Stella's Restaurant.

Camping: Snowshoe and Twin Lakes campsites in Waterton Lakes National Park require a backcountry permit. Sage Pass, Font Creek and Jutland Creek sites in the forest district do not require a pass. Random camping is allowed outside the national park.

Information sources: Rocky Mountain Forest District (BC) and Alberta Parks.

Resupply stations: Castle Ski Resort.

Special notes: If you park in Waterton Lakes National Park, your park entrance permit gives your vehicle a week of free parking. If you choose not to stay overnight in the national park, you do not require additional permits.

However, you should stop by the park information centre to find out current trail conditions and tell the attendants how long your vehicle will be at the Red Rock Canyon trailhead. Horses are permitted, but you will likely end up walking your horse up and down several steep and shale-covered peaks. Bikes are technically permitted, but you would end up carrying and pushing it most of the way.

Additional reading: *Waterton Lakes National Park Visitors Guide*, available for free at the Waterton information centre or online at waterton.ca/wp-content/uploads/2015/03/43253-Visitors-Guide-for-Web.pdf.

Sage Pass to unnamed pass north of Font Mountain (9.2km, 421m up, 540m down)

Entering the Rocky Mountain Forest District in BC, a trail contours 500m to a T-junction. This trail had new blazes in 2014 and is obvious now. In fact, the recent trail work continues all the way to Scarpe Pass at waypoint a25. At the T-junction, 50m to the left, is a small campsite with a fire ring, in sparse forest. Beside the camp is a small stream. The next water source is 7km north. To the right from the T-junction, the trail continues up a moderate ascent. Eventually the ascent becomes a steep switchback up to a ridge crest (2220, 1.2, a18) on the Divide, high above Lost Lake. The steep ascent continues up the BC side of the Divide and contours below Peak 2434 for just over a kilometre, reaching a highpoint of 2360m before rejoining the crest. Descend and follow the crest through a peculiar ridgetop canyon to the edge of a boulder field. The trail descends steeply to the right and skirts the boulder field at timberline. Switchbacks bring you down to the Font Creek campsite (2080, 5.4, a19) in a large meadow near the head of Font Creek. The camp has a fire ring and a spring nearby. The spring, which runs late into the season, is 7km from the previously mentioned water source and 6km from the next one.

Leave the campsite and immediately cross the creek, aiming for the peak of Font Mountain through a subalpine meadow. Shortly the trail goes to the right and climbs moderately through trees gaining the northeast ridge crest (2105, 1.0, a20) of Font Mountain. The trail rollercoasters a bit before descending steeply into the broad valley north of Font Mountain. Where the trail reaches a junction in 500m, keep left and head west. The GDT follows a faint path that climbs to the west through an expansive meadow to the unnamed pass (2075, 1.6, a21) between Mount Matkin and Font Mountain. You should find a seasonal creek flowing 300m before reaching this pass.

Font Mountain seen from a curious, crest-top canyon on the Divide. Photo: Bob Hodges.

Unnamed pass north of Font Mountain to La Coulotte Peak (9.7km, 943m up, 601m down)

The trail is vague on the Alberta side of the pass but well defined on the BC side. Look for the trail at the northern extremity of the pass if you have lost sight of it. The route contours to the west, below Mount Matkin, through a previously burnt area that now has many young trees. A brief but steep ascent brings you to an unnamed, treed pass (2100, 2.7, a22). Ignore the overgrown trail that immediately descends into the forest from the pass and turn west to find good trail on the ridge. Follow this for 200m and then descend steeply through forest another 200m to a narrow meadow. In this meadow you'll find a spring that is 6km from the last water source and 3km to the next one, which happens to be up to 500m off-route. Go downstream if you don't immediately see water here. On the other side of the spring is Jutland Creek campsite, with a fire ring. NOBOS should stay here to wait out any electrical storms before proceeding north. Before crossing the spring, turn left and follow the trail upstream into a meadow. Climb a steep grade to a forested ridge crest (2195, 1.1, a23). The path follows the crest back to the Divide and crosses into BC. Descend to a small circular meadow on Scarpe Pass (2095, 1.5, a24) at the head of Scarpe Creek.

If you need water there is a source roughly 500m downhill on the Scarpe Creek trail, but if you are lucky there might still be a spring at the base of the nearby boulder field. The previous water source is 3km south and the next is in 12km on the main route and 12km on the alternate. The rough Scarpe Creek trail later joins a seismic line and eventually the South Castle road if you need to exit the GDT in an emergency. NOBOS, make sure you have enough water and energy at this point for one of the most

This terrain typifies much of the Barnaby Ridge alternate route. The peak is the 2430m summit referenced in the route description.

arduous climbs on the whole GDT, and be prepared to wander back and forth across the crest to pick your way up this daunting route.

From the unnamed pass stay on the Divide and climb the very steep mountainside to the west, encountering some scree closer to the La Coulotte Ridge crest (2225, 0.7, a25). SOBOS, you should descend from the last summit of La Coulotte Ridge on the Alberta side of the crest and look for the round meadow on Scarpe Pass. Look for a faint trail crossing the meadow; this is the GDT.

La Coulotte Ridge has a windswept shale crest with sparse vegetation. You can pass obstacles such as small bluffs on the BC side of the Divide. Initially the ascent is moderate, becoming steeper as it nears a 2375m summit. Descend steeply on the crest to a col at 2200m and climb to a 2305m summit. You can spot the craggy fingers of the Starvation Range to the south, near the United States border. Also in view is much of the alternate along the rim of Waterton Lakes National Park. The cross-country route continues down to a pass at 2115m, and a final push over difficult scree brings you to the summit of La Coulotte Peak (2430, 3.7, a26) on the Continental Divide. In 2016 a GDTA member installed an orange summit register in the cairn at this location. I urge you to visit this summit and not try to side-hill around the south side of it – hikers report that this is just as hard as going over the peak.

BARNABY RIDGE ALTERNATE ROUTE – 22.4KM INSTEAD OF 24.8KM. NO HORSES. NO BIKES. MAKE SURE YOU CAN ASSIST YOUR DOG ON STEEP CLIFF STEPS. DO NOT ATTEMPT THIS ROUTE IN A STORM!

The ridge crest north offers some of the most exquisite views along this section, especially in contrast to the main route of the GDT, which crawls along the adjacent river valley bottom. This traverse is challenging enough that I can't endorse it as the main route. Three scrambles on the sharp crest are beyond the scope of most hikers except those who are confident with heights. However, if heights don't bother you and you have some experience scrambling, I highly recommend it. Plan on taking significantly longer if you take this alternate – perhaps twice as long as following the main route.

After a short scramble, continue down the ridge crest north of La Coulotte Peak. Traverse two summits over the next 5km and then climb the steep 2390m unnamed summit south of Ruby Lake. The parallel crests of Barnaby Ridge and Lys Ridge extend to the north, with Grizzly Creek flowing along the floor of this enormous bathtub formed between. From the summit, the route goes left, down the crestline to a col. It is possible to descend to Ruby Lake by a difficult steep scramble, but it is better to visit the next lake as a water source, as it is nearer the route and less trouble to access. Visible from the crest is the Grizzly Creek trail that goes 16km from Ruby Lake to the Castle River, where it joins the South Castle forest service road at a point 10km south of Highway 774.

The Barnaby Ridge alter- nate route south of Peak 2471.

From the col above Ruby Lake, follow the crest north. In 2km, the route passes high above Grizzly Lake and a shoreline campsite. This lake is 12km from the last water source and 15km to the next. There is an emergency water source in 9km off-route but hikers report it is unappealing, with large amounts of algae in it. From the lowest point on the crest above the lake, a steep trail descends the reddish scree to the campsite. (A trail from the camp joins the Grizzly Creek trail.) The crest is thickly forested as you follow it north over two more summits over the next 2km. Beware: if you reach a questionable cliff over the second summit, you should backtrack 50m and look for a better break in the rocks, on the NE side of the ridge. Hikers also report a passage on the west side that involved handing packs down. Either way, this leads down through some tight bushwhacking to a broad pass at 1895m. There is a minor scramble down the northeastern side of the second peak. Leaving the trees for open shale, the route climbs the crest of Barnaby Ridge. Approximately 2km north you start a scramble along a 500m-long section of very narrow and rocky crest. Take your time and watch for loose rock! The route reaches a 2420m summit above a small lake 1km after the scramble. The route stays on the rim of the lake's bowl for 2km, ascending one peak but descending to the north, off the crest, before reaching Peak 2471, the last peak around the bowl. You can access the small lake by continuing toward Peak 2471 and descending the scree straight down. This lake is a steep kilometre off-route and 9km from the last water source. It isn't worth the effort unless it's an emergency to get that water. The next lake is 6km north.

Bypassing a minor summit, the route follows the crest 2km to a 2460m unnamed peak. Scramble down shale-covered rock steps on the crest to the northwest (left). After 2km you climb to the summit of 2370m Southfork Mountain. Proceed north on the crest; at a convenient location,

Southfork Lakes on the Barnaby Ridge alternate route.

nearly 500m farther, leave the crestline to the right and descend to the east through a sparse larch forest. Aiming for the Upper Southfork Lake, descend 1km on a broad ridge, cross-country. This uppermost of three lakes is 6km from the last water source, but beyond here sources of water are not as scarce. The Southfork Lakes trail runs along the western shore of the three lakes and the outflow creek.

Follow the maintained Southfork Lakes trail 3km down through dense forest over a shallow saddle to a broad, sparsely forested bench. The trail used to be littered with blown-down trees but was in good repair at the time of writing. The trail turns abruptly left at the lightly forested ridge and descends steeply 1km to the west, down an open ridge crest. Near the West Castle River, the Southfork Lakes trail joins two seismic lines; turn left at the first one, marked with a blue diamond, and do not follow any sign for "syncline parking." Follow this for 1km and then ford the river. This ford would be difficult early in the season. If you are SOBO, trying to find this trailhead from across the river will be problematic, as it is over-grown and unmarked. Directly across the river from the trailhead are a campsite and a rough, one-lane dirt track. The track goes through forest to an intersection in a meadow. To the left is a university field station. Go straight to another intersection on the edge of the meadow and keep to the left to reach Highway 774. The dirt track meets the road where the overhead power lines cross from one side of the road to the other. This intersection is 300m from the river ford and 22.4km from La Coulotte Peak at the beginning of the alternate route. On Highway 774 you can turn right for the Suicide Creek bridge in 1.9km, or turn left and go 4km to the Castle Ski Resort (and T-Bar Pub).

End Barnaby Ridge alternate route – 22.4km instead of 24.8km

Descending from La Coulotte to the unnamed pass at way-point a27. Photo: Bob Hodges.

La Coulotte Summit to Unnamed Pass
(4.0km, 373m up, 581m down)

Still following the Continental Divide westward, you will find that descending La Coulotte Peak is not as easy as it looks from the summit. Near the end of the steep descent, there is a cliff band blocking the route on the crest. Avoid this obstacle by contouring to the southeast (on the BC side of the Divide), nearly 200m across steep and vegetated slopes, before resuming the descent. The steep ascent up to the crest of the next unnamed peak to the west brings you to a long summit ridge, in 2.2km at 2360m, followed by a moderate descent over that summit. The final ascent of the segment, to a peak at 2310m, is very steep. Leaving the summit, the cross-country route follows the Continental Divide to the west and descends to an unnamed pass (2160, 4.0, a27) where an OHV trail dead-ends. The pass, situated on the Divide, straddles the sources of the West Castle River in Alberta and Commerce Creek in British Columbia.

Unnamed Pass to Castle Ski Resort
(16.8, 135m up, 862m down)

An obvious and deactivated OHV track starts from the pass. This rocky track contours above the head of the West Castle River before descending steeply into forest. The washed-out track encounters a creek in 2.3km. This is the first water source along the route since Scarpe Creek (off-route by up to 500m), 12 very strenuous kilometres to the south. If you cannot find any water where the track crosses the creek, then make your way about 150m upstream to where a spring lingers even at the end of a dry summer. The OHV track resumes a moderate descent. The descent eases as the track becomes more overgrown. Within 100m after passing an old logging road that branches to the left, you reach a creek ford (1610, 4.2, a28) with a good camping spot nearby. The OHV track is visibly wider from this point on, despite having to push through bushes in places. This previously logged area has many tracks that branch off, so be careful to stay on the main one. Walk straight through any junctions, keeping to the obvious track. Leaving the creek, the wide track descends to another creek ford in 1.6km. In 200m past that creek, you may find a gate which, from April 20 to December 1, closes the road you just descended. Soon you arrive at a narrow, metal OHV bridge (1520, 5.4, a29) over the West Castle River. Continue down the valley on the east side of the river on a gravel road to a log bridge (1430, 7.1, a30) over the West Castle River. Located on the other side of the bridge is a forestry recreation campground with fire rings and vehicle access. The campground sits on the periphery of the Castle Ski Resort. The small resort town has a public telephone and the T-Bar Pub, which is open Fridays 4–9pm, Saturdays 10am–6pm, and Sundays 9–2. The Castle Ski Lodge and Hostel operates every day, year-round, but you should contact them in advance if you are interested in accommodations or sending a resupply package there. Rates start at $25 per person. The Huckleberry Fest runs in late August and features food and live entertainment (festivalseekers.com/abrockies/huckleberryfestival). There is an Air B&B in Beaver Mines at Stella's Restaurant, about 30km up the road, if you can manage a ride.

View of segment 4 from the Barnaby Ridge alternate route. The Suicide Creek trail angles up from the middle of the photo, up to the left, to the highpoint at waypoint a32.

Segment 4 – Castle Ski Resort to Lynx Creek campground (20.1km)

Easy hiking on wide trails. Horses and bikes permitted.

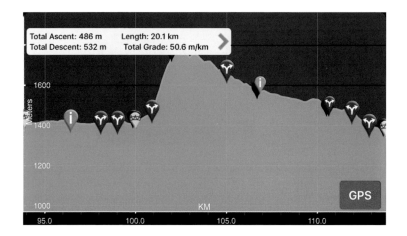

Total Ascent: 486 m Length: 20.1 km
Total Descent: 532 m Total Grade: 50.6 m/km

This low-elevation amble through mixed forest has modest views and gentle walking. The trail system in this area between the West Castle and Carbondale rivers is extensive and potentially bewildering to any hiker. The trails normally host motorized visitors, which may change as the area is now part of the new Castle Wildland provincial park established by the Alberta government in 2016.

Maps: 82 G/8 Beaver Mines and 82 G/9 Blairmore.

Jurisdiction: Alberta Parks.

South access: Castle Ski Resort is at the western end of the 30km-long Highway 774, most of which is paved. Highway 774 intersects with Highway 507 just east of the small village of Beaver Mines. Castle Ski Resort is 30km west of this intersection. If you are approaching the area from BC or from north of the Crowsnest Pass, turn south onto 507 at Burmis, on Crowsnest Highway 3. If you're coming from the east or from the U.S., turn west onto 507 from Pincher Creek. Starting from either Burmis or Pincher Creek it is approximately 50km to the ski resort.

North access: The Lynx Creek campground shares the same access as the Castle Ski Resort. The difference is you must turn north from Highway 774 at the Castle ranger station, roughly 12km before the ski resort and 1km after passing an intersection for Beaver Mines Lake. This two-lane gravel road is in good enough condition to accommodate all vehicles. The road

Looking across the valley at the Suicide Creek trail and the Divide in the distance.

crosses the Castle River and passes the Castle River Bridge campground. Turn left onto the Mount Haig road soon after passing the campground. In another 10km, keep to the right where the Carbondale haul road intersects. The Lynx Creek campground is on the right in another kilometre. (The road continuing past the campground is Adanac Road, which in 16km leads to Hillcrest Mines just off Crowsnest Highway 3. The Lynx Creek road goes over Willoughby Ridge and descends to Blairmore on Highway 3 in roughly 20km.)

Car campgrounds and accommodations: There is a lot of free camping to choose from in the area if you only need a place to park and set up a tent. The two forestry campgrounds that do have facilities require a $10 fee. These are the Lynx Creek and Castle River Bridge campgrounds. Read the North Access description for this segment if you are interested in finding them. I recommend staying at the Lynx Creek campground. Accommodations include the Castle Ski Resort and an Air B&B in Beaver Mines at Stella's Restaurant.

Camping: Random camping and Lynx Creek campground.

Information sources: Alberta Parks.

Resupply stations: Castle Ski Resort.

Special notes: A solid red diamond indicates a trail that is open for motorized vehicle use all year long. If the red diamond has a black bar in the centre, the trail is only for summer use, while a white bar designates winter use. From the Castle Ski Resort to Coleman, the GDT follows nearly 50km of motorized trails. The best days to schedule this part of the route are mid-week when there are fewer OHVS. This is subject to change as this

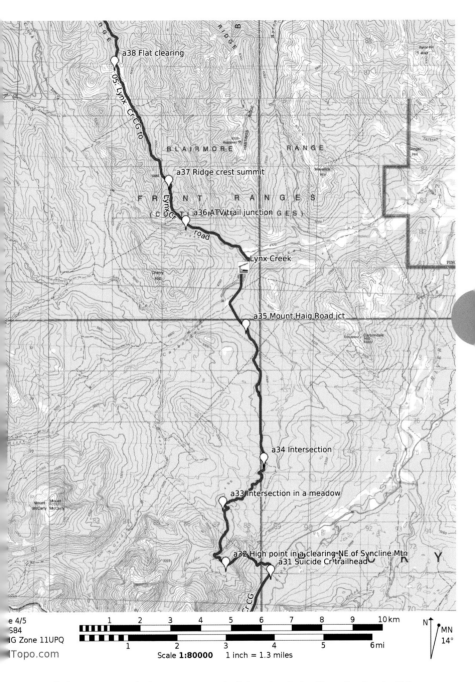

a38 Flat clearing

BLAIRMORE RANGE

a37 Ridge crest summit

FRONT RANGES

a36 ATV trail junction

road

Lynx Creek

a35 Mount Haig Road jct

a34 Intersection

a33 Intersection in a meadow

a32 High point in a clearing NE of Syncline Mtn
a31 Suicide Cr trailhead

Scale **1:80000**   1 inch = 1.3 miles

N
MN
14°

whole area recently became a provincial park. Find wifi at the Castle Ski Resort hostel.

Additional reading: Refer to the Alberta Parks website for Castle and

Castle Wildland provincial parks. Currently, there are plans to upgrade the road to the ski resort and even build a new provincial parks info centre. Thanks to the GDTA, the route is a recognized trail in the new parks and will hopefully benefit from some upgrades, markers and trailheads.

Castle Ski Resort to Syncline Mountain bench
(8.0km, 418m up, 63m down)

Follow Highway 774 from the ski resort. There are OHV trails that parallel the road no more than 100m away that offer more pleasant walking than the road. At 4km, you pass the dirt spur road (where the overhead power lines cross Highway 774) that accesses the northern end of a considerable Barnaby Ridge alternate route. Refer to the previous segment for more information. Whether following the road or one of the parallel OHV trails, you will reach the Suicide Creek bridge (1410, 6.1, a31). Looking west from the bridge, the trail you will be on looks like a gash across the face of the forested mountainside. Continue walking over the bridge; immediately on the left is an obvious pullout. Follow an OHV track marked with a red diamond into the forest, not the more obvious and steeper dirt road that goes uphill – although both go to the same destination. At first, this trail diverges from the creek. At a junction in 100m, the path rejoins the steep dirt road. In another 100m, turn left as the more prominent dirt road heads to the northeast (and not where you want to go). Our route heads west through forest toward Suicide Creek and crosses it in 400m. At a junction in another 300m, avoid following the obvious path that heads north, back to the creek. Instead, follow the straight, brushy path northwest. In a long meadow, walk parallel to the creek, upstream, exiting the meadow on an overgrown cutline that ascends steeply up the mountainside. Providing a convenient drainage channel over the years, the cutline makes for an awkward climb, especially in places where it is overgrown, but it is worth the views across the valley. When the ascent eases, veer left and climb the gash that was apparent from the Suicide Creek Bridge below. The route ascends to a level clearing and dirt road (1770, 2.1, a32), northeast of Syncline Mountain. NOBO hikers, turn right. (SOBO hikers must look around a bit for the trail at this point, which is 600m from where you last crossed Suicide Creek.)

Syncline Mountain bench to Lynx Creek campground
(12.1km, 68m up, 469m down)

The route between the West Castle and Carbondale rivers follows an OHV trunk route, one side of the O'Hagen Loop trail, which eventually joins the Mount Haig road. It is an enjoyable walk provided there are few vehicles and little mud. The O'Hagen Loop trail intersects many spur trails

Walking a forestry road near the end of segment 4.

that are all potential points for you to go astray. The side of the O'Hagen Loop trail that the GDT follows goes due north and is usually easy to identify as a very well-used route.

Turn right on the dirt road and follow it over the bench for 600m to a hop across Suicide Creek. Within 100m you pass a spur trail that heads uphill to the left. The main track remains obvious as it crosses seismic lines and goes around a couple of sharp bends before reaching a junction (1650, 2.9, a33) in a meadow. The O'Hagen Loop trail continues straight through the intersection to the northeast and re-enters the forest. The GDT contours down to a good spring in 1.7km. Still in trees, the O'Hagen Loop trail intersects with a larger, signed dirt road 24 (1560, 2.2, a34). Turn left and head north. You soon cross a couple of seismic lines and after 1.5km a spring. The track is in poor condition with the potential for large pools and a lot of mud. In some places, the O'Hagen Loop trail is washed-out. In another 2km, the track goes straight through a minor junction. Just 300m farther, you follow a 50m-wide seismic line for about 50m northeast before turning left (north) back onto the dirt road and enter forest again. A gentle descent delivers the O'Hagen Loop trail to a junction with the Mount Haig road (1460, 4.7, a35). At this trailhead, there is a large red diamond containing the number 32 in black and white. Across the two-lane gravel road is a metre-high post with the number 2 on it. Follow the Mount Haig road downhill for 1km to where it joins the Carbondale haul road. There is a trail info kiosk next to this intersection. Turn right and follow the Carbondale road over a bridge in 900m. In 400m more you reach the entrance to the Lynx Creek campground, which occupies both sides of the road. This recreation site caters to car-campers and can be noisy on weekends. The fee is $7 for a site that has a table, outhouse access and fire pit. Of special interest to hikers is a water pump in the centre of the campground.

SEGMENT 5 – Lynx Creek campground to Lynx Creek road on Willoughby Ridge (15.5km)

This is an easy hike with moderate ascents. Horses and bikes permitted.

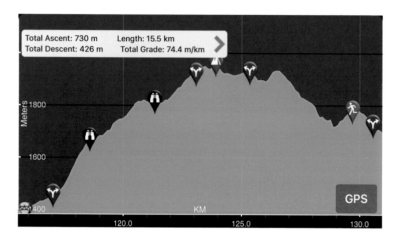

This is a superb walk along a panoramic ridge crest, parallel to the Continental Divide. The GDT follows the Willoughby Ridge trail between easily accessible points. A large forest fire severely affected this area in 2003 but the trails have reopened since then.

Maps: 82 G/8 Beaver Mines and 82 G/9 Blairmore.

Jurisdictions: Alberta Parks and Castle Forest District (Alberta).

South access: The Lynx Creek campground shares the same access as the Castle Ski Resort. The difference is you must turn north from Highway 774 at the Castle ranger station, roughly 12km before the ski resort and 1km after passing an intersection for Beaver Mines Lake. This two-lane gravel road is in good enough condition to accommodate all vehicles. The road crosses the Castle River and passes the Castle River Bridge campground. Turn left onto the Mount Haig road soon after passing the campground. In another 10km, keep to the right where the Carbondale haul road inter-sects. The Lynx Creek campground is on the right in another kilometre. (The road continuing past the campground is Adanac Road, which in 16km leads to Hillcrest Mines just off Crowsnest Highway 3. The Lynx Creek road goes over Willoughby Ridge and descends to Blairmore on Highway 3 in roughly 20km.)

North access: Follow the Lynx Creek road 10km south from Blairmore to the crest of Willoughby Ridge. You should park well off the road near the ridge crest if you plan to leave a car there.

Car campgrounds and accommodations: The Lynx Creek campground at the start of the segment is a great spot. The fee is $7 and there are 28 vehicle sites with picnic tables, outhouse, water pump, firewood, and a day-use area. In Blairmore you will find the Lost Lemon RV park and campground at the eastern end of Main Street (just beyond the avenue where you turn right to find Lynx Creek Road). This campground has everything, including a telephone, laundry, swimming pool, hot tub, and showers, but a simple tent site is $30, with a $10 reservation fee if you book in advance.

Camping: Random camping.

Information source: Alberta Parks.

Resupply stations: None.

Special notes: See the special notes for segment 4.

Lynx Creek campground to Willoughby Ridge summit (12.4km, 647m up and 249m down)

Continue northeast on the Carbondale haul road from the Lynx Creek campground and cross the Lynx Creek bridge in 200m at 1360m elevation. Turn left on Lynx Creek Road within 100m after the bridge. The road ascends gently and stays well above the northeast bank of the creek. In 1.5km from the intersection, you cross another bridge with a camping area just beyond it. Ignore the dirt road that heads north off Lynx Creek Road 500m past the bridge and continue another 500m to the Willoughby Ridge OHV trail junction (1460, 5.1, a36). There is a large boulder standing on end 50m before this junction, beside the road. Some hikers report seeing a sign just up from the junction that reads "Whiskey Ridge." There is usually no water for the next 11km (and that source may run dry in the late season). Turn right and follow the OHV track. Follow this well-used track up the ridge crest. It's a moderate climb up to a ridge crest summit (1705, 1.6, a37).

The OHV track joins an old logging road that ascends and generally follows the crest of Willoughby Ridge through a burnt forest. Views of the Divide to the west abound as the route ascends a spur to a flat clearing and minor junction and campsite (1925, 4.5, a38). The track continues on the crest of Willoughby Ridge 900m before reaching a steep descent through trees. Climb the open ridge crest to a minor summit (1940, 1.8, a39) that has a panoramic view. In 400m you pass an OHV trail junction that branches downhill to the west (which eventually reaches the Lynx Creek road in 2km near the confluence of Lynx and Snowshoe creeks).

Our OHV track continues along the crest of Willoughby Ridge to the

Willoughby Ridge has an open, grass-covered crest. It is a pleasure to hike.

The author looking north from the northern-most summit of Willoughby Ridge.

last prominent summit (1975, 1.7, a40). From here, you can see the Lynx Creek road where it crests Willoughby Ridge. Following a bearing of 280 degrees you could make your way straight there. However, there is a better trail that heads down a ridge crest to the north.

Willoughby Ridge summit to Lynx Creek Road (3.1km, 83m up and 177m down)

The OHV trail that descends to Lynx Creek Road is better than in previous years, owing to more traffic since the 2003 fire. Depart the summit to the north-northwest and then descend along the ridge crest directly north through burnt forest and a patch that escaped being burned. In 500m the trail curves in the remnant forest before turning sharply right

The GDT follows this gravel road into Coleman. Highway 3 and part of Coleman are visible.

and descending parallel to the north-trending ridge crest. Pass straight through a couple of obscure junctions with old logging roads before coming to a four-way intersection (1865, 1.7, a41). Turn left and head down to the southwest on the OHV trail. The trail gently descends to a creek gully (1800, 0.7, a42). Avoid the road going downstream and hop the creek, the first water source in 11km. The grass-covered roadbed now contours through the forest and then regains some elevation before it reaches the Lynx Creek road (1785, 0.7, a43). At this waypoint, the Lynx Creek road crests Willoughby Ridge. You will see a Texas gate and a fence with a sign marking the forestry district boundary.

From here the GDT turns left and follows a pleasant OHV trail down the York Creek drainage and descends an active gravel road into Coleman, Alberta.

BLAIRMORE ALTERNATE ROUTE – 15.5KM INSTEAD OF 15.4KM

This alternate route departs at kilometre 129.7 and rejoins the main route at kilometre 145.1 in Coleman. There are more amenities in Blairmore than in Coleman. There's a campground with showers and laundry. However, it is easy enough to catch a ride if passing through Coleman, especially if you stay at A Safe Haven B&B. Walking on the Lynx Creek road into Blairmore can be unpleasant on a hot day and there is a lot of traffic on weekends. If you do take this route, follow a nice municipal trail system that parallels Highway 3 between the two towns.

End Blairmore alternate route.

SEGMENT 6 – Lynx Creek Road to Coleman (16.2km)

Easy walk on OHV trails and a gravel road. Horses and bikes permitted.

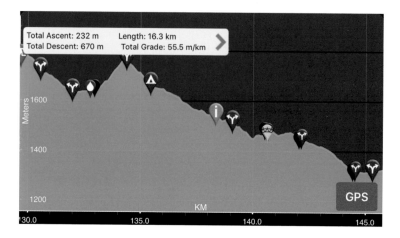

Total Ascent: 232 m   Length: 16.3 km
Total Descent: 670 m   Total Grade: 55.5 m/km

The GDT seems like it should follow the crest of the Flathead Range to the west of this section. The ridges on the Divide seem like the best place for the GDT if it weren't for the fact that they are so precipitous and difficult to access. My hope is that one day the GDT will follow the Divide in segments 5 and 6. With that said, the Willoughby Ridge route in the preceding section, linked with the trails described in this segment, make for some interesting hiking and a convenient resupply for thru-hikers. If you are mailing packages in advance of hiking, following the main route through Coleman makes the most sense. However, if you plan to buy food along the way, take the alternate route mentioned at the end of the preceding segment through Blairmore, where you can buy reasonably priced food.

Maps: 82 G/9 Blairmore and 82 G/10 Crowsnest.

Jurisdiction: Castle Forest District (Alberta).

South access: Follow the Lynx Creek road 10km south from Blairmore to the Willoughby Ridge crest. A kilometre farther on the right you will see two red diamonds marking the OHV trailhead, one with the number 39 in it. You should park off the trailhead or on the crest of Willoughby Ridge to avoid conflicts with OHVs and logging trucks.

North access: Coleman is a small mining town on Crowsnest Highway 3, 5km west of Blairmore and 15km east of the Crowsnest Pass on the British Columbia and Alberta boundary. Refer to the route description to find the entrance to the York Creek road if you would like to eliminate some of the road walking.

Car campgrounds and accommodations: Coleman has a limited tourist industry and does not have a campsite within the town. The alternative to finding a motel room or B&B in Coleman is to camp on the GDT outside the town limits. McGillivray Creek campground is 6km north of the town and there is a small campsite en route 10km south of Coleman. There are some motel accommodations in Coleman and Blairmore. While Coleman only has a convenience store, Blairmore has a supermarket. Hikers recommend A Safe Haven B&B in Coleman, which caters to hikers with special rates and excellent service such as a laundry and a hiker's box for exchanging unneeded supplies. They are truly 'trail angels.'

Camping: Random camping.

Information source: Alberta Parks.

Resupply stations: Coleman Remedy'sRx Postal Services or A Safe Haven B&B.

Special notes: For southbound hikers, a solid red diamond indicates a trail that is open for motorized vehicle use all year long. If the diamond has a black bar in the centre, the trail is only for summer use, while a white bar designates winter use.

Additional reading: See *Hiking the Historic Crowsnest Pass* (2nd ed., 2001), by Jane Ross and William Tracy, to learn more about other trails in the region and the local history.

Lynx Creek road on Willoughby Ridge to Lynx and York Creek Pass (4.7km, 153m up, 158m down)

The route follows the Lynx Creek road west and downhill to an OHV trail junction (1740, 0.9, a44) marked with two red diamonds, one with the number 39 in it. To the east of the pass, the Lynx Creek road descends 10km to the town of Blairmore (see the alternate route description at the end of the previous segment). Turn right and gently descend the wide and rocky track past a creek in 100m. After 1.4km there is an OHV trail junction marked with the number 40. Take the uphill track on the right. The trail curves to the west and in 900m steps across the head of Lynx Creek, the first reliable water source in 15km. Climb past the creek to a junction with a marked winter trail. Turn right and follow this narrow trail to the north and up a moderate grade to a junction (1770, 3.8, a45) with a summer trail on a broad, forested and unnamed pass between Lynx and York creeks.

Lynx Creek and York Creek pass to Coleman
(11.5km, 79m up, 512m down)

Keep right and descend the OHV track to the north into the York Creek valley from the pass. Staying on the trunk trail, continue past several signed junctions for spur trails that head west across York Creek, most of which have a red diamond marking them. In 1.1km the route crosses a bridge where there is a possible campsite before arriving in Coleman. In 4.0km you should pass a small spring. Another 700m brings you to a hairpin turn where it meets the York Creek road. The trailhead is marked with a red diamond. The route follows this road down a couple of switchbacks to the York Creek bridge (1570, 5.8, a46).

The road gently ascends from the bridge and then starts a long descent to Crowsnest Highway 3. York Creek Road continues to a Texas gate (1385, 3.0, a47) at a fence, where a sign indicates you are leaving the Rocky Mountain Forest Reserve. The road becomes the asphalt 13th Avenue in Coleman. The easiest way to get to the post office at the centre of town is to follow 13th Avenue and turn left on 83rd Street, which crosses the Crowsnest River. The street comes to a T-intersection at the railway tracks. Go nearly two blocks to the left on 15th Avenue, cross the tracks and then turn right on 16th Avenue. This is where the northern end of Blairmore alternate route rejoins the main route. See the end of the preceding segment. Continue uphill past a hotel to Highway 3. Some 200m, to the left on Highway 3 is the Coleman Remedy'sRx Postal Services (1345, 2.7, a48) on the right side of the highway (also called 20th Avenue). The town of Blairmore, 5km east of Coleman, has more amenities, such as a large grocery store, campground and motels.

The last segment is 900m short of the section 1 end noted in the Atlas Guides GDT app.

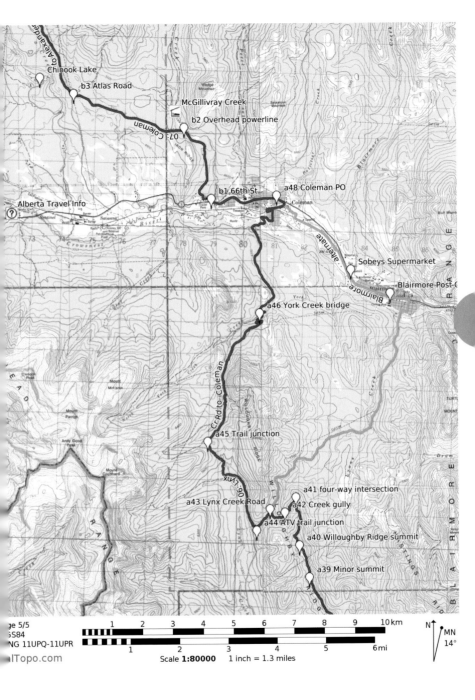

Chinook Lake
b3 Atlas Road
McGillivray Creek
b2 Overhead powerline
Coleman
b1 66th St.
a48 Coleman PO
Alberta Travel Info
Sobeys Supermarket
Blairmore Post
a46 York Creek bridge
a45 Trail junction
a41 four-way intersection
a43 Lynx Creek Road
a42 Creek gully
a44 ATV trail junction
a40 Willoughby Ridge summit
a39 Minor summit

ge 5/5
SS84
NG 11UPQ-11UPR
ITopo.com

1 2 3 4 5 6 7 8 9 10 km
1 2 3 4 5 6 mi
Scale 1:80000   1 inch = 1.3 miles

N
MN
14°

SECTION B: *Coleman to Kananaskis (Elk Pass trailhead)*

Segments 7–13, 197.3 km

Location	Near waypoint	NOBO km	SOBO km
McGillivray Creek car campground*	b2	151.8	981.4
Deadman Pass	b5	164.7	968.5
Alexander Creek campground	b6	170.1	963.1
The Crown (highpoint)	b10	187.0	946.2
Dutch Creek campsite	b15	210.9	922.3
Tornado Saddle	b17	215.9	917.3
South Hidden Creek campsite	b18	219.7	913.5
Hidden Creek campsite	b19	223.5	909.7
Cache Creek campsite	b21	234.1	899.1
Soda Creek campsite*	b22	239.9	893.3
Oldman campsite	b24	248.6	884.6
High Rock campsite	b25	253.8	879.4
Lost Creek campsite	b27	265.7	867.5
Cataract Creek campsite	b28	274.3	858.9
Etherington Creek campsite	b29	280.9	852.3
James Lake campsite	b30	286.8	846.4
Fording River Pass campsite	b31	292.8	840.4
Aldridge Creek campsite	b32	302.6	830.6
Weary Creek car campground*	b33	310.7	822.5
Riverside car campground	b38	321.0	812.2
Tobermory Creek car campground	b38	327.3	805.9
Lower Elk Lake campsite (BC Parks)	b38	334.3	798.9
Mount Sarrail walk-in campground*	b40	344.0	789.2
Boulton Creek car campground*	b40	344.0	789.2
RESUPPLY: Peter Lougheed visitor centre*	b40	344.0	789.2

Introduction

As this is the only section entirely outside the national parks on the GDT route, it makes sense that the GDTA would select this area for the first portion of the official GDT to be constructed since the 1980s. The new section is called High Rock Trail and construction began in 2016. Not only will the estimated 30km of trail divert the existing main route away from the contested property of the Line Creek mine, in BC, it will set the standard for future trail-building efforts and hopefully galvanize hikers from

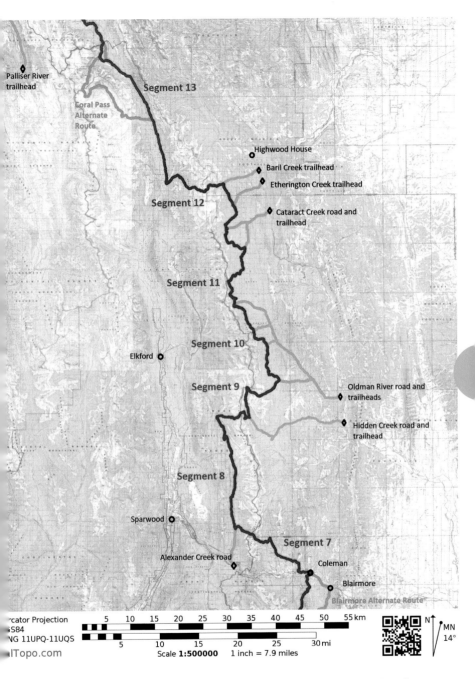

Palliser River trailhead

Segment 13

Coral Pass Alternate Route

Highwood House

Baril Creek trailhead

Etherington Creek trailhead

Segment 12

Cataract Creek road and trailhead

Segment 11

Segment 10

Elkford

Segment 9

Oldman River road and trailheads

Hidden Creek road and trailhead

Segment 8

Sparwood

Segment 7

Alexander Creek road

Coleman

Blairmore

Blairmore Alternate Route

...rcator Projection
...S84
...NG 11UPQ-11UQS
...lTopo.com

| 5 | 10 | 15 | 20 | 25 | 30 | 35 | 40 | 45 | 50 | 55 km |

| 5 | 10 | 15 | 20 | 25 | 30 mi |

Scale **1:500000**   1 inch = 7.9 miles

N
MN
14°

the local area and far and wide to participate in the grand dream of establishing the entire trail one day.

High Rock Trail will extend the centrepiece of the section, which is the

95.7km 'original Great Divide Trail,' built by the first incarnation of the GDTA over 30 years ago. Recently the GDTA has led several trail maintenance and bridge building trips to this area, including the upper Cataract Creek, Baril Creek, the upper Oldman River, Lost Creek, Hidden Creek, Aldridge Creek, and Etherington Creek.

To get to the start of the original Great Divide Trail from Coleman, the route relies on 40km of motorized trails and 20km of active roads. The lack of hiking trail is discouraging but it is still a wilderness route. During my second hike over Deadman Pass, I encountered a grizzly sow and her cub. I followed grizzly bear tracks for most of the Alexander Creek valley. And when the High Rock route is completed, by sometime in 2022, this section of the GDT will shine.

The original Great Divide Trail at the heart of this section is worth the walk along roads and OHV trails. It follows the Divide in Alberta and reaches some truly intriguing areas. The northern spur of Beehive Mountain, for example, has a captivating view of the High Rock Range. Panoramic, grass-covered crests characterize the highpoints, while each valley offers a retreat from the dry ridges beside clear headwaters. Fording River Pass at the northern end of the original Great Divide Trail is an expansive alpine haven. You would need several days to explore the whole area. I had a knee-quaking encounter on Fording River Pass with the largest grizzly I have ever seen. This after I awoke at dawn and howled unintelligible answers to a coyote pack.

Experienced hikers should consider the 30.5km Coral Pass alternate. It offers a spectacular high-country route that avoids some lengthy road walking north of the original GDT. While I see the road walking as a drawback, several hikers have attested to how much they liked the scenery and unimpeded foot travel offered by the road – I guess it depends on your point of view. Of course, these comments surfaced back in the day, when the Aldridge Creek trail was a bushwhack.

The Coral Pass alternate route is very strenuous, involving some committed bushwhacking along Cadorna Creek and some dangerous footing beside the Nivelle Creek gorge. That is, if you can even start, depending on the depth of the Elk River ford. This alternate has many rewards, though. There are spectacular views of 3300m-high Mount Abruzzi and other spires, and there are so many coral fossils over the pass that a day in the alpine here seems like a day at the beach. The isolation of Coral Pass can give you an awe-inspiring sense of remoteness. Compared to the straightforwardness of the road below, the Coral Pass alternate is exhilarating and worth the extra effort.

Segment 7 – Coleman to Alexander Creek campground (23.4km)

Easy walking along wide trails and gravel roads. Horses and bikes permitted.

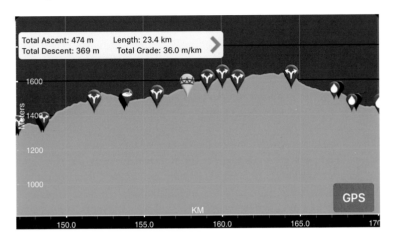

This leg of the GDT depends on OHV trails and gravel roads. Although the ideal route for hikers would lie nearer the Continental Divide, the segment does have some redeeming qualities. The OHV trail cresting the Divide over Deadman Pass is an enjoyable walk. The prominent features such as the castellated spires of Seven Sisters and Crowsnest Peak are ever-present and scenic companions.

Map: 82 G/10 Crowsnest.

Jurisdiction: Bow/Crow Forest District (Alberta).

South access: Coleman is a small mining town on Crowsnest Highway 3, 5km west of Blairmore and 15km east of the Crowsnest Pass and the Alberta–British Columbia boundary. Refer to the route description in this segment if you plan to drive the initial leg to the McGillivray campground.

Other access: Travel 3km west of Coleman on Highway 3 to the Allison Creek road intersection. Turn right and follow the gravel road north. In 3km you pass the Chinook Lake turnoff on the left. In another 5km you reach waypoint b4, not far from the unsigned Allison Creek horse campground and corral mentioned in the route description. Driving past b4, you may see a sign for 'Western Adventures' within 1km. From there a road goes southwest over Allison Creek to the confusing 4-way junction mentioned in the route description. Essentially, what used to be a public campground has turned into a private outfitter's horse camp near Allison Creek.

North access: Turn north onto the Alexander Creek road from Highway 3 about 3km west of the Alberta–British Columbia boundary. This forestry road is not suitable for some cars with low clearance and is likely closed during periods of active logging. If it's open, drive carefully, staying alert for logging trucks. Keep right at a fork 6km from the highway and then cross a major bridge over Alexander Creek. Within another 1km keep right again at another fork. This road continues 1km to the sharp turn on the main route of the GDT, just south of waypoint b6.

Car campgrounds and accommodations: Coleman has a limited tourist industry and does not have a campsite within the town. The alternative to finding a motel room in Coleman is to camp on the GDT outside the town limits. McGillivray Creek campground is 6km north of town, and there is a small campsite en route 10km south of Coleman. There are some motel accommodations in Coleman and Blairmore. While Coleman only has a convenience store, Blairmore has a supermarket. Hikers recommend A Safe Haven B&B in Coleman, which caters to hikers with special rates and excellent service such as a laundry and a hiker's box for exchanging unneeded supplies. They are truly 'trail angels.'

Camping: Forest Service campgrounds at McGillivray Creek, Allison Creek and Alexander Creek and random camping.

Information sources: Travel Alberta's Crowsnest Pass Visitor Information Centre is located on Highway 3, west of Coleman. Call 1-800-252-3782. Check the Alberta Parks website; much of the area in this segment is in the proposed High Rock Wildland Provincial Park.

Resupply stations: Coleman Remedy'sRx Postal Services or A Safe Haven B&B.

Special notes: From waypoint b4 on the Allison Creek/Atlas road it is possible to bypass most of this segment and all of segment 8, to meet up with the southern terminus of the original GDT in segment 9. It might be more appealing to hikers to road walk this section rather than deal with possible trespassing issues in segment 8 at the Line Creek mine. In this case, continue following the Atlas road 14km to a junction. There, turn left and go another 11km due north to meet up with the Dutch Creek road described in 'Other access' for segment 9. Turn left and follow the Dutch Creek road up to the GDT in 7.5km, meeting the route at kilometre 206.9. The road walk is 33km long, replacing 47.8km of the main route. I'm not listing this as an alternate route, because within a few years the new High Rock Trail being built by the GDTA will replace much of segments 7 and 8 (and the

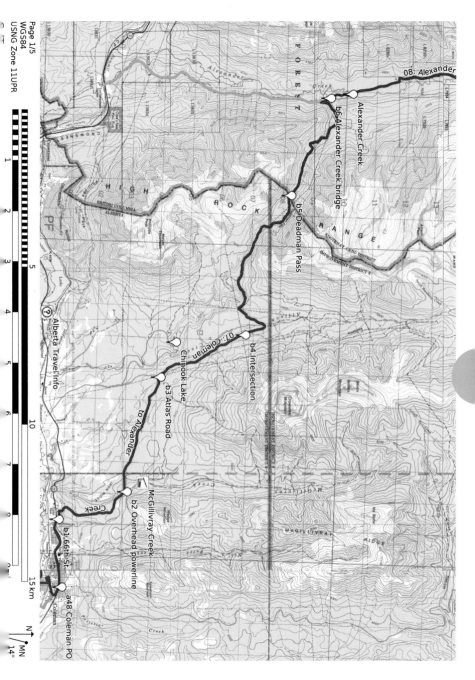

alternate road walk). I don't recommend the road walking but you should be aware of it.

Additional reading: *Hiking the Historic Crowsnest Pass* (2nd ed., 2001), by Jane Ross and William Tracy, gives detailed information on other trails in the region and on local history.

Coleman to McGillivray Creek campground
(5.4km, 170m up, 44m down)

Follow Highway 3 west from Coleman (1345, 0, a44). Although the highway shoulders are wide, the heavy volume of traffic can make even the briefest walk perilous. After crossing McGillivray Creek, turn right at the 66th Street intersection (1350, 2.2, b1). Walk uphill another 100m and turn left on 22nd Avenue. In 300m turn right onto 23rd Avenue (which soon becomes 63rd Street, aka McGillivray Creek Road) and follow it uphill to the north. After skirting around the east side of Iron Ridge, the gravel road passes beneath an overhead power line (1480, 3.2, b2). If you were to continue north on this road for 500m, you would come to the McGillivray Creek campground at the foot of Wedge Mountain.

McGillivray Creek campground junction to Allison Creek
horse campground (7.6km, 179m up, 77m down)

There are many OHV trails around the McGillivray Creek recreation area, some of which go to the Atlas/Allison Creek road to the west. The most navigable of these follows the wet terrain beneath the power line westward to start. Within 1km the road veers north of the power line, heading west-northwest toward a red and white communications tower. There is a water source in a steep ravine in 2.4km. You reach the Atlas/Allison Creek road (1480, 4, b3) after passing through recent clear-cuts and crossing a signed underground pipeline. Turn right and follow the Atlas/Allison Creek road. (At this point, the town of Coleman is roughly 7km by way of Allison Creek Road and Highway 3.) The road stays on the east side of Allison Creek and you will likely see several RVs parked in this area. A trail that parallels the road on the left may offer better walking when the road is busy or muddy. The route follows the Atlas/Allison Creek road north to an intersection (1560, 3.3, b4) immediately after crossing an obvious seismic line. Turn left on the unattractive cutline going west-southwest and descend 300m to the Allison Creek horse campground and corral.

Allison Creek campground to Deadman Pass
(5km, 101m up, 60m down)

The road to Allison Creek campground turns into an OHV track that fords Allison Creek. In 700m beyond the creek, you will arrive at a confusing 4-way junction. Moreover, there are two roads heading north-north-west. If you take the westernmost of these two tracks, it should start to descend and veer away from the other one. This rocky track follows

Slash pile over Deadman Pass. The GDTA is building a new trail that will avoid the industrial activity in segments 7 and 8.

A fresh grizzly bear track near Deadman Pass.

a drainage and gradually ascends in forest through the northern part of the Allison–Chinook cross-country ski area. Stay on the main track, ignoring other signed ski trails. Nearing the pass the trail criss-crosses a long east–west seismic line several times. The final crossing is at 5km from

Julia Lynx hikes through Alexander Creek in flood.

waypoint b4, just 300m before reaching Deadman Pass (1590, 5.3, b5) on the Continental Divide. (You can continue following this seismic line, as it does meet up with the main route again in 2.7km and is reportedly drier than the main route.)

Deadman Pass to Alexander Creek campsite (5.4km, 24m up, 188m down)

The descent from the pass is mostly gentle. In 2.6km you reach a wade-across ford of a creek. On the other side of the creek is a small camp. Within 100m past this crossing, you encounter a newly constructed logging road which is at the end of the seismic line you criss-crossed on the other side of Deadman Pass. (You could follow the seismic line SOBO to meet up with the main route in 2.7km if you like.) In 2016 hikers reported seeing a 'No Trespassing' sign here warning that people weren't permitted to pass through the area during active logging. The logging happens only on weekdays, though, and may have been underway only during that season. Turn left and follow the road downhill 1km to a new steel bridge. Keep following the road over the bridge another 600m to a hairpin turn and a junction. Turn sharply right at this Y-junction and follow the road 200m to a bridged crossing. Continue for another 900m to a substantial ford of Alexander Creek (1430, 5.4, b6) that could be an issue in early season or after a lot of precipitation. Cross the creek and reach the Alexander Creek campsite near a private bridge and a private cabin that can be quite raucous and busy at times.

SEGMENT 8 – Alexander Creek campsite to South Line Creek road (26.9km)

Easy hiking with some moderate climbs and navigational challenges. Horses and bikes permitted – read special notes.

The hiking is enjoyable near the headwaters of Alexander Creek. The GDT mostly follows OHV trails but you do get the opportunity to do some straightforward cross-country travel. Adjacent to the Continental Divide the view from the route is panoramic. Hikers report seeing moose and bears in this segment but they have also reported issues with Line Creek mine security staff near waypoint b12 (see image below). Normally there is no issue if you don't try to use the private roads (inside the pink area) and stick to the main route. This is the reason why the GDTA is building the new High Rock Trail on the eastern side of the Divide from this location. The new trail will avoid much road walking and this trespassing issue.

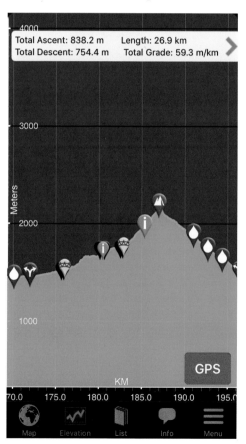

Maps: 82 G/10 Crowsnest and 82 G/15 Tornado Mountain.

Jurisdiction: Rocky Mountain Forest District (BC).

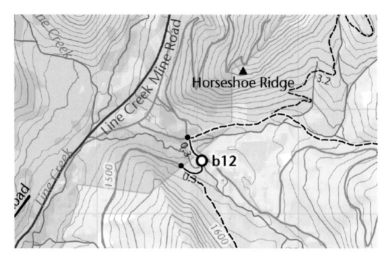

Waypoint b12 map, showing Line Creek mine private property in red. Map credit: Ryan Silk

The Line Creek mine in segment 8.

South access: Turn north onto the Alexander Creek road from Highway 3 about 3km west of the Alberta–British Columbia boundary. This forestry road is not suitable for some cars with low clearance and is likely closed during periods of active logging. If it's open, drive carefully, staying alert for logging trucks. Keep right at the fork in 6km and then cross a major bridge over Alexander Creek. Within another 1km keep right again at another fork. This road continues 1km to the sharp turn on the main route of the GDT, just south of waypoint b6.

North access: Access is restricted by Teck, the company that operates the Line Creek mine. You need permission from Teck to proceed toward the South Line Creek road near waypoint b12 (which they aren't likely to grant). I describe this access for emergencies only. Just east of Sparwood on

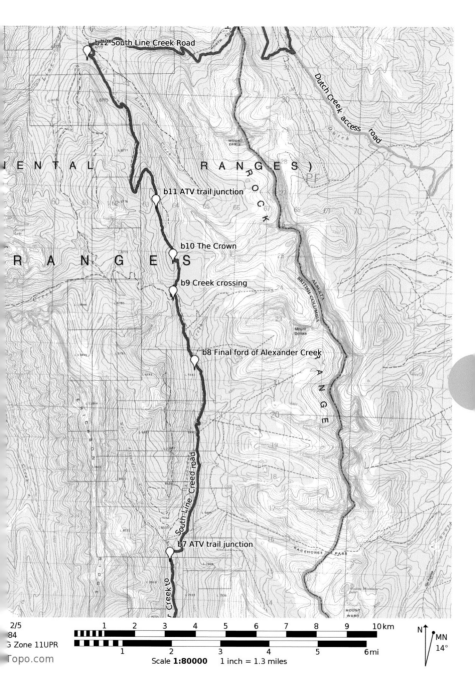

b12 South Line Creek Road

b11 ATV trail junction

b10 The Crown

b9 Creek crossing

b8 Final ford of Alexander Creek

b7 ATV trail junction

Dutch Creek access road

(IENTAL   R A N G E S)

R A N G E S

South Line Creek road

Creek to

2/5
84
G Zone 11UPR
Topo.com

| 1 | 2 | 3 | 4 | 5 | 6 | 7 | 8 | 9 | 10km |

| 1 | 2 | 3 | 4 | 5 | 6mi |

Scale **1:80000**   1 inch = 1.3 miles

N
MN
14°

Highway 3, turn north on Highway 43 and travel toward Elkford. Roughly
20km north, turn right on a minor road for Grave Lake and the Line Creek
mine. After crossing the Elk River, turn left on the Fording River road, go

Washout on a seismic line up the Alexander Creek valley.

The Divide from near the Crown.

another 2km and turn right on the Line Creek road toward the mine. In approximately 10km turn right to cross the Line Creek bridge. Over the bridge turn left onto the South Line Creek road.

Car campgrounds and accommodations: None. However, if you are passing through the Crowsnest, read the campground and accommodation info for segment 7 if you plan to stay in Coleman or Blairmore. Elkford has limited accommodations, but there are many car campgrounds on the Elk River road north of Elkford, described in segments 12 and 13.

Camping: Alexander Creek campsite and random camping.

Information source: Rocky Mountain Forest District.

Resupply stations: None.

Special notes: As noted in the introduction to this segment, beware of the trespass issue around waypoint b12 and the Line Creek mine. Although the route barely crosses the legal boundaries of the mine property, you may see 'No Trespassing' signs well up the GDT route north and south. Hikers advise to 'not get caught.' However, if approached by security staff, be reasonable and keep calm. Explain what you are doing and where you are going. Don't use b12 as an access point unless it's for an emergency, in which case I would flag down anyone in the area for help. This applies to equestrians and cyclists as well.

Alexander Creek campsite to the Crown
(16.9km, 809m up, 72m down)

From the campsite, follow the road along the west side of the creek for 1.9km to the Alexander Creek road. Turn right and follow that road. At 100m before reaching a bridged crossing of Alexander Creek, the route comes to a Y-junction (1530, 5.9, b7) with an OHV trail. Turn right and cross the bridge. There is a campsite near the bridge. Follow the road east and cross another bridge in 200m. The road starts gaining elevation, turns abruptly north and soon heads northeast 800m to another Y-junction. Keep going north, past the road on the right (SOBOs keep right, heading down to the creek). You will cross several small tributaries. In another 3.4km from the junction, you reach a large, nearly square clear-cut. The route exits through the northern corner of the clear-cut and goes steeply down an embankment to another road that immediately contours around a drainage. The OHV road continues north, diverging from Alexander Creek. In 2.5km from the square clear-cut, you cross Alexander Creek on a bridge (1750, 6.9, b8). The OHV track continues up to a signed junction in 200m. The sign reads 'No Unauthorized Vehicles.' Turn right and then left in less than 100m. A moderate ascent continues 2.2km up the east side of a tributary until crossing the creek near a campsite (2180, 2.5, b9).

After crossing the creek, the OHV track does an unnecessary switchback to the south before resuming the ascent to the north. The track follows the west side of the small tributary to a highpoint known locally as the Crown (2145, 1.6, b10). This pass is northeast of Crown Mountain and is a popular area for motorized recreation.

The Crown to South Line Creek Road
(10km, 29m up, 682m down)

The route descends moderately, almost directly north, on the left side of a creek, roughly paralleling it but never crossing it. Likewise the GDT stays to the right of a parallel ridge crest. The route descends to an OHV trail (2030, 2.0, b11) and follows it around the top of a clear-cut, then around the ridge crest below that clear-cut to a creek crossing in 2km. The trail continues down the creek drainage, which you cross again in 1.7km. The route continues a moderate descent down the east side of the creek 1.6km to another crossing. Afterwards the trail gently descends north-north-west 2.2km to an important junction at a hairpin turn (1480, 7.5, b12). From the hairpin road junction, turn sharply to the right. In 200m cross a large bridge and then keep left at the next junction, within 100m. Follow this road north for almost 250m over a bridge to the South Line Creek road junction.

SEGMENT 9 – South Line Creek road to Hidden Creek campsite (27.3km)

Strenuous hike over three passes with steep climbs and descents. Horses and bikes permitted – read special notes.

Map: 82 G/15 Tornado Mountain.

Jurisdictions: Rocky Mountain Forest District (BC) and Bow/Crow Forest District (Alberta).

South access: Access is restricted by Teck, the company that operates the Line Creek mine. You need permission from Teck to proceed toward the South Line Creek road near waypoint b12 (which isn't likely to be granted). I describe this access for emergencies only. Just east of Sparwood on Highway 3, turn north on Highway 43 and travel toward Elkford. Roughly 20km north, turn right on a minor road for Grave Lake and the Line Creek mine. After crossing the Elk River, turn left on the Fording River road, go another 2km and turn right on the Line Creek road toward the mine. In approximately 10km turn right to cross the Line Creek bridge. Over the bridge turn left onto the South Line Creek road.

Other access: From Highway 40 where it crosses Dutch Creek, follow the Dutch Creek road west for 25km to meet the GDT. Highway 40 is well travelled but the upper Dutch Creek road conditions are only suitable for OHVs.

North access: From Highway 40, follow the Oldman River road approximately 8km to the Hidden Creek trailhead at the confluence of Hidden Creek with the Oldman River. Cross the river and hike roughly 9km up the Hidden Creek trail to join the GDT 800m downstream from the Hidden Creek campsite.

Car campgrounds and accommodations: On Highway 40 in Kananaskis Country there are two campgrounds, at Etherington Creek and Cataract Creek, 10km and 20km respectively south of Highwood House. There is a $15 fee at each campground. Cataract Creek campground has shelters in the day-use area. Call 403-591-7226 for more information.

Camping: Forest Service campsites at Dutch Creek, South Hidden Creek and Hidden Creek, plus random camping.

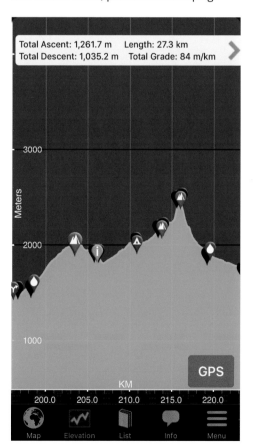

Information sources: Rocky Mountain Forest District, GDTA website and Alberta Parks (Beehive Natural Area).

Resupply stations: None.

Special notes: Beware of the trespass issue around waypoint b12 and the Line Creek mine. Although the route barely crosses the legal boundaries of the mine property, you may see 'No Trespassing' signs well up the GDT route north and south. Hikers advise to 'not get caught.' However, if approached by security staff, be reasonable and keep calm. Explain what you are doing and where you are going. Don't use b12 as an access point unless it's for

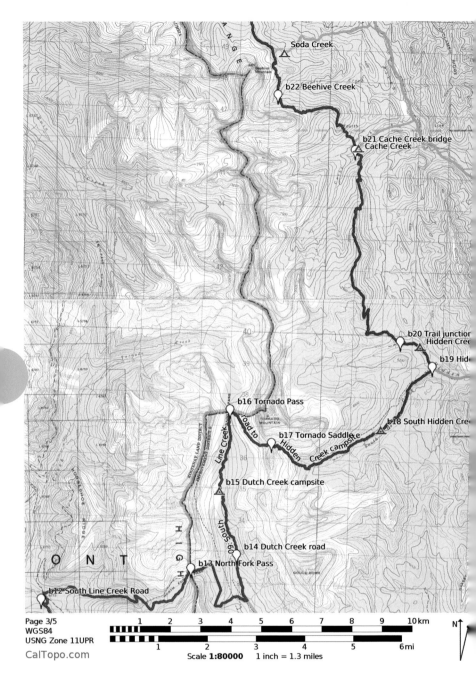

Soda Creek
b22 Beehive Creek
b21 Cache Creek bridge
Cache Creek
b20 Trail junction
Hidden Creek
b19 Hid
b16 Tornado Pass
b18 South Hidden Cre
b17 Tornado Saddle
Road to Hidden
Creek campsite
b15 Dutch Creek campsite
Line Creek
b14 Dutch Creek road
b13 North Fork Pass
b12 South Line Creek Road

1   2   3   4   5   6   7   8   9   10 km
1   2   3   4   5   6 mi
Scale **1:80000**   1 inch = 1.3 miles

N↑

an emergency, in which case I would flag down anyone in the area for help. This applies to equestrians and cyclists as well.

soвo hikers, refer to the 'Special notes' for segment 7 to learn of a road walk alternate route to bypass segment 8 and much of 7. I don't recommend road walking, so I'm not listing it as an alternate route. You should be aware of it, though.

The original Great Divide Trail uses special markings that you should learn to recognize. Along the route, one orange blaze signifies that the trail continues straight ahead, while two orange rectangles, one above the other, signify an imminent change in direction. The blazes are usually head height and painted on trees. There are some surviving trail registers en route that aid navigation and give you the opportunity to communicate with fellow hikers. I would suggest carrying your own pen and paper if you would like to make use of the registers.

Additional reading: For stories about the original Great Divide Trail and its construction there are a couple of good sources. The May 1977 issue of the Sierra Club *Bulletin* had an interesting article by Pat Kariel titled "Waterton to Banff: Canada's Proposed Great Divide Trail." And in the July/August 1989 *Explore* magazine, Marcia Farquhar recounts her previous summer's hike in "The Great Divide Trail Revisited." Highway 40, south of Highwood House is still labelled as 940 on some maps.

South Line Creek Road to North Fork Pass (6.4km, 501m up, 32m down)

At the South Line Creek road junction turn right (east). If you miss turning at this junction, you will be walking right into the mining operations and will probably be approached by security personnel. There is likely a sign warning 'Danger, Active Mining Area, No Trespassing' that will indicate you've gone too far past the junction.

Going east, toward North Fork Pass, keep right at a junction in 800m. The route follows the creek and then crosses it in another 400m.

Skeleton on the trail, North Fork Pass area.

The road degenerates into a seldom used OHV track and reaches the next creek crossing in 700m. The next water source is 8km away, at Dutch Creek, so you should fill up here. In 300m go straight through a junction (the other road heads to a clear-cut). Beyond this point the trail is rough, with frequent washouts, which makes for difficult walking. A poor trail climbs gradually into meadows before reaching the signed North Fork Pass (2000, 6.9, b13) on the Divide. This pass is the southern terminus of the original Great Divide Trail. Look for an old sign in the pass and stay alert for orange blazes on trees marking the trail for the next 100km.

North Fork Pass to Dutch Creek campsite (7.5km, 258m up, 239m down)

From the pass, follow the most obvious OHV track downhill. The track weaves through old clear-cuts. It can be steep and very muddy. Eventually the track fords Dutch Creek in 3.3km and joins the Dutch Creek road in 200m. SOBOs, you should fill your water bottles here, since there's no water for 8km. Refer to the 'Other access' description at the beginning of this segment if you plan to use this road as an access for the Great Divide Trail. Turn left and head upstream, following the track northward. Within 2km you will reach the first blazed stretch of the GDT, on Dutch Creek (1830, 4.5, b14).

The original GDT follows the Dutch Creek road north, up the valley. The trail, in good condition, continues through the forest. Pass the edge of a large area of avalanche debris and arrive at the Dutch Creek campsite (2000, 3.0, b15). The campsite is situated on the edge of a large boulder field, with a nearby spring and a clear view of the valley above and below.

Dutch Creek campsite to Tornado Mountain saddle (5.0km, 480m up, 18m down)

After leaving the campsite the trail crosses a creek in 500m and then several more times before starting a moderate climb up to Tornado Pass (2166, 2.8, b16). At Tornado Pass a crumbled monument marks the Divide and the boundary between Alberta and British Columbia. The now obscure trail turns away from the Divide and heads back into Alberta. East of the monument a noticeable trail enters the trees and gently descends to the southeast. After contouring around debris chutes, you begin a moderate ascent toward the obvious col south of Tornado Mountain. Eventually the path fades and a cross-country leg brings you into the alpine at the foot of scree leading up to the pass. You may see a remnant trail heading up through the scree, but if not it is easy enough to pick your own way up. The steep ascent brings you to the Tornado Mountain saddle (2266, 2.2, b17).

The hike from Tornado Pass to Tornado Mountain Saddle starts gently enough.

Julia Lynx reads some of the inscriptions etched on the Tornado Pass provincial boundary marker in 1996. The obelisk has since disintegrated.

Leaving steep scree for firmer ground, Julia nears the Tornado Mountain saddle.

Julia looks over her shoulder from the Tornado Mountain saddle to the pass.

Tornado Mountain saddle to South Hidden Creek campsite (3.8km, 1m up, 594m down)

The descent to the east of the unnamed col is nearly as steep as the western side but the trail is evident thanks to some recent work by the GDTA in 2014. Cairns mark the switchback descent. Lower down, the trail tends to stay along the north side of the meadow, near the major drainage. The original GDT becomes easily visible on a small ridge that parallels the southern bank of South Hidden Creek. Ford the creek in 2km and descend through forest. Look for the orange blazes. After a gentle descent, you reach a junction with an OHV track. Turn left and take the track for 400m to another junction. Ignore the road leading downhill and go straight through this second junction near the South Hidden Creek campsite (1860, 3.8, b18).

South Hidden Creek campsite to Hidden Creek campsite (4.6km, 22m up, 152m down)

The trail continues descending along the creek, crossing it twice on footbridges. While there is an OHV trail above this section of the original GDT, it isn't recommended. The GDTA did a trail maintenance trip in this area too in 2014, fixing the footbridges and clearing the trail. The marked trail reaches a junction with OHV trail 115 at a bridge over Hidden Creek (1720, 3.8, b19). Turn left and follow the track upstream 800m, avoiding a road that goes back down to the creek, to the well-maintained Hidden Creek campsite.

Beehive Mountain in the Beehive Natural Area, part of the High Rock Range that forms the Continental Divide.

SEGMENT 10 – Hidden Creek campsite to Oldman River Road (23.8km)

Moderate hiking on good trail with two strenuous ascents. Horses and bikes permitted.

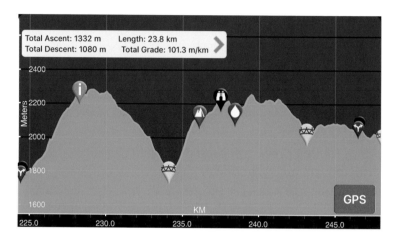

Total Ascent: 1332 m   Length: 23.8 km
Total Descent: 1080 m   Total Grade: 101.3 m/km

The original Great Divide Trail traverses the Beehive Natural Area at timberline. Much of the route stays on ridge crests, giving you the opportunity to stay in view of Beehive Mountain and the High Rock Range. The hiking is superb throughout this segment.

Maps: 82 G/15 Tornado Mountain and 82 J/2 Fording River.

Jurisdiction: Bow/Crow Forest District (Alberta), Alberta Parks.

South access: From Highway 40, follow the Oldman River road approximately 8km to the Hidden Creek trailhead at the confluence of Hidden Creek with the Oldman River. Cross the river and hike roughly 9km up the Hidden Creek trail to join the GDT, 800m downstream from the Hidden Creek campsite.

Other access: There are two routes from the Great Divide Trail to the Oldman River road that link up with Highway 40: (1) From the Beehive Natural Area, a trail leads downstream 2km along Cache Creek to the Oldman River road. The road connects with Highway 40 in approximately 20km. This is the easiest access to the original Great Divide Trail. (2) Past the Beehive Mountain saddle, you can turn right at the Soda Creek trail junction and follow it 4km to the Oldman River road at a point 25km from Highway 40.

North access: You can safely drive a car from Highway 40 up the Oldman

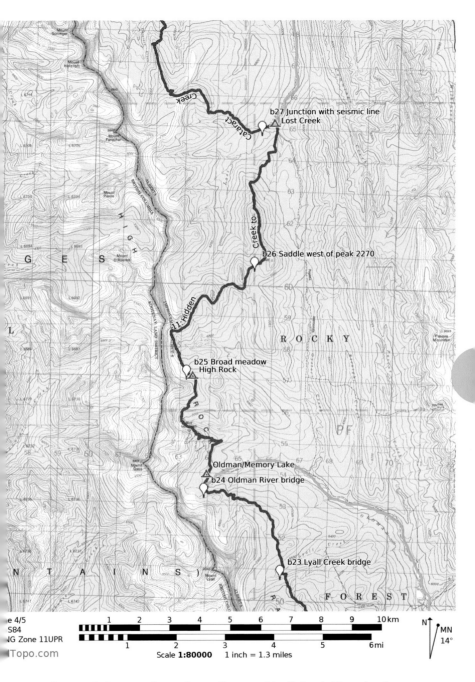

b27 Junction with seismic line
Lost Creek

b26 Saddle west of peak 2270

b25 Broad meadow
High Rock

Oldman/Memory Lake
b24 Oldman River bridge

b23 Lyall Creek bridge

Cataract Creek

Creek to

11: Hidden

G E S   H I G H

L

R O C K Y

F

N   T   A   I   N   S

F O R E S T

e 4/5
S84
NG Zone 11UPR
Topo.com

	1	2	3	4	5	6	7	8	9	10km

	1	2	3	4	5	6mi

Scale **1:80000**   1 inch = 1.3 miles

N
MN
14°

River road almost as far as the confluence of Lyall Creek. There is a large
clearing 2km past the Soda Creek trail access, where you can park and

Much of the original GDT is below timberline, punctuated by brief forays into the alpine. This is the view north from Beehive Mountain.

Our tent perched below Beehive.

hike another 9km to the Great Divide Trail. OHVs can reach the Great Divide Trail on the Oldman River road.

Car campgrounds and accommodations: On Highway 40 in Kananaskis Country there are two campgrounds: Etherington Creek and Cataract Creek, 10km and 20km south of Highwood House. There is a $15 fee at each. Cataract Creek campground has shelters in its day-use area. Call 403-591-7226 for more information.

Camping: Hidden Creek campsite, Cache Creek campsite, and Soda Creek campsite, which is 900m off-route. Random camping.

Information sources: Alberta Parks (Beehive Natural Area) and the GDTA website.

View of the Divide from south of Cache Creek.

Resupply stations: None.

Special notes: Along the original GDT, one orange blaze means the trail continues straight ahead, while two orange rectangles, one above the other, signify an imminent change in direction. The blazes are usually head height and painted on trees. Highway 40 south of Highwood House is still labelled as the 940 on some maps.

Hidden Creek campsite to Cache Creek campsite (9.8km, 560m up, 539m down)

From the Hidden Creek campsite, continue up Hidden Creek. In 300m, where the route encounters a Y-intersection, turn left, staying near the northern bank of Hidden Creek. Consider gathering water here. The next reliable water source is 10km north. In another 500m the trail reaches a marked junction (1720, 1.6, b20); turn right and take the well-used trail that starts a moderate ascent. During dry years, there is no water for the next 9km for NOBO hikers. Switchbacks and a steep ascent bring you to the edge of a long meadow on a ridge crest. The original GDT follows the crest line over a minor peak – a highpoint of 2260m – and then along a contour east of a larger, forested peak. The marked trail rejoins the crest line and gently descends through meadows. A moderate descent through trees brings the trail off the ridge crest down to a bridge (1790, 9.0, b21) over Cache Creek in the Beehive Natural Area. The Cache Creek campsite is on the Cache Creek trail 200m to the right, downstream. See 'Other access' in this segment for the Cache Creek trail. During dry years, SOBO hikers should collect water before leaving the creek.

Cache Creek campsite to Soda Creek trail junction (5.8km, 582m up, 163m down)

Starting out as a deceptively gentle ascent, the trail leaves Cache Creek and soon crosses a seismic line. Climb switchbacks steeply up to a forested

The original GDT south of Cache Creek.

Ridge walking south of Cache Creek.

ridge crest, reaching a highpoint of 2120m in 2km. An undulating path traces the crest and then traverses open slopes with excellent panoramic views. The trail descends steeply to Beehive Creek (2135, 4.3, b22), where there is a campsite next to a spring. Climb gradually through trees for 1km to a 2230m saddle east of Beehive Mountain. Contour 500m from the saddle to the Soda Creek trail junction. Read 'Other access' in this segment for the Soda Creek trail. If you do need to use the Soda Creek trail, there is a campsite 900m down the trail.

Soda Creek trail junction to Oldman River road (8.2km, 190m up, 378m down)

Continue straight past the junction and through meadows before descending to a bridge at Lyall Creek (2016, 4.7, b23). There is a nice campsite next to the bridge. Climb a moderate 100m elevation gain through forest over a ridge, cross a seasonal creek in 1.4km and gently descend to another tributary and trail junction for Memory Lake in 3.6km. Turn right and avoid the better trail that goes uphill 1km to the lake – although, if you do take that trail, there is a good campsite at the lake. Eventually, you reach a footbridge over the Oldman River (2010, 4.9, b24) on the northern boundary of the Beehive Natural Area. There is a campsite in 500m – see the route description in segment 11.

SEGMENT 11 – Oldman River road to Cataract Creek campsite (26.2km)

Moderate hiking on good trail. Horses and bikes permitted.

This is the heart of the original Great Divide Trail. It is in a lofty position on crests adjacent to the High Rock Range and the Divide. Most of the trail is in good condition; it is well marked and is an overwhelming pleasure to hike.

Maps: 82 J/2 Fording River and 82 J/7 Mount Head; Gemtrek #9 Highwood & Cataract Creek.

Jurisdictions: Bow/Crow Forest District (Alberta) and Kananaskis Country (Alberta Parks).

South access: You can safely drive a car from Highway 40 up the Oldman River road almost as far as the confluence of Lyall Creek. There is a large clearing 2km past the Soda Creek trail access, where you can park and hike another 9km to the Great Divide Trail. OHVs can reach the Great Divide Trail on the Oldman River road.

Other access: Follow the Cataract Creek road described in 'North access' just below. In 4.5km you cross the bridge over Cataract Creek and continue up the Lost Creek road 5.5km to the seismic line mentioned in the main trail description below. Turn right on the prominent line and reach the trail in 400m.

North access: Drive 18km south of Highwood House to a trailhead parking area just before the Cataract Creek campsite on Highway 40. The trailhead jointly accesses a fire lookout hike and an access road up Cataract Creek. Leaving your car at the trailhead, you walk around the gate that restricts access to the Cataract Creek road and follow this gravel road. In 4km you pass an old sawmill on the right. Turn right and leave the Cataract Creek road 500m farther on before crossing a bridge. Continue following an OHV trail alongside the northern bank of Cataract Creek 4km upstream to reach the GDT. A new haul road goes along the northern bank of Cataract Creek but the OHV trail is nicer walking.

Car campgrounds and accommodations: On Highway 40 in Kananaskis Country there are two campgrounds, Etherington Creek and Cataract Creek, 10km and 20km south of Highwood House. There is a $15 fee at each. Cataract Creek campground has shelters in its day-use area. Call 403-591-7226 for more information.

Camping: High Rock, Lost Creek and Cataract Creek campsites. Random camping.

Information source: GDTA website.

Resupply stations: None.

Special notes: Along the original GDT, one orange blaze means the trail continues straight ahead, while two orange rectangles, one above the other, signify an imminent change in direction. The blazes are usually head height and painted on trees. Highway 40 south of Highwood House is still labelled as 940 on some maps.

Oldman River road to High Rock campsite (5.7km, 318m up, 151m down)

The route north of the Oldman River can be confusing with all the OHV tracks. Orange blazes remain the best indication of where the trail goes. A wide trail leaves the Oldman River bridge and crosses a seismic line that is a continuation of the Oldman River road. You reach the eastern end of the shallow lake below Mount Gass in 500m, at the other end of which is a small campsite with a fire ring.

Follow the original GDT past the shallow lake. The trail soon meets the access road for the abandoned Galena Miracle mine, which it follows on and off for the next kilometre, shortcutting long switchbacks in the road.

Looking south along the GDT. The abandoned Galena Miracle mine is on the other side of the summit.

The route ascends Mount Gass in conjunction with the road gaining a total of 200m elevation. At the end of a switchback in the mining road, the trail leaves the road for good. Cross a ridge crest and descend steeply toward a creek ford in a cirque. From the creek, the trail ascends a broad ridge before descending to a spur trail junction (2194, 5.7, b25) for the High Rock campsite.

High Rock campsite to Peak 2270 saddle
(6.2km, 274m up, 268m down)

Five hundred metres past the High Rock campsite you come to a broad meadow at the foot of the High Rock Range escarpment. Climb up from the meadow and gain a contour line that takes you south of a minor peak. The trail traverses alpine slopes below three summits at timberline before reaching a saddle west of Peak 2270 (2190, 6.2, b26).

Peak 2270 saddle to Lost Creek campsite
(5.7km, 91m up, 454m down)

The original GDT goes north from the saddle and joins the northern ridge of Peak 2270. Ascend a minor summit on the crest. The route descends along the crest and stays in a tree corridor between forestry cut blocks lower down. Before arriving at Lost Creek you come to a junction. Turn right on this new section of the trail, a grass-covered road, and follow it 250m down to another junction, where you continue north. Look for orange blazes in this area and cross Lost Creek, which was considerably impacted by the 2013 floods. Continue north and in 100m from the main creek drainage you'll arrive at the Lost Creek campsite (1850, 5.7, b27). To the right a seismic line joins the Lost Creek road and in 10km reaches Highway 40. See 'Other access' for this segment.

A recent clear-cut sits adjacent to the original Great Divide Trail near Cataract Creek.

Lost Creek campsite to Cataract Creek campsite (8.6km, 422m up, 385m down)

Turn left (west) on the seismic line at the Lost Creek campsite and follow it 900m almost in a direct line, crossing a creek along the way. Look for the orange blazes of the original GDT. At the far end of the straight trail, the route begins a moderate ascent up a ridgeline of Mount Farquhar. You reach the top of the climb in 3.3km and 330m of hard won elevation. There is a GDT marker here – turn right (north). Descend to a dry creekbed and climb the 2250m summit directly east of Mount Holcroft, which is on the Divide. Following the ridge crest, you descend 1.5km until you drop off the ridge to the right (east) at a large cairn and re-enter forest. Continue along marked trail to a bridge over Cataract Creek (1859, 8.5, b28). The Cataract Creek campsite is off-route, 100m to the right, on the Cataract Creek trail.

SEGMENT 12 – Cataract Creek campsite to Elk River Road (36.4km)

Strenuous hiking on good trail with much elevation gain and loss. Horses and bikes permitted.

The route drapes across bald ridge crests and the vast alpine meadows of Fording River Pass. This pass was the northern terminus of the original Great Divide Trail but it isn't the end of good hiking to the north. The route continues down Aldridge Creek to the Elk River valley bottom on worthwhile trail.

Maps: 82 J/7 Mount Head; Gemtrek #9 Highwood & Cataract Creek.

Jurisdiction: Kananaskis Country (Alberta Parks).

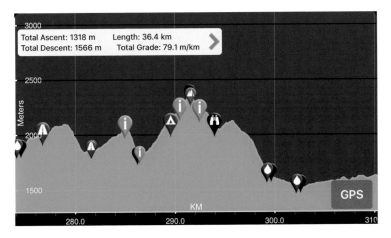

Total Ascent: 1318 m	Length: 36.4 km
Total Descent: 1566 m	Total Grade: 79.1 m/km

South access: Drive 18km south of Highwood House to a trailhead parking area just before the Cataract Creek campground on Highway 40. The trail-head jointly accesses a fire lookout hike and an access road up Cataract Creek. Leaving your car at the trailhead, you walk around the gate that restricts access to the Cataract Creek road and follow this gravel road. In 4km you pass an old sawmill on the right. Turn right and leave the Cataract Creek road 500m farther before crossing a bridge. Continue following an OHV trail alongside the northern bank of Cataract Creek 4km upstream to reach the GDT. A new haul road goes along the northern bank of Cataract Creek but the OHV trail is nicer walking.

Other access: The Etherington Creek trail starts at the Etherington Creek campground on Highway 40, 10km south of Highwood House. Walk the trail 9km up Etherington Creek to meet the Great Divide Trail.

The Baril Creek trailhead is 2km south of Highwood House on Highway 40. You can hike 9km up Baril Creek to intercept the Great Divide Trail at a point that is 5km from Fording River Pass.

North access: In British Columbia, drive 34km north on Highway 43 from Sparwood to Elkford. Continuing on Highway 43 through Elkford, this paved road becomes the gravel Elk River road. Follow the road another 46km north to the intersection with the Kananaskis Power Line road. This intersection is 1km north of where the road crossed from the west side of the Elk River to the east side. Turn right on the Kananaskis Power Line road and drive as far as your vehicle will permit. The Aldridge Creek trailhead is 8.1km ahead, on the left.

Car campgrounds and accommodations: On Highway 40 in Kananaskis Country there are two campgrounds: Etherington Creek and Cataract Creek, 10km and 20km south of Highwood House. There is a $15 fee at each. Cataract Creek campground has shelters in its day-use area. Call 403-591-7226 for more information. There are several BC recreation sites up the Elk River forest service road north of Elkford. The Weary Creek campground is at the bridge over the Elk River at the 144km marker of the road, 1km before the intersection with the Kananaskis Power Line road mentioned above in 'North access.'

Camping: Forest Service campsites at Cataract Creek, Etherington Creek, Baril Creek and Fording River Pass. Random camping.

Information sources: Alberta Parks; GDTA website.

Resupply stations: None.

Special notes: Along the original Great Divide Trail, one orange blaze signifies that the trail continues straight ahead, while two orange rectangles, one above the other, signify an imminent change in direction. The blazes are usually head height and painted on trees. Highway 40 south of Highwood House is still labelled as 940 on some maps.

Additional reading: Gillean Daffern describes many of the trails of the Highwood area, including the original Great Divide Trail, in her *Kananaskis Country Trail Guide, Volume 2.*

Cataract Creek campsite to Etherington Creek campsite (6.7km, 259m up, 283m down)

Over the bridge, turn left at the junction marked with a blue rectangle. The campground is to the right. The trail parallels the northern bank of Cataract Creek to the west for 200m and then turns north, following the eastern side of a tributary. The trail reaches an old road in 400m where you follow the markers and turn left. An additional 500m brings you to a better road; turn right. The route follows this road for 350m, then turns left at a signed junction. In 1.5km you reach a major junction and continue straight through. Near the top of Rye Ridge the trail becomes distinguishable from the snowmobile track and follows the sparsely treed crest to a 2090m summit east of Mount Etherington. The trail follows the ridge crest meadow north, then descends steeply to the Etherington Creek footbridge (1830, 6.7, b29). From the bridge you will find the campsite 75m northwest, on the other side of a meadow, just inside the treeline.

Etherington Creek campsite to Fording River Pass (10.6km, 771m up, 276m down)

The original GDT curves to the west through meadows past Etherington Creek for 200m before turning north and reaching a tributary in 1km. At this small creek the route joins a marked OHV trail. If you were to turn right, you would get to Highway 40 in about 9km (read 'Other access').

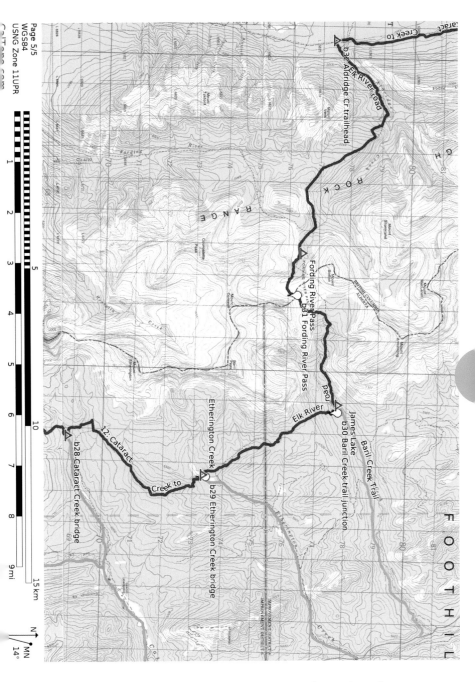

b32 Elk River road
b32 Aldridge Cr trailhead

Fording River Pass
b31 Fording River Pass

Elk River
b30 Baril Creek trail junction
James Lake

Baril Creek Trail

12. Cataract
b28 Cataract Creek bridge

Etherington Creek

Creek to
b29 Etherington Creek bridge

Creek to

ROCK RANGE

FOOTHIL

N
MN
14°

Turn left and follow the washed-out track to the northwest through a narrow meadow for 600m. After leaving the track and parallel tributary, the trail disappears at a clearing in another 500m. Look for the trail across the clearing to the right or continue straight across and into the trees, bush-whacking, to pick up the route again in 100m. The trail climbs to a maximum altitude of 2070m on a bald summit affectionately dubbed Lunch Stop Meadow by the GDTA crews who built the trail through the area. The path disappears over the highpoint but picks up again as you follow a ridge down the other side. Descend steeply to Baril Creek and continue 50m to the right to a signed trail junction (1805, 5.6, b30). The trail going downstream joins the Baril Creek trail, which leads to Highway 40 in 11km (read 'Other access'). Turn left and follow the trail as it meanders through forest past James Lake in 200m. The James Lake campsite is near the small lake's outflow. In 800m climb to a junction with the Baril Creek trail and join it, turning left, uphill. The trail stays north of Baril Creek until it reaches a primitive campsite in 2.1km, where it crosses a final time. The ascent continues 500m up switchbacks and becomes gentler as it reaches the alpine. At this point, turn left, leaving the old roadbed at a marked trail junction. The trail climbs through meadows to the south of a small lake and crosses the Divide into British Columbia at Fording River Pass (2305, 5.1, b31). You can make camp at the small lake or continue over the pass 1.5km to another lake with a suitable site that is just 200m off route, to the north. At the junction for that lake is where the trail rejoins the old road bed.

Fording River Pass to Elk River Road
(19.1km, 288m up, 1025m down)

Once the trail tops Fording River Pass and descends into British Columbia, the GDT starts following a long chain of seismic lines down the Aldridge Creek valley. The first of these descends steeply southwest through a forest of stunted trees. The trail departs from this line in 400m but soon cuts back to it. Once the gradient eases, the route joins another seismic line heading west-northwest that is a washout with difficult footing. To the right, 1km down from the pass, you will find a small lake and the Fording River campsite. The route passes south of the small lake and an adjacent hill to the west, descending to a three-way junction near Aldridge Creek, 1.3km past the lake. Turn left down to a boulder-strewn slope and start a moderate climb on recently cleared trail. After passing a spring and encountering a last steep ascent, you descend good trail on a ridge crest to Aldridge Creek in 5.1km. The trail is washed out in spots as it continues downstream to a ford in 800m after reaching the creek. Stay on the north bank for 700m before refording the creek. Follow the trail 300m past the ford to the Kananaskis Power Line road (1535, 11.0, b32), where there is a GDT sign. Turn right on the road, ford Aldridge Creek again in 300m, and follow the decent Kananaskis Power Line road north to an intersection

Camping beside one of the several lakes dotting the expansive alpine meadows of Fording River Pass.

(1610, 8.1, b33) with the Elk River road. The Weary Creek campground is off-route 1km to the left on the Elk River road, just before the Elk River

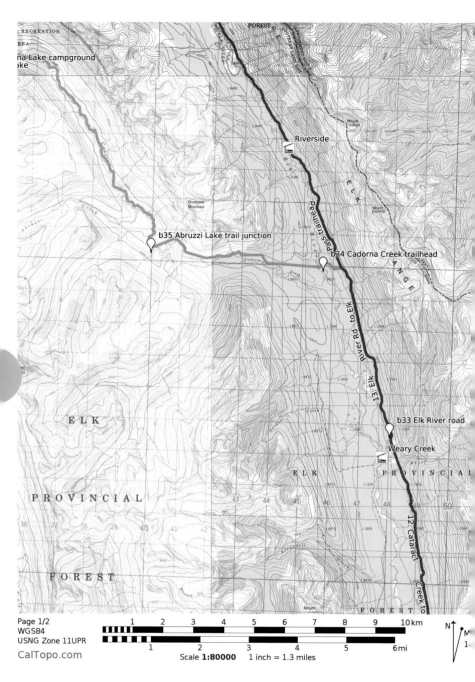

Page 1/2
WGS84
USNG Zone 11UPR

CalTopo.com

Scale **1:80000**   1 inch = 1.3 miles

bridge. There is a self-registration fee of $8 per night. Turn right, however, to follow the GDT route.

SEGMENT 13 – Elk River road to Elk Pass trailhead (33.3km)

Easy road walk with a gentle climb on hiking trail over West Elk Pass. Horses not permitted. Bikes permitted – see 'Special notes'.

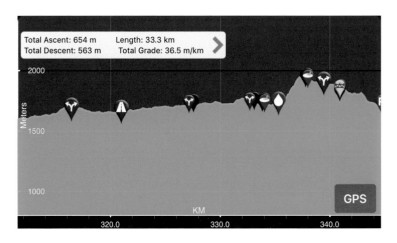

This is a segment of possible extremes. You have a choice of strolling along the Elk River road on the main route or boldly forging cross-country over the Coral Pass alternate. Without a trail linking the heads of Cadorna and Nivelle creeks, the route-finding over Coral Pass is difficult and potentially dangerous. The alternate is 30.5km, most of which is cross-country travel and worth the effort for expert hikers. The decision will be easier for NOBOs, who can gauge the water level at the Elk River ford before even starting the alternate route. SOBO hikers must commit to that ford or face an unpleasant decision of backtracking 30km if they find the river too high. Breaking with convention, waypoints b34 to b37 are on the Coral Pass alternate route.

From Elk Lakes Provincial Park to Mount Robson and beyond, the GDT route is within protected areas where OHV travel, for instance, is prohibited. Industrial activities are also prohibited, with few exceptions. However, from Elk Lakes south to the Castle provincial and wilderness parks, the GDT route weaves in and out of park jurisdictions that have varying degrees of environmental protection. Logging, oil and gas exploration, hunting, and OHVs share the landscape with the GDT.

Maps: 82 J/7 Mount Head and 82 J/11 Kananaskis Lakes; Gemtrek #7 Kananaskis Lakes and #9 Highwood & Cataract Creek.

Jurisdictions: Rocky Mountain Forest District (BC), Elk Lakes Provincial

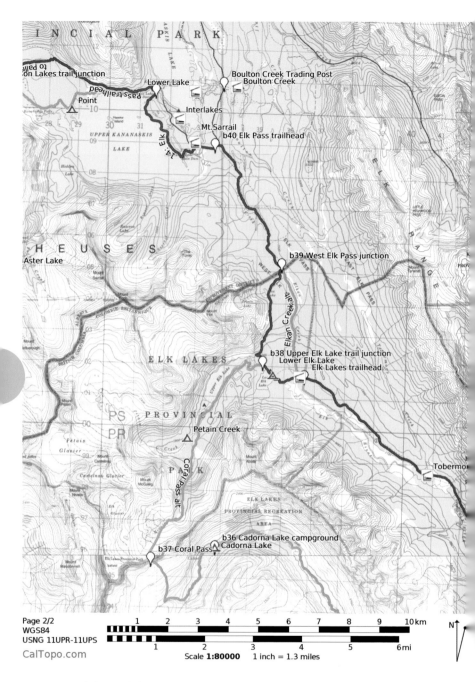

Scale **1:80000**   1 inch = 1.3 miles

N

Park (BC Parks), and Kananaskis Country – Peter Lougheed Provincial Park (Alberta Parks).

South access: In British Columbia, drive 34km north on Highway 43 from

Sparwood to Elkford. Continuing on Highway 43 through Elkford, this paved road becomes the gravel Elk River road. Follow this for another 46km north to the intersection with the Kananaskis Power Line road. This intersection is 1km north of where the road crossed from the west side of the Elk River to the east side. Turn right on the Kananaskis Power Line road and drive as far as your vehicle will permit. The Aldridge Creek trailhead is 8.1km ahead, on the left.

North access: From the junction of Trans-Canada Highway 1 and Highway 40 (aka Kananaskis Trail), head 50km south to the Kananaskis Lakes Trail junction. Turn right and follow this road. Reach the signed Elk Pass trailhead parking area in 12km on the left, 2km past the Boulton Creek Trading Post. You can also access Kananaskis Lakes Trail by driving 70km south on the gravel Smith-Dorrien/Spray Trail from the Trans-Canada Highway at Canmore. In Canmore, follow signs for the Nordic Centre through town to find the start of the Smith-Dorrien/Spray Trail. The gravel road is suitable for all vehicles. From the junction of the Smith-Dorrien/Spray Trail (Hwy. 742) with Kananaskis Lakes Trail, turn right and proceed 8km to the Elk Pass trailhead parking area.

Car campgrounds and accommodations: The Weary Creek campground is at the bridge over the Elk River at the 144km marker of the road, 1km before the intersection with Kananaskis Power Line Road mentioned in 'South access'. Near the end of the Elk River road there are two BC Forest Service campgrounds of interest: Riverside and Tobermory Creek. I suggest staying at the Lower Elk Lake campsite in Elk Lakes Provincial Park. This campsite is for hikers only, and it is 1km from the Elk Lakes trailhead parking area on the GDT. There is a self-registration fee of $5 per night.

There are three campgrounds in Peter Lougheed Provincial Park close to the GDT. Mount Sarrail (walk-in tenting) and Interlakes campgrounds are both en route and cost $26 per night. Both have secure food storage and an on-site manager that can take Visa and MasterCard. If you would like a hot shower and flush toilets, you should book the Boulton Creek campground in advance for a $12 fee and $26 per night for an unserviced tenting site. Refer to page 340 for contact info.

Camping: Lower Elk Lake campsite and alternatively Cadorna Lake campsite and the Upper Elk Lake campsite, plus random camping. The Upper and Lower Elk Lake campsites require a fee of $5 through self-registration. These are first come, first served campsites that do fill up on weekends in the summer months. Rangers patrol these sites regularly. You can also reserve the ACC Elk Lakes cabin through the club, alpineclubofcanada.ca. The Elk Lakes cabin is located at the very start of this section, not far from the trailhead parking, and has a wood stove, propane stoves, cooking utensils, mattresses and a nearby water source. The fee is $25 per night and you don't have to be an ACC member to book. Dogs aren't permitted at any ACC hut.

Information sources: Peter Lougheed Provincial Park information centre, albertaparks.ca, and Rocky Mountain Forest District (BC). The Barrier Lake information centre on Highway 40 near the entrance to Kananaskis Country can also be helpful if you are driving from the Trans-Canada Highway.

Resupply stations: The closest resupply is the Peter Lougheed Provincial Park information centre, 8.7km north on Kananaskis Lakes Trail. The info centre is open 8:30 to 4:30 (5:30 on weekends) and has several amenities, including a sitting room with fireplace, sink and kettle, and wifi that remains accessible even after hours. The Boulton Creek Trading Post is only 2.5km away but doesn't accept packages. It has a restaurant and a store with limited food and supplies for people staying at the nearby campground (like mac and cheese and soups). While you could find enough food there for a few days' travel, it will cost twice as much as a grocery store elsewhere. The store is open from 9am to 10pm daily during the summer. The store does not have wifi.

Special notes: Bikes aren't permitted on most of the Elk Pass trail described as the main route, through Elk Lakes and Peter Lougheed provincial parks. However, there is a parallel trail (a road really) that heads north from a point 300m south of the Elk Lakes parking area, over the pass to the same Elk Pass trailhead as in the trail description. The presence of this alternate route means that all of section B is permitted for cyclists.

Unfortunately, Elk Lakes and Peter Lougheed provincial parks don't allow horse travel to Elk Pass. This is why the GDTA is working on an alternate horse route that crosses the Divide farther south. I don't describe that route in this book, but you can request more information from the GDTA.

Additional reading: Obtain all the maps and Kananaskis Country brochures you would like at the Boulton Creek Trading Post or the Peter Lougheed Provincial Park information centre. Janice Strong has a good section on Elk Lakes Provincial Park in *Mountain Footsteps* and Gillean Daffern describes the Coral Pass alternate route in her *Kananaskis Country Trail Guide, Volume 1*.

Elk River road to Upper Elk Lake trail junction (24.1km, 381m up, 290m down)

From the intersection (1610, b33) of the Elk River forest service road with the Kananaskis Power Line road, turn right and follow the Elk River road north. The road is two-lane gravel that follows along the eastern side of

The head-waters of Cadorna Creek on the Coral Pass alternate route.

the Elk River. In 5.7km you reach the trailhead for the Coral Pass alternate on the left. Though it used to be signed, this might not be the case when you reach it, so watch your GPS for the exact distance from the last waypoint.

CORAL PASS ALTERNATE ROUTE — 30.5KM COMPARED TO 18.9KM. HIKERS (AND DOGS) ONLY.

Turn left onto the gravel access road for the Cadorna Creek trailhead. The trailhead parking area is 800m down the access road on the bank of the Elk River. You may find a registration box at the Cadorna Creek trailhead (1610, 6.5, b34). Immediately, the trail fords the potentially formidable Elk River and follows a winding track to the start of a long seismic line. The wide seismic line continues due west for 2km toward Cadorna Creek. The trail stays on the north side of the creek, encountering a couple of minor washouts, and arrives at a trail junction (1770, 6.2, b35) for Abruzzi Lake and a nearby outfitter's camp. Continue to the right, staying on the same (north) side of the creek. The trail narrows through a boggy area. Eventually it arrives at the Cadorna Lake campsite (1910, 10.7, b36) on the eastern end of Cadorna Lake.

There is no trail up to the pass. The most navigable route seems to be above the long rock band on the north side of the lake. Follow this to the small inflow stream at the other end of the lake. A well-defined animal track follows this small creek steeply up to timberline. From the wide, boulder-strewn meadow you can see a pass to the north. Travel cross-country as directly as possible to Coral Pass (2520, 4.4, b37). The final bit of the ascent is a steep slope covered with loose shale. Remnant snow persists through the summer on the north side of this high pass.

Descend northeast 1.5km from the pass along ridges of recessional

The view of West Elk Pass and Upper Elk Lake from the Coral Pass alternate route.

moraine to the head of Nivelle Creek, still in the alpine. Look for bighorn coral along this stretch. Some of the fossils have eroded out of the rock and lay scattered on the bedrock in this region (collect pictures only). A rough trail that stays on the south side of Nivelle Creek leads 300m east to the base of a wide talus slope and enters forest. The trail follows the drainage as it turns north for 1.1km through forest, staying on the east side of the creek. Now at an impressive height above the rock-walled gorge, a flagged trail makes its way back toward Nivelle Creek. A short and easy scramble brings the route down the narrowest part of the substantial cliff band not far from the edge of the gorge. Turn right and leave the gorge, following the base of the cliff band you just down-climbed for 200m along a narrow trail. At this point the flagged route makes its way down a series of bushy rock steps. This difficult terrain is even worse when the rocks and tree roots are slick with fresh rainfall. The vegetation thickens as the route nears a sharp bend in Nivelle Creek just below the gorge. Starting by the creek bend, follow the flagged route along gravel bars to the north. After a minor creek ford, you reach the Pétain Creek campsite near the confluence of Pétain and Nivelle creeks in 2.2km (5.5km from the pass). A fair trail continues across gravel washes and then along the eastern side of Upper Elk Lake 2.9km to a trail junction (1765, 8.4, b38) just past a bridge over the lake's outflow.

End Coral Pass alternate route.

The main route of the GDT stays on the Elk River road and continues north from this junction. In another 4.5km you pass the spur road for the Riverside forestry recreation site and in 6.4km after that you reach the Tobermory Creek forestry recreation site, where there is supposed to be a cabin open for public use. Continuing on the Elk River road another 5.7km, you reach the Elk Lakes Provincial Park boundary at the Elk Lakes trailhead parking area. **Note:** cyclists turn right 300m before this parking lot to follow a power line trail over Elk Pass into Peter Lougheed Provincial Park in Alberta. The main route follows the Lower Elk Lake trail for 1.3km past the ACC hut to the Lower Elk Lake campsite. You will pass the Elkan Creek trail by design – it's just not as interesting as the main route through this park. It does shave off a couple of kilometres if you decide to follow it to West Elk Pass. There is a $5 self-registration fee at the Lower Elk Lake campsite, and it is first come, first served. (You can pay in advance for BC Parks campsites such as this one, at discovercamping.ca/Backcountry.) The good trail continues past the lake and in 500m reaches the Upper Elk Lake trail junction (1765, 24.1, b38). This waypoint on the main route continues from b33. Waypoints b34 to b38 describe the Coral Pass alternate route. This is the only exception to the use of waypoints on the main route. I originally did this to encourage the use of the Coral Pass alternate and have kept it in this edition of the guidebook. The view over Upper Elk Lake is worth it.

Upper Elk Lake trail junction to West Elk Pass (4.0km, 229m up, 54m down)

The trail continues straight through the junction and climbs steeply through forest and open slide paths with great views to a highpoint of 1945m. Pass the Fox Lake trail junction in 2.9km. In another 900m keep right at the Frozen Lake trail junction and head west 200m to the West Elk Pass trail junction (1975, 4.0, b39), on the Divide. This is where the Elkan Creek trail meets the main route if you decided to follow this other, more direct trail.

West Elk Pass to the Elk Pass trailhead (5.2km, 44m up, 219m down)

The GDT follows the trail to the northwest, into Alberta. You leave Elk Lakes Provincial Park and continue on the well-maintained Elk Pass trail into Peter Lougheed Provincial Park. In 500m, turn left at the first trail junction. At this point the trail is more like a gravel road. This is a popular cross-country ski area with a virtual maze of trails. In general the trail follows Fox Creek for the next kilometre, and then follows the obvious overhead power lines northwest for the rest of the way, down to the Elk Pass trailhead parking lot (1720, 5.2, b40) on the Kananaskis Lakes Trail road. If you are headed to the Boulton Creek Trading Post, there is a shortcut trail 400m before you reach the trailhead. It is 3km north to the trading post from there. It is a shorter walk on the road – 2.5km.

Section C: *Kananaskis to Field*

Segments 14–20, 208.5 km

Location	Near waypoint	NOBO km	SOBO km
Elk Pass Trailhead	b40	344.0	789.2
Point campsite (AB Parks)* (see note below)	c1	350.8	782.4
Forks campsite (AB Parks) (see note below)	c2	356.3	776.9
Turbine Canyon campsite (AB Parks) (see note below)	c3	364.0	769.2
Palliser Pass campsite	c5	376.2	757.0
Burstall Us18 campsite (Banff NP)	c6	385.0	748.2
Birdwood Us15 campsite (Banff NP)	c6	388.8	744.4
Watridge Lake Junction, Access	c7	397.4	735.8
Big Springs Br9 campsite (Banff NP)	c8	400.8	732.4
Marvel Lake Trail Junction	c8a	404.2	729.0
Bryant Creek Shelter*	c8a	404.2	729.0
McBride's Camp Br14 campsite (Banff NP)*	c8a	404.2	729.0
Marvel Lake Br13 campsite (Banff NP)	c8a	404.7	728.5
Wonder Pass	c9	414.2	719.0
Naiset Cabins (BC Parks)	c10	416.9	716.3
RESUPPLY: Assiniboine Lodge	c10	417.4	715.8
Lake Magog campsite (BC Parks)*	c10	417.4	715.8
Og Lake campsite (BC Parks)	c11	422.2	711.0
Porcupine campsite (BC Parks)*	c12	427.7	705.5
Howard Douglas Lake Su8 Camp (Banff NP)	c14	438.0	695.2
RESUPPLY: Sunshine Village Ski Area*	c15	442.6	690.6
Healy Creek E5 campsite (Banff NP)*	c17	449.6	683.6
Egypt Lake E13 campsite (Banff NP)	c19	456.8	676.4
Egypt Lake Shelter	c19	456.8	676.4
Ball Pass Junction Re21 campsite (Banff NP)	c21	465.3	667.9
Flow Lake #12 campsite (Kootenay NP)	c26	486.9	646.3
Numa Creek #11 campsite (Kootenay NP)	c29	496.1	637.1
Tumbling Creek #10 campsite (Kootenay NP)	c31	503.8	629.4
Wolverine Pass random campsite	c32	506.5	626.7
Helmet Falls #6 campsite (Kootenay NP)	c35	515.4	617.8
McArthur Creek campsite (Yoho NP)	c37	528.9	604.3
RESUPPLY: Field, BC	c39	552.4	580.8
NOTE: Peter Lougheed PP requires reservations.			

Introduction

For many, this section of the Great Divide Trail is the most attractive.

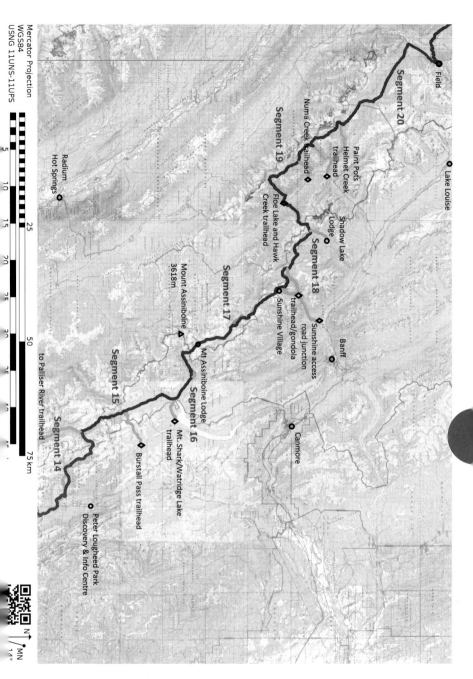

The route traverses three national parks and three provincial parks with well-maintained trails, frequent campsites and hardly any road walking.

The main range of the Canadian Rockies becomes more dominant during the length of this section. High peaks like Mount Assiniboine are more common and glaciers are more numerous than to the south. The effect of glaciation along the Rockwall trail in Kootenay National Park is dramatic. Masses of ice such as Tumbling Glacier cling to sheer, kilometre-high headwalls. The Rockwall trail diverges from this impressive bulwark at stunning Helmet Falls, one of the highest waterfalls in the Canadian Rockies.

This is a long section. The trek is 10 days at a pace of 20km/day. However, there are numerous access points where you can arrange for resupply – two of which are Assiniboine Lodge and Sunshine Village, accessible by helicopter and tour bus respectively. Resupplying at these intermediate points is expensive but may save your back.

This is a popular section. With the exception of the Height of the Rockies Provincial Park, camping is permitted in designated sites only, meaning you will have to plan your itinerary well and reserve in advance, especially for the Rockwall trail in Kootenay National Park and around Sunshine Meadows in Banff National Park.

I see this part of the GDT as a first pick for anyone who has backpacking experience and wants to hike an entire section. The excellent trail means you will encounter few serious navigational worries. If you cannot stay ahead of your blisters, there are plenty of realistic bailout points. Moreover, except at Palliser Pass, you are never very isolated from other hikers. Considering the renowned backcountry destinations such as Mount Assiniboine, Sunshine Meadows, Egypt Lake and the Rockwall trail, you will probably find enough reason to hike even if you do get blisters.

There is very little cycling access in the national parks from this point to the extended northern terminus in Kakwa Provincial Park. The exceptions are usually access trails. I will make a note of where they are permitted. The alternate equestrian route overlaps the GDT in this section on the Palliser, Spray and Bryant Creek trails and terminates in the town of Banff. It isn't within the scope of this book to describe that entirely alternate trail but more information is available from the GDTA website.

SEGMENT 14 – Elk Pass trailhead to Palliser River (27.5km)

Moderate climb on good hiking trail with a potentially difficult ford of the Palliser River. Bikes and horses not permitted.

This segment of the GDT leads you into the secluded Height of the Rockies Provincial Park at the head of the Palliser River. Starting in Peter Lougheed Provincial Park, you trace the northern side of Upper Kananaskis Lake.

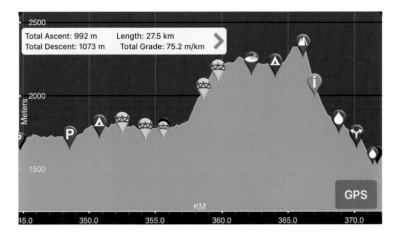

The constant view of the dramatic peaks surrounding the lake and the excellent hiking trail is very enjoyable. The trail remains in very good shape up to North Kananaskis Pass on the Divide. An interesting feature en route is Turbine Canyon, a deep incision in the mountainside concealing waterfalls and shady pools.

There is some talk of an alternate route through South Kananaskis Pass. However, I have only found one link-up that works (which is almost as far down as the Palliser River) and in my opinion it isn't any better than the main route and in fact entails more bushwhacking than the upper LeRoy Creek drainage that draws so many complaints by thru-hikers.

Maps: 82 J/11 Kananaskis Lakes; Gemtrek #7 Kananaskis Lakes.

Jurisdictions: Peter Lougheed Provincial Park (Alberta Parks) and Height of the Rockies Provincial Park (BC Parks).

South access: From the junction of Trans-Canada Highway 1 and Highway 40 (aka Kananaskis Trail), head 50km south to the Kananaskis Lakes Trail junction. Turn right and follow this road. Reach the signed Elk Pass trailhead parking area in 12km on the left, 2km past the Boulton Creek Trading Post. You can also access the Kananaskis Lakes Trail by driving 70km south on the Smith-Dorrien/Spray Trail (Hwy. 742) from the Trans-Canada Highway at Canmore, Alberta. In Canmore, follow signs for the Nordic Centre through town to find the start of the gravel Smith-Dorrien/Spray Trail, which is suitable for all vehicles. From the junction of the Smith-Dorrien/Spray Trail with Kananaskis Lakes Trail, turn right and proceed 8km to the Elk Pass trailhead parking area.

North access: From Highway 93 in Kootenay National Park, turn south onto Settlers Road in the southeastern corner of the park. You will leave Kootenay National Park and turn left to cross the Kootenay River bridge.

Fall near Upper Kananaskis Lake turns the aspens yellow.

Turn right onto Palliser River Road. Follow the gravel road to its terminus at Joffre Creek. On foot, go north on the Palliser River trail and ford Joffre Creek. Within 2km ford the Palliser River to the western bank. You pass a cabin in 7km and meet the LeRoy Creek trail in 14km in total. Be warned: this access includes 80km of gravel forestry roads. I include this access mostly for trail runners who need a support crew, but equestrians travelling the alternate GDT could use it as well.

Car campgrounds and accommodations: There are three campgrounds in Peter Lougheed Provincial Park close to the GDT. Mount Sarrail (walk-in tenting) and Interlakes campgrounds are both en route and cost $26 per night. Both have secure food storage and an on-site manager that can take Visa and MasterCard. If you would like a hot shower and flush toilets, you should book the Boulton Creek campground in advance for a $12 fee and $26 per night for an unserviced tenting site. Refer to page 340 for contact details. If you decide to use the northern access, there are several places to pull over and camp en route.

Camping: Kananaskis Country backcountry campsites Point, Forks and Turbine Canyon – see 'Special notes' below. Random camping in Height of the Rockies Provincial Park only.

Information sources: Peter Lougheed Provincial Park information centre, Invermere Forest District, BC Parks Kootenay District.

Resupply stations: The closest resupply is the Peter Lougheed Provincial Park visitor information centre, 8.7km north on Kananaskis Lakes Trail. The Boulton Creek Trading Post is only 2.5km away but doesn't accept packages. It has a restaurant and a store with limited food and supplies for people staying at the nearby campground (like mac and cheese and soups). While you could find enough food to purchase for a few days' travel, it will cost twice as much as a grocery store elsewhere. The store is open from 9am to 10pm daily during the summer months. It doesn't have wifi but the park visitor centre does.

Special notes: In Peter Lougheed Provincial Park there is a per night cost for backcountry campsites. You must stay in designated campsites. Passes are available through the Peter Lougheed Provincial Park information centre, by phone and at albertaparks.ca. In Height of the Rockies Provincial Park there are no established campsites, so please practise no-trace random camping.

Elk Pass trailhead to North Interlakes trailhead (4.5km, 104m up, 113m down)

From the Elk Pass trailhead (1725, 0, b40), leave the parking lot and turn left on the Kananaskis Lakes Trail road. Follow it over the spillway for 800m to a trailhead turnoff for the Upper Kananaskis Lake trail (the actual trail, not the road. Confusing, I know). Turn left and follow the road 200m to the parking area. Follow excellent trail from this point. Though

Mount Lyautey over Upper Kananaskis Lake from the North Interlakes trailhead.

longer than the road, the trail is highly scenic and worth the extra distance. The trail follows the lakeside to arrive at the North Interlakes trailhead (1715, 4.5, c1) beside a dam. There is a pay phone, outhouse, picnic area and trailhead information at this location. It is a busy trailhead during summer weekends because it is the main access point for most of the backcountry campsites in the park. Inform the visitor centre in advance if you intend to leave a car here for an extended time.

North Interlakes trailhead to Forks campsite (7.8km, 202m up, 121m down)

Follow the Three Isle Lake trail over the dam and head west, below the jutting flank of Mount Indefatigable. In 800m, pass a junction for the Upper Lake circuit trail and a second junction for the same trail in another 1.4km. Here you have a choice to travel 1.3km off route to the Point campsite, if you couldn't get a booking at the Forks campsite on route. Continue straight past both junctions to stay on the main route. Cross a bridge in 1.7km and another bridge 1.8km farther. The Three Isle Lake trail follows the river upstream to a third bridged crossing in 1.4km. From here the trail veers away from Three Isle Creek to head northwest alongside the Upper Kananaskis River. In 600m you reach a trail junction at the Forks campsite (1780, 7.8, c2).

Forks campsite to Turbine Canyon campsite (7.7km, 527m up, 66m down)

Avoid the turnoff to Three Isle Lake and follow the Maude–Lawson trail north, through Forks campsite. The trail stays near the river at first but soon begins a long, moderate ascent across a large avalanche slope. It

Mateo Antonelli straddles Turbine Canyon near North Kananaskis Pass. The rough trail that follows the canyon downhill is worth exploring.

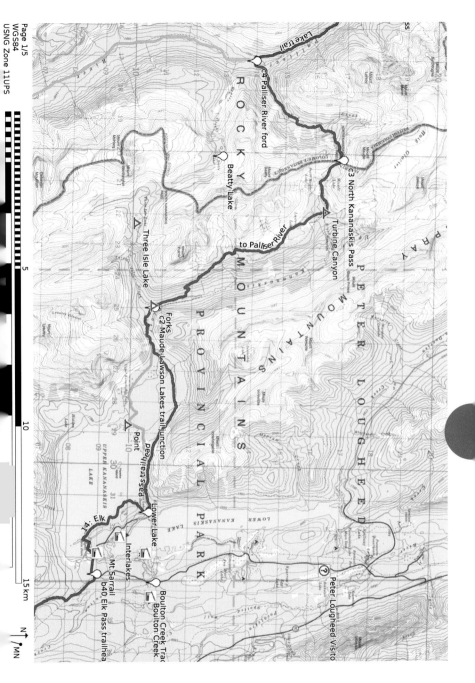

climbs steeply up a switchback on the eastern side of Mount Putnik. Cross a bridge in 2.3km as the trail levels out in the subalpine. The trail reaches Lawson Lake in mostly open terrain in 3.6km and the Turbine Canyon campsite 1.8km farther, just on the northern side of Maude Brook. The GDT goes to the left but the trail going downstream is worthwhile. If you walk just 200m down this path you will approach the brink of the awesome Turbine Canyon. You can straddle the narrow canyon where the water begins to plummet out of sight.

Turbine Canyon campsite to North Kananaskis Pass (2.1km, 149m up, 4m down)

The Maude–Lawson trail follows Maude Brook upstream to Maude Lake. Follow the southeastern edge of the water to reach North Kananaskis Pass (2360, 9.8, c3) on the Continental Divide. At the boundary, you enter Height of the Rockies Provincial Park in British Columbia and trade maintained trails for wilderness ones (meaning that only the passage of the odd hiker or lone elk keeps the trail recognizable). There are flat areas for camping over the pass if you couldn't reserve one at Turbine Canyon campsite.

North Kananaskis Pass to Palliser River (5.4km, 10m up, 769m down)

A faint trail marked by cairns descends along a feeder stream of LeRoy Creek west of the pass. The steep descent has several ruts and rocky sections before getting down to a gentler slope alongside LeRoy Creek. Once out of the alpine, the route becomes extremely brushy. In 1.8km from the pass, cross to the northern bank of LeRoy Creek in a boulder field if you aren't already on the north side. Keep following the northern side of LeRoy Creek 2.7km to the Palliser River. Ford the Palliser River just upstream from its confluence with LeRoy Creek (1585, 5.4, c4).

SEGMENT 15 – Palliser River to Watridge Lake trail junction (25.9km)

Vigorous climb over a high pass with some route-finding necessary at the head of the Palliser River. Horses permitted. Bikes prohibited.

Palliser Pass, the extreme southern boundary of Banff National Park, draws few visitors and yet you will find some of the most beautiful lakes and alpine scenery of the park here. The trail up the Palliser River to the pass is narrow and rarely travelled, while north of the pass the Spray River valley has a flat bottom and more visitation.

Maps: 82 J/11 Kananaskis Lakes and 82 J/14 Spray Lakes Reservoir; Gemtrek #5 Banff & Mount Assiniboine and #7 Kananaskis Lakes.

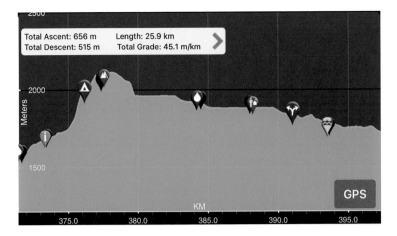

Total Ascent: 656 m Length: 25.9 km
Total Descent: 515 m Total Grade: 45.1 m/km

Jurisdictions: Height of the Rockies Provincial Park (BC Parks) and Banff National Park.

South access: From Highway 93 in Kootenay National Park turn south onto Settlers Road in the southeastern corner of the park. You will leave Kootenay National Park and turn left to cross the Kootenay River bridge. Turn right onto the Palliser River road. Follow the gravel road to its terminus at Joffre Creek. On foot, go north on the Palliser River trail and ford Joffre Creek. Within 2km ford the Palliser River to the western bank. You pass a cabin in 7km and meet the LeRoy Creek trail in 14km in total. Be warned, this access includes 80km of gravel forestry roads. I include this access mostly for trail runners who need a support crew, but equestrians travelling the alternate GDT could use it as well.

Other access: The Burstall Pass trailhead parking area is on the gravel Smith-Dorrien/Spray Trail (Hwy. 742) at 45km south of Canmore and 20km north of the Kananaskis Lakes Trail intersection. From the Burstall Pass trailhead you climb to a viewpoint in 8km over a 400m gain in elevation. The trail down to the Spray River is seldom used but in good shape. Leave the Burstall Pass viewpoint trail near a large depression and follow a gully downhill. Long switchbacks bring the trail another 4km down into the valley to meet the Spray River trail.

North access: Follow signs for the Nordic Centre through Canmore. Continue past the Nordic Centre turnoff and stay on Smith-Dorrien/Spray Trail (Hwy. 742) as it becomes a gravel road and heads uphill. This road is suitable for all vehicles. In 35km, look for signs indicating Mount Shark and the Mount Engadine Lodge turnoff, to the right. Follow the signs for Mount Shark and travel 5km to the trailhead at the end of this road. If you are approaching from Calgary, turn off the Trans-Canada onto Highway 40 and

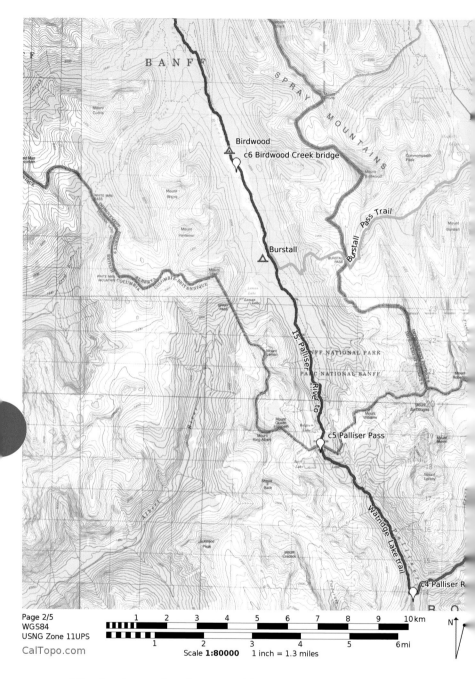

Birdwood

c6 Birdwood Creek bridge

Burstall

Burstall Pass Trail

BANFF

SPRAY MOUNTAINS

15: Palliser River to

BANFF NATIONAL PARK

PARC NATIONAL BANFF

c5 Palliser Pass

Watridge Lake trail

C4 Palliser R

| 1 | 2 | 3 | 4 | 5 | 6 | 7 | 8 | 9 | 10 km |

| 1 | 2 | 3 | 4 | 5 | 6 mi |

Scale **1:80000**   1 inch = 1.3 miles

N

follow it 50km south to the Kananaskis Lakes Trail junction. Turn right and follow this road 2km to a junction. Turn right onto Smith-Dorrien/Spray Trail (Hwy. 742). The turnoff for Mount Shark and Mount Engadine Lodge is

26.5km north. Drive the remaining 5km, following signs to the Mount Shark trailhead. Hike 6km on the Watridge Lake trail into Banff National Park to meet the Spray River trail at waypoint c7.

Car campgrounds and accommodations: The Spray Lakes West campground is midway between Canmore and the Mount Shark turnoff on Smith-Dorrien/Spray Trail (Hwy. 742). Just south of the Spray Lakes ranger station (public telephone), turn toward the reservoir and cross Three Sisters Dam. There are 50 sites to choose from along the lakeshore. The fee is $26, collected by an on-site manager/caretaker. The Canyon campground is on the Kananaskis Lakes Trail road, 2km past the junction for Smith-Dorrien/Spray Trail (Hwy. 742) and the Kananaskis Lakes Trail road. It is also $26 per night for an unserviced campsite.

There are several vehicle campgrounds and pullouts where you can camp on the roads described above in 'South access.'

Camping: Banff National Park backcountry campsites Burstall (Us18) and Birdwood Creek (Us15). Random camping in Height of the Rockies Provincial Park.

Information sources: Invermere Forest District, BC Parks Kootenay District, Banff National Park visitor information centre.

Resupply stations: None.

Special notes: There are no established campsites in Height of the Rockies Provincial Park. You must practise no-trace random camping. This segment is on the alternate GDT horse route and does have several signed stretches of horse trail that diverge from and rejoin the main trail in the national park.

Additional reading: The June 1973 issue of *National Geographic* has an insightful article by Mike Edwards called "Hiking the Backbone of the Canadian Rockies." Besides offering a good narrative of this thru-hike, Edwards discusses some of the challenges that kept the GDT from becoming an official hiking trail through the national parks. You will find a good map and excellent photographs, of course. Relevant to this segment, Edwards started his northbound hike of the GDT at Palliser Pass.

Palliser River to Palliser Pass (6.5km, 543m up, 46m down)

Ford the Palliser River above its confluence with LeRoy Creek. Ignore the faint trail that heads upstream on the west bank of the river. Instead, continue 300m west- northwest through a small meadow – crossing a tributary stream – to a well-defined horse trail. Don't be tempted to walk up the river; find the horse trail. It's there. Turn right and follow the horse trail north. This trail stays on the west side of the river and ascends through forest and along the bottom of open slide paths

The Palliser River valley.

It can snow at any time in summer on the GDT. This is near Palliser Pass.

that can be brushy at times. In 2km you reach a ford of the river itself. The Palliser River trail levels out for nearly a kilometre and stays on the right (east) side of the river. The trail ascends moderately and diverges from the Palliser River, following a tributary to a campsite in 2.5km. In 750m past the campsite, you reach a false pass before descending another 500m to Palliser Lake. There is a potential campsite here but it can be wet and buggy. Continue 500m on level ground to Palliser Pass (2170, 6.5, c5). Palliser Pass sits on the Divide at the edge of a large meadow. This pass is the southernmost boundary of Banff National Park. From this point onward you are permitted to stay in designated backcountry campsites only.

Palliser Pass to Burstall campsite junction
(7km, 42m up, 224m down)

In Banff National Park you join the signed Spray River trail. Start your descent of the Spray River valley by first passing between the Belgium Lakes at the northern end of the meadow beyond Palliser Pass. The trail re-enters the forest and descends steeply through bushy sections from the lakes to the gravel bars of the Spray River. When you first reach the Spray River flood plain in 2km, cross to the west side of the river through a small meadow and unofficial campsite to reach a good trail near the tree-line. For the most part you are walking in the open with a clear view of the valley walls. Stay on the west side of the river until the trail crosses back over the river in 2km. In 700m after the crossing, the trail reaches the signed junction with the Burstall Pass trail mentioned in 'Other access' at the beginning of this segment. Burstall campsite is 300m to the left on the Leman Creek trail. The Leman Creek trail appears to be an easy access point to southern Banff National Park but it is a rough road at the end of a confusing array of gravel forestry roads. If you need to leave the trail (or join it) at this point, definitely take the Burstall Pass trail.

Burstall campsite junction to Birdwood Creek campsite
(3.8km, 8m up, 16m down)

Stay on the east (right) side of the river. The rutted, wet and sometimes bushy trail now improves as you follow it north. Continue downriver through long meadows and cross the bridged Birdwood Creek (1840, 14, c6) near the Palliser warden cabin. The Birdwood Creek campsite is another 700m north of here, on the right side of the Spray River trail.

The Spray River valley is flat and wide. Palliser Pass is at the head of the river, on the right side of this photo.

Birdwood Creek campsite to Watridge Lake trail junction (8.6km, 63m up, 229m down)

The trail reaches the White Man Pass Trail junction in 2.2km past the campsite. Continue straight on the Spray River trail. In another 2.7km, you cross a bridge to the west side of the Spray River. In 200m there is another bridge, this time over Currie Creek. Turn right and continue downriver at the trail junction, staying on the western bank of the Spray. Continue walking north on excellent trail to the signed Watridge Lake trail junction (1715, 9.3, c7) near a bridge over the Spray River.

SEGMENT 16 – Watridge Lake trail junction to Mount Assiniboine Lodge (20.0km)

Uphill all the way for northbound hikers, with some steep sections. Horses permitted. Bikes prohibited. See 'Special notes.'

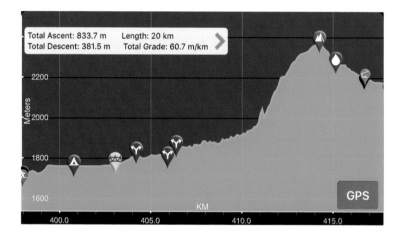

Mount Assiniboine Provincial Park can be a busy backcountry area during the summer. This is a well-known destination for hikers and for a very good reason: the view of Mount Assiniboine is captivating. The trail up Bryant Creek is a nice walk with plenty of views higher up the valley. Wonder Pass is the highlight of this segment. It is a spectacular pass and the most awe-inspiring way to enter Mount Assiniboine Provincial Park.

Maps: 82 J/14 Spray Lakes Reservoir and 82 J/13 Mount Assiniboine; Gemtrek #5 Banff & Mount Assiniboine.

Jurisdictions: Banff National Park and Mount Assiniboine Provincial Park (BC Parks).

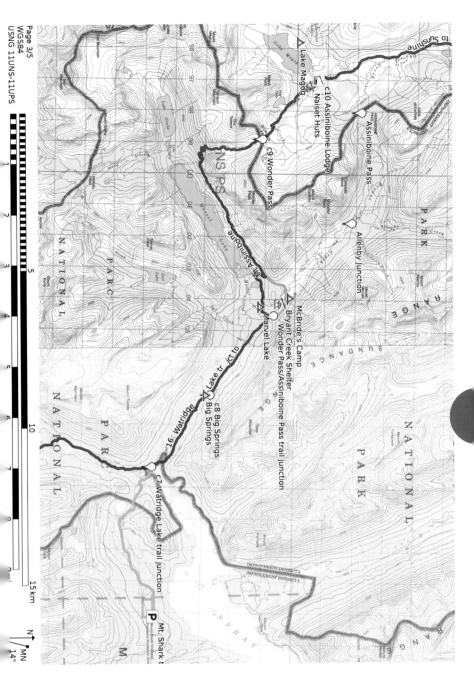

South access: Follow signs for the Nordic Centre through Canmore. Continue past the Nordic Centre turnoff and stay on Smith-Dorrien/Spray

Relaxing in the sunshine near the Watridge Lake trail junction. Cone Mountain stands above the point where the Spray River flows into the Spray Lakes reservoir.

Trail (Hwy. 742) as it becomes a gravel road and heads uphill. This road is suitable for all vehicles. In 35km, look for signs indicating Mount Shark and the Mount Engadine Lodge turnoff, to the right. Follow signs for Mount Shark and travel 5km to the trailhead at the end of this road. If you are approaching from Calgary, turn off the Trans-Canada onto Highway 40 and follow it 50km south to the Kananaskis Lakes Trail junction. Turn right and follow this road 2km to a junction. Turn right onto Smith-Dorrien/Spray Trail (Hwy. 742). The turnoff for Mount Shark and Mount Engadine Lodge is 26.5km north. Drive the remaining 5km following signs to the Mount Shark trailhead. Hike 6km on the Watridge Lake trail into Banff National Park to meet the Spray River trail at waypoint c7.

North access: The GDT follows the two most popular trails that access the heart of Mount Assiniboine Provincial Park (BC). You can also access the area by hiking 30km from Kootenay National Park, starting at the Simpson River trailhead on Highway 93. Follow the river and then Surprise Creek over Ferro Pass. The easiest way to arrive at Lake Magog is by helicopter. Helicopters service Mount Assiniboine Lodge from Canmore and a helipad near the Mount Shark trailhead. Contact Alpine Helicopters and consult Assiniboine Lodge assiniboinelodge.com/general-info/flying.

Car campgrounds and accommodations: The Spray Lakes West campground is midway between Canmore and the Mount Shark turnoff, on Smith-Dorrien/Spray Trail (Highway 742). Just south of the Spray Lakes ranger station (public telephone), turn toward the reservoir and cross the Three Sisters Dam. There are 50 sites to choose from along the lakeshore. The fee is $26, collected by an on-site manager/caretaker. The Canyon campground is on the Kananaskis Lakes Trail road at 2km past the junction for Smith-Dorrien/Spray Trail (Hwy. 742) and the Kananaskis Lakes Trail road. It is also $26 per night for an unserviced campsite.

Mount Assiniboine Lodge has rustic rooms and cabins that you can reserve (well in advance). You can stay in one of the five Naiset huts (first come, first served) near the lodge for a $20 drop-in fee or $25 in advance. If you stay at the huts, you can use the Wonder Lodge cooking shelter, which has two propane stoves, fuel, utensils and tables.

Camping: National park campsites: Big Springs (Br9), Marvel Lake (Br13), McBride's Camp (Br14), and the Bryant Creek shelter (near Br14). Naiset Huts, Mount Assiniboine Lodge, and Lake Magog campsite in Mount Assiniboine Provincial Park. Bring $10 cash to pay the fee for either Lake Magog or Og Lake campsites. While neither of these two campsites can be reserved, you can pay in advance at discovercamping.ca/backcountry.

You can reserve the Bryant Creek shelter on the Bryant Creek trail through the Banff Information Centre when you get the permits for your trip. The cost is $6.80 a night per person and spaces can be reserved up to three months in advance (which will likely switch to January of each year when the new electronic reservations system is implemented in 2017–18 for Banff National Park).

Information sources: Banff National Park Visitor Information Centre in Banff, BC Parks, Mount Assiniboine Lodge, and Alpine Helicopters. (Check out the lodge's webcam at assiniboinelodge.com/general-info/webcam for a view of Mount Assiniboine while you plan your hike!)

Resupply stations: Mount Assiniboine Lodge. Contact the lodge in advance to arrange for a helicopter to deliver your resupply parcel. The $3 per pound cost isn't that prohibitive once you consider the convenience of it. Just use your lightest, dehydrated food for this resupply.

Special notes: The Mount Assiniboine area can be busy during the summer. Don't be alarmed. Try to enjoy the view and move on.

Banff National Park has placed restrictions on the Bryant Creek and Allenby Pass trails from August 1st to September 30th annually in order to reduce human and bear conflicts during the berry season. This doesn't affect hikers or their dogs who stay on the main route of the GDT; it only affects equestrians on the alternate GDT horse route that goes over Allenby Pass. During this time, riders must be in groups of two and no dogs are permitted.

Watridge Lake trail junction to Big Springs campsite (3.4km, 58m up, 22m down)

Continue straight through the Watridge Lake trail junction and head north on the Bryant Creek trail. In 600m you cross a footbridge over Bryant Creek and follow the Bryant Creek trail northwest up the valley on excellent trail. Within the first kilometre you pass the Trail Centre warden cabin on the left. The well-maintained trail reaches a bridged tributary beside the Big Springs campsite (1720, 3.4, c8) in forest cover.

Big Springs campsite to the Marvel Lake campsite Br13 (4.0km, 51m up, 19m down)

Continuing on the Bryant Creek trail, cross a bridge in 2.3km. In another 1.1km you arrive at the Marvel Lake and Wonder Pass trail junction. If you have booked Bryant Creek Shelter or McBride's Camp, continue straight for 600m and 1.2km respectively. (There is a cut-off trail from McBride's Camp travelling southwest to join the Marvel Lake trail in 1.1km, so you don't have to backtrack if you decide to stay there.) Turn left at the Marvel Lake trail junction (1805, 3.4, c8a) and reach the Marvel Lake campsite in 600m.

Marvel Lake campsite Br13 to Wonder Pass (9.4km, 722m up, 139m down)

The trail heads west and comes to a junction in 1.1km. Take the spur trail a short distance down to the lake at this point to fill your water reserves for the hike over Wonder Pass. NOBO hikers, there is no other dependable water source for the next 9km. Continue 500m up the trail to a signed trail junction with the cut-off trail from McBride's Camp. Turn left and

continue southwest on good trail. Reach a junction with the Marvel Pass trail in 4.5km at the end of Marvel Lake. Be sure to continue right, uphill. A steep climb brings the route 3.3km farther, up to Wonder Pass (2380, 10.0, c9). On the Divide the route leaves Banff National Park in Alberta for Assiniboine Provincial Park in British Columbia.

The indisputable highlight of segment 16 is the world-famous view of Mount Assiniboine from Lake Magog.

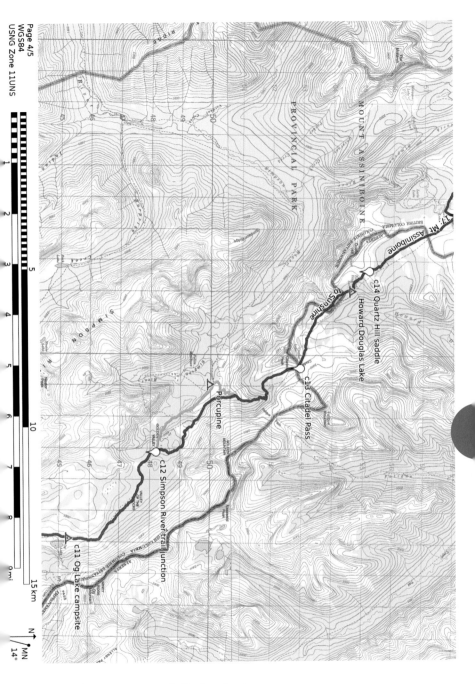

Wonder Pass to Assiniboine Lodge
(3.2km, 3m up, 202m down)

Descend open alpine slopes to a bridge over Magog Creek in 900m. SOBO

Looking down at Wonder Pass and Gog Lake from the Wonder Peak traverse. "Isabelle" is spelled with rocks in the foreground in commemoration of a departed friend.

Wonder Pass in the fading light above Lake Magog from the BC Parks campsite.

hikers should fill their water bottles here because the next water source is in 9km. The trail continues gently downhill, going through some patches of sparse forest, passing the Wonder Lodge cooking shelter in 1.7km. The Naiset huts are in this area. There is a drop-in rate of $20 to stay at one of these basic cabins – check at Assiniboine Lodge if you wish to stay there. Good trail and boardwalks bring the route 500m to Assiniboine Lodge (2175, 3.2, C10). The lodge offers a daily teatime to the public from 4pm to 5pm. To get to the Lake Magog campsite, turn left and follow the Lake Magog trail 1.4km around the north side of the lake. You will find signs and distances at each trail junction. There is an open-sided cook shelter at the Lake Magog campsite where hikers and climbers tend to congregate – it's a good place to meet kindred spirits. A spring runs beside the campsite all summer. It is $10 cash for the self-registration fee to stay overnight.

Segment 17 – Mount Assiniboine Lodge to Sunshine Village junction (25.2km)

Moderate hiking on good trail with a long climb over Citadel Pass. Horses and bikes not permitted.

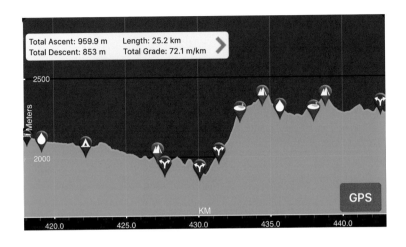

Total Ascent: 959.9 m
Total Descent: 853 m
Length: 25.2 km
Total Grade: 72.1 m/km

Mount Assiniboine from the Niblet on the Nub Peak trail. If you have the time, this is a worthwhile side trip.

Sunshine Meadows is a popular destination, near the end of segment 17.

Rolling alpine meadows are the hallmark of this leg of the GDT – so too is the view of Mount Assiniboine. After a winding hike through the Valley of the Rocks, you climb up to Citadel Pass and traverse the renowned Sunshine Meadows. This is the epitome of alpine hiking and running trails.

Maps: 82 J/13 Mount Assiniboine and 82 O/4 Banff; Gemtrek #5 Banff & Mount Assiniboine and #17 Banff Egypt Lake.

Jurisdictions: Mount Assiniboine Provincial Park (BC Parks) and Banff National Park.

South access: The GDT follows the two most popular trails that access the heart of Mount Assiniboine Provincial Park. You can also access the area by hiking 30km from Kootenay National Park, starting at the Simpson River trailhead on Highway 93. Follow the river and then Surprise Creek over Ferro Pass. The easiest way to arrive at Lake Magog is by helicopter. Helicopters service Mount Assiniboine Lodge from Canmore and a helipad near the Mount Shark trailhead. Contact Alpine Helicopters and consult Assiniboine Lodge at assiniboinelodge.com/general-info/flying.

North access: Drive to the Sunshine ski area exit, 9km west of Banff on Trans-Canada Highway 1. Follow the Sunshine Village road another 9km to the parking lot. Sunshine Village is 6km up the restricted gondola access (gravel) road. From June 30 to September 24 there is a shuttle bus that goes to and from Banff and a gondola that operates on odd days. Check the schedule and rates at sunshinemeadowsbanff.com. Currently, a one-way bus ride is only $10.

Car campgrounds and accommodations: Mount Assiniboine Lodge has rustic rooms and cabins you can reserve (well in advance). You can stay in one of the Naiset huts (first come, first served) near the lodge for $20 drop-in fee or $25 in advance. If you stay at the huts, you can use the Wonder Lodge cooking shelter, which has two propane stoves, fuel, utensils and tables.

Sunshine Village offers a gondola sightseeing and shuttle bus service that started in 2017. The gondola ride is prohibitively expensive for the 'tour' but they will likely allow you to ride the lift down for half price. Once you are down at the gondola base station, they offer a $12 return shuttle bus to Banff. Alternatively you could choose to stay at Sunshine Mountain Lodge. The resort now offers summer accommodations from June 30 to September 23 – see sunshinemountainlodge.com/summer-at-sunshine.

Banff has all services and amenities, but book in advance if you are planning to stay overnight there. If you haven't booked in advance, you might be able to find an open bed at one of three hostels in town: Banff International, Banff Hostel, or Hosteling International Banff – see the 'Contacts' appendix starting on page 340. Otherwise, Tunnel Mountain campground, operated by Parks Canada, charges $36 and has showers. Banff and Canmore have a local transit system called Roam. These buses run on a regular schedule to all key points in the two towns and a day pass costs just $5: roamtransit.com.

Camping: *National park campsites*: Howard Douglas Lake (Su8).

BC Parks campsites: Lake Magog, Og Lake, and Porcupine (off-route by 1.5km); $10 self-registration. Hikers indicate a preference for Magog over Og because it has more sites, better tree cover and access to the lodge. Hikers also recommend Magog as a basecamp to do other interesting hikes in the area, such as the famed 'Nub Peak.'

Information sources: Banff National Park Visitor Information Centre, BC Parks, Mount Assiniboine Lodge, and Alpine Helicopters.

Resupply stations: White Mountain Adventures provides a service to thru-hikers: they will take parcels delivered to their company office in Banff to Bruno's Cafe at (upper) Sunshine Village. Bruno's is open daily from 11:30am to 6:30pm. Failing that, contact Sunshine Mountain Lodge through their website, sunshinemountainlodge.com.

Special notes: The Mount Assiniboine area can be busy during the summer. Don't be alarmed. Try to enjoy the view and move on. Sunshine Meadows and the Sunshine Village area can also be busy. There is an alternate route that bypasses Sunshine Village if you aren't planning on a resupply (or pub stop).

Helicopters service Assiniboine Lodge, which makes for a convenient resupply.

Assiniboine Lodge to Og Lake campsite (4.8km, 14m up, 135m down)

From Assiniboine Lodge, continue on amazing trail north. Follow signs for the Og *Lake* trail (there is also an Og *Pass* trail). In 800m travel through the junction for the Assiniboine Pass trail. In another 400m, turn left at the Og Pass trail junction down along the creek. The trail quickly leaves the trees and crosses to the western bank of Og Creek 600m farther. Stay on the west (left) side of the creek through the impressive Og Meadows. Remember to look over your shoulder to take in the view of Mount Assiniboine. In another 3km you arrive at the Og Lake campsite (2050, 4.8, C11), where there is a $10 self-registration per person for overnighting.

Og Lake campsite to Porcupine campsite trail junction (5.5km, 98m up, 194m down)

Make sure you have water before leaving. NOBO hikers, the next water source is 11km north. Ascending from Og Lake, traverse a broad pass and descend into the dry Valley of the Rocks amidst trees and heaps of boulders. This is the winding Citadel Pass trail that eventually reaches the Simpson River trail junction (1935, 5.5, C12) above a small seasonal lake in a deep depression.

PORCUPINE CAMPSITE ALTERNATE ROUTE – 4.0KM INSTEAD OF 3.7KM

Choose this alternate route if you plan to stay at Porcupine. Keep to the left at the Y-junction and follow the Simpson River trail. In 3.0km go straight through the Police Meadows trail junction to reach the Porcupine campground within 300m. Continue through the campground and keep

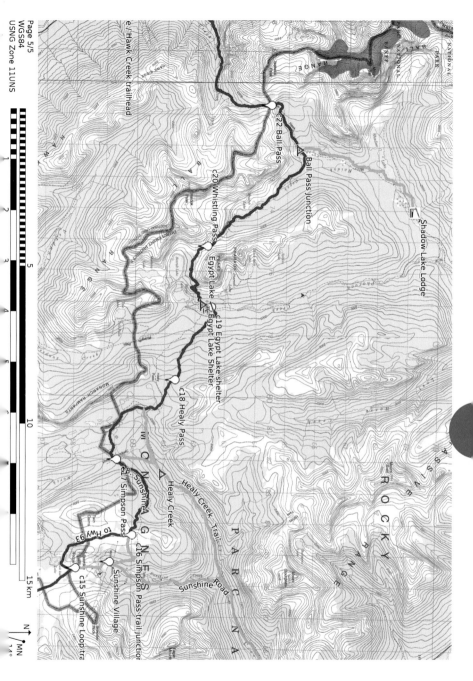

to the right at a trail junction for Citadel Pass. Turn right and climb to join the GDT on the Citadel Pass trail in 700m up switchbacks. If you are considering staying at the Police Meadows shelter shown on the map – don't. It's not worth the side trip unless you need to escape the worst weather.

End Porcupine campsite alternate route

Porcupine campsite trail junction to Citadel Pass (6.8km, 583m up, 162m down)

Turn right at the trail junction, leaving tree cover for the exposed slopes of Golden Mountain on the northeastern side of the valley. Gently ascend 3.7km to the northern Porcupine campsite trail junction, on the lip of a hanging valley (the alternate Porcupine campsite route goes steeply downhill to the left). The main route ascends to the north through sparse trees before coming to a pond in 1.5km. SOBO hikers, the next water source

The author on an out-and-back run to Citadel Pass. Sunshine Village to the Mount Shark trailhead (segments 16 and 17) is a classic trail run. Photo: Jerry Auld.

Dustin and Julia approach Citadel Pass. Mount Assiniboine stands on the horizon. Photo: Doug Mouser.

Howard Douglas Lake below Citadel Peak. Mount Assiniboine is visible in the distance.

is in 11km. Turn west and climb the steep switchbacks to the northwest. The switchbacks relent as the trail reaches a small lake. The route reaches Citadel Pass (2365, 6.8, c13) through alpine meadows and re-enters Banff National Park in Alberta.

Citadel Pass to Howard Douglas Lake campground (3.5km, 90m up, 198m down)

The route follows good trail through undulating meadows past Citadel Peak, with some muddy sections. Cross a small stream in 1.2km. The Howard Douglas Lake campsite is reached in another 2.3km, just before starting a steep climb over Quartz Hill to the northwest.

Howard Douglas Lake campsite to Sunshine Loop trail junction (4.6km, 175m up, 164m down)

After a steep 800m climb up to Quartz Hill saddle (2380, 4.3, c14), descend through meadows and hop across a small creek. Start a gentle climb toward Standish Ridge, crossing the Continental Divide back into Mount Assiniboine Provincial Park. When you reach the signed Sunshine Loop trail junction (2290, 3.8, c15), turn left and follow the Sunshine Loop trail toward Rock Isle Lake. If you turned right, you would descend to Sunshine Village.

SUNSHINE VILLAGE ALTERNATE ROUTE – 3KM INSTEAD OF 3.3KM

Plan to take this route if you mean to resupply at or use Sunshine Village facilities. At the Sunshine Loop trail junction with the Citadel Pass trail, turn right. A built-up trail crosses the Divide and descends toward the

Julia heading down the wide and well-used trail on the Sunshine Village alternate route.

Sunshine Village ski resort. The trail passes the avalanche control cabin and becomes a gravel road. The day lodge has a cafeteria, washrooms and a telephone. This is also where you will find Trapper's Saloon, Bruno's Cafe and a good store. Continue past the day lodge. The trail starts again below the Wawa T-bar lift on the northern side of Larix House. The gravel path ascends through sparse trees with frequent footbridges to reach the Simpson Pass trail junction (2360, 3.3, c16) described in the next segment.

End Sunshine Village alternate route

SEGMENT 18 - Sunshine to Highway 93 (34.1km)

Strenuous hiking on good trails with long climbs over three high passes. Horses and bikes prohibited.

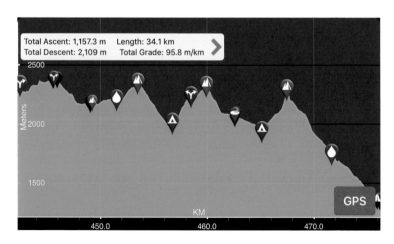

Total Ascent: 1,157.3 m Length: 34.1 km
Total Descent: 2,109 m Total Grade: 95.8 m/km

The Egypt Lake area in Banff National Park is a popular backcountry destination, though not as busy as Mount Assiniboine. The GDT descends to Egypt Lake from the stunning Healy Pass, where you can get a good view of the Pharaoh Creek valley and Egypt Lake. Whistling and Ball passes are unlike the alpine haven of Healy; they are precipitous gateways poised between high rock walls and summits. For the weekend hiker, there are many exquisite loops that all seem to centre around Pharaoh Peaks, for good reason; it's an enchanting area.

Maps: 82 O/4 Banff and 82 N/1 Mount Goodsir; Gemtrek #10 Kootenay National Park, #5 Banff & Mount Assiniboine and #17 Banff Egypt Lake.

Jurisdictions: Banff and Kootenay national parks.

South access: Drive to the Sunshine ski area exit, 9km west of Banff on Trans-Canada Highway 1. Follow the Sunshine Village road another 9km to the parking lot. Sunshine Village is 6km up the restricted gondola access (gravel) road. From June 30 to September 24, there is a shuttle bus that goes to and from Banff and a gondola that operates on odd-numbered days. Check the schedule and rates at sunshinemeadowsbanff.com. Currently, a one-way bus ride is only $10.

Other access: At the Sunshine Village parking area, look for the signed Healy Pass trailhead. The trail crosses a bridge and then follows Healy Creek upstream. You will come to the Healy Creek campsite in 5km and then reach a trail junction 800m farther. If you turn left, you will reach the GDT in 1.3km, at Simpson Pass. Continue straight through the junction and there is another junction with the Simpson Pass trail (the GDT) in 1.9km.

Via Redearth Creek: Drive to the Redearth Creek trailhead on Trans-Canada Highway 1, 20km west of Banff and 10km east of Castle Junction, on the south side of the highway. Hike 7km up the Redearth Creek trail to the Lost Horse campsite. In another 3.5km you reach the Pharaoh Creek trail junction. If you turn left, toward Egypt Lakes, you will get to the GDT in 9km at the Egypt Lake campsite. If you continue ahead on the Redearth Creek trail, you will pass Shadow Lake Lodge and campsite in 2.5km and find the Ball Pass trail junction in another kilometre. Turn left at the junction and reach the GDT in 5km at the Ball Pass Junction campsite. In total you will either hike 19.5km to the Egypt Lake campsite or 19km to the Ball Pass Junction campsite to reach the GDT.

North access: Drive to Castle Junction on Trans-Canada Highway 1. Head south on Highway 93 (Banff–Radium) for 32km to the Floe Lake and Hawk Creek trailhead parking area, on the southwest side of the highway. Alternatively, you can drive north from Radium on Highway 93 and get to the trailhead parking area in 72km. You will find toilets and a trailhead information kiosk at the parking lot.

Car campgrounds and accommodations: *Sunshine Village* offers a gondola sightseeing and shuttle bus service that started in 2017. The gondola ride is prohibitively expensive for the 'tour' but they will likely allow you to ride the lift down for half price. Once you are down at the gondola base station, they offer a $12 return shuttle bus to Banff. Alternatively you could choose to stay at Sunshine Mountain Lodge. The resort now offers summer accommodations from June 30 to September 23 – see sunshinemountainlodge.com/summer-at-sunshine.

Banff has all services and amenities, but book in advance if you are planning to stay overnight there. If you haven't booked in advance, you might be able to find an open bed at one of three hostels in town: Banff International, Banff Hostel, or Hosteling International Banff – see the 'Contacts' appendix starting on page 340. Otherwise, Tunnel Mountain campground, operated by Parks Canada, charges $36 and has showers. Banff and Canmore have a local transit system called Roam. These buses run on a regular schedule to all key points in the two towns and a day pass costs just $5: roamtransit.com.

Kootenay National Park has three campgrounds, the closest one to the GDT being Marble Canyon, 17km south of Castle Junction on Highway 93. The campground charges $21.50 and has no showers. You can find accommodations at Castle Junction if you go north to the Bow Valley Parkway 1A instead of south on Highway 93. Contact the Castle Mountain HI youth hostel.

Shadow Lake Lodge is a backcountry accommodation 5.3km off-route from the Ball Pass–Shadow Lake trail junction. The lodge has several cabins and they serve three meals a day, including an afternoon tea. The stay is expensive but might be more appealing for you than a roadside layover elsewhere on the GDT. The teatime may figure into your resupply plans – it is quite a spread for a flat price of $15. No dogs. See shadowlakelodge.com.

Camping: National park campsites: Healy Creek (E5) off-route by 2.1km, Egypt Lake campsite (E13) and Egypt Lake Shelter, Ball Pass Junction campsite (Re21), Shadow Lake Lodge off-route by 5.3km.

Information sources: Banff National Park Visitor Information Centre, Kootenay National Park Visitor Information Centre, Lake Louise Visitor Information Centre.

Resupply stations: White Mountain Adventures provides a service for thru-hikers: they will take parcels delivered to their company office in Banff to Bruno's Cafe at (upper) Sunshine Village. Bruno's is open daily from 11:30am to 6:30pm. Failing that, contact Sunshine Mountain Lodge through their website, sunshinemountainlodge.com.

Julia Lynx and Doug Mouser standing at waypoint c16, where the Sunshine Village alternate route rejoins the main route.

Sunshine Loop trail junction to Healy Pass
(11.0km, 417m up, 357m down)

Staying on the main route of the GDT, head south toward Rock Isle Lake from the Sunshine Loop trail junction. Within 800m you pass by Rock Isle Lake and then the Larix Lake trail junctions on the left. In another 300m you pass the Standish Ridge trail junction on the right. From that junction the Sunshine Loop trail heads north. The trail crosses the Divide again on the way to the Simpson Pass trail junction (2360, 3.3, c16) in the alpine. SOBO hikers, the alternate route to the Sunshine Village and Trapper's Pub descends from here – see segment 17 for the trail description. Turn left, descend to the west over a broad ridge into forest, and contour along steep slopes. The trail crosses and recrosses the Divide on the descent to Simpson Pass (2150, 3.4, c17). From the first of two trail junctions in the pass you can descend north 2.1km to the Healy Creek campsite (see 'Camping'). In 900m pass a junction where the Eohippus Lake trail branches off to the left, and continue up the other side of Simpson Pass. Ascending steeply at first, the trail climbs through trees past a pond.

Doug Mouser plows his way up to Whistling Pass. Snowfall blanketed the area the night before.

Off route, Julia Lynx looks down onto the Ball Pass trail, which sits on the Divide between Banff and Kootenay national parks.

Follow a minor tributary downstream, cross the bridged Healy Creek and join the Healy Pass trail (read 'Other access'). Turn left and follow the Healy Pass trail. The trail leaves Healy Creek in the alpine and a moderate ascent leads to Healy Pass (2340, 4.3, c18).

Healy Pass to Egypt Lake shelter and campsite (3.2km, 5m up, 338m down)

On Healy Pass you can nearly touch the Continental Divide as it traces the crest of the Monarch Ramparts to the south. Leave the alpine and descend down a long, moderate trail to the Egypt Lake warden cabin. Cross a bridge over Pharaoh Creek to a junction with the Pharaoh Creek trail (read 'Other access'). Turn left to the Egypt Lake campsite and shelter (2000, 3.2, c19). The shelter has bunks, tables, clotheslines and a wood-burning stove. You can reserve the Egypt Lake shelter for $6.80 per night. I've stayed there several nights and enjoyed the bountiful wood supply in conjunction with the stove in winter.

Egypt Lake shelter and campsite to Whistling Pass (3.3km, 355m up, 48m down)

Walk through the campsite to the Whistling Pass trail junction, away from Pharaoh Creek. The ascent is gradual as the trail negotiates some short boardwalks through a boggy area. Suddenly the Whistling Pass trail begins a steep climb through trees and cliff bands. Pass the trail junction for Mummy Lake in 1.8km. Traverse talus above timberline with good views of Scarab and Mummy lakes. Whistling Pass (2310, 3.3, c20) is huddled below Pharaoh Peaks to the north and the Divide to the south.

Whistling Pass to Ball Pass Junction campsite (5.2km, 2m up, 393m down)

A moderate descent leads across talus to the shore of Haiduk Lake in 2.1km. A shoreline path continues north along the eastern side of the lake and crosses the outflow on a bridge in 800m. The descent to the Ball Pass Junction campsite (1900, 5.2, c21) has partial views of Whistling Valley. The trail going downstream joins the Redearth Creek trail (read 'Other access') and reaches Shadow Lake Lodge in 5.3km.

Ball Pass Junction campsite to Ball Pass (2.3km, 301m up, 2m down)

Turn left at the Ball Pass Junction campsite and follow the Ball Pass trail upstream. The sometimes rutted trail follows the northern bank of the creek, ascending moderately to the southwest. NOBO hikers, pick up water while you are close to the stream. The next water source is 7km distant.

Cross over the head of the creek. The final and short leg up to Ball Pass (2280, 2.3, c22) is steep, make no mistake. The impressive 3306m Mount Ball and its precarious ice cap stand in clear view to the north from the pass.

Ball Pass to Floe Lake and Hawk Creek trailhead (9.1km, 78m up, 967m down)

Descend through forest along a minor tributary to Hawk Creek. The trail follows the northern wall of the Hawk Creek valley. Walk across a small log bridge over a tributary in 4.2 km. SOBO hikers should get water here. The next water is in 6km, over the other side of the pass. Despite devastation from a 2003 fire, the trail is in good shape. A steep descent leads to a reclaimed fire road and then gently descends to Banff–Radium Highway 93, where Hawk Creek meets the highway. Turn left and use the highway shoulder to cross the creek. Follow a gravel path that parallels the northern side of the road for 400m. Cross the sometimes busy thoroughfare and arrive at the Floe Lake and Hawk Creek trailhead parking area (1340, 9.1, c23). SOBO hikers face nearly a full kilometre of elevation gain up to Ball Pass – this is one of the most sustained climbs of the GDT.

SEGMENT 19 – Highway 93 to Helmet Falls campsite (38.7km)

Strenuous climbs over several passes on a well-travelled trail. Horses and bikes prohibited.

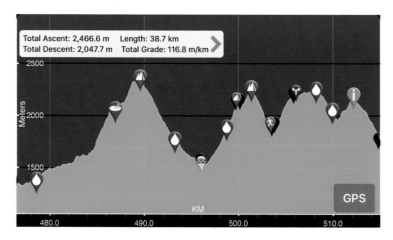

Welcome to the world-renowned Rockwall trail in Kootenay National Park. This is a busy but extremely gorgeous and worthwhile hiking destination.

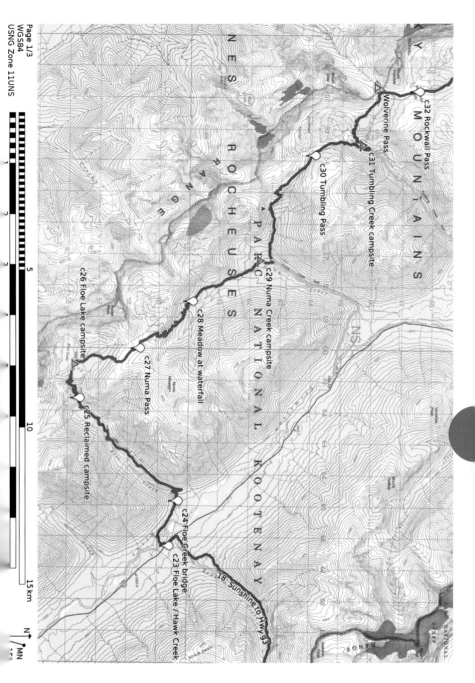

During some years, the snow does not completely vanish from the trail until August. The short season condenses many of the trail users into one month, so getting a wilderness permit can be more challenging than

Julia Lynx and Dustin Lynx below Numa Creek falls on the Rockwall trail in Kootenay National Park. Photo: Doug Mouser.

hiking the mountainous terrain. The GDT follows the Rockwall trail along the foot of a kilometre-high escarpment for nearly 30km over high alpine passes. This is a particularly popular trail for trail runners in recent years. Though the footing can be technical, the setting is perfect for a long run.

Maps: 82 N/1 Mount Goodsir; Gemtrek #10 Kootenay National Park.

Jurisdiction: Kootenay National Park.

South access: Drive to Castle Junction on Trans-Canada Highway 1. Head south on Banff–Radium Highway 93 for 32km to the Floe Lake and Hawk Creek trailhead parking area, on the southwest side of the highway. Alternatively you can drive north from Radium on Highway 93 and get to the trailhead parking area in 72km. You will find toilets and a trailhead information kiosk at the parking lot.

North and other access: *Via Numa Creek*: drive 24.5km south from the Highway 1 and Highway 93 South junction to the Numa Falls picnic area on the south side of the highway. Walk across the Vermilion River footbridge and hike 6.4km to intersect the GDT on the Rockwall trail. The Numa Creek campsite is to the left.

Via Helmet Creek: drive 19.8km south from the Highway 1 and Highway 93 South junction to the Paint Pots trailhead parking (2.6km past the Marble Canyon parking lot). Follow the Paint Pots trail over the Vermilion River bridge to join the Helmet Creek trail. Continue along Helmet Creek 2.4km to the Tumbling Creek trail junction. If you turned left here, you would reach the GDT in 6.6km. Continue through the junction, up Helmet Creek and pass the Helmet–Ochre Junction campsite in 2.3km. Continuing through this campsite, you will reach the Helmet Falls campsite in another 8.0km on the Rockwall trail, at the foot of Helmet Falls.

Car campgrounds and accommodations: *Kootenay National Park* has three campgrounds, the closest one to the GDT being Marble Canyon's, 17km south from the Highway 1 and Highway 93 South junction. The campground charges $21.50 and has no showers. You can find accommodations at Castle Junction if you go north to Bow Valley Parkway 1A instead of south on Highway 93. Contact the Castle Mountain HI youth hostel.

Kootenay Park Lodge is 40km south from the Highway 1 and Highway 93 South junction at Vermilion Crossing (8.6km south on the highway from the GDT) and has a store and gift shop as well as cabins that rent for $175/night. Book well in advance.

Camping: National park campsites at Floe Lake (#12), Numa Creek (#11), Tumbling Creek (#10) and Helmet Falls (#6). Random camping 250m off route at Wolverine Pass (between Tumbling and Helmet Falls).

Information sources: Kootenay National Park Visitor Information Centre and Lake Louise Visitor Information Centre. You can reserve campsites in Kootenay from either of the visitor centres in Banff National Park or online.

Resupply stations: None.

Special notes: The Kootenay Information Centre in Radium doesn't open until May 18 each year. You can reserve online, however.

Floe Lake trailhead to Floe Lake campsite (10.2km, 840m up, 128m down)

The excellent Floe Lake trail descends 500m southward from the trailhead parking area to a footbridge spanning the Vermilion River. The trail turns northwest, travelling 1.4km farther to the Floe Creek bridge (1350, 1.9, C24). NOBO hikers, get water here for the potential 9km of waterless ascent to follow. Long, moderate switchbacks bring the trail up to a traverse above Floe Creek, passing through debris chutes before getting to a good viewpoint (1665, 5.7, C25) just beyond a normally dry creek drainage. After encountering a steep section of switchbacks, you top out on a broad ridge crest above Floe Lake at the Floe Lake campsite (2030, 2.6, C26), in full view of the Rockwall and Foster Peak. SOBO hikers should take up water at the lake for the 9km waterless descent. This is a particularly beautiful setting for a campsite. A warden station is nearby.

Floe Lake campsite to Numa Creek campsite (9.2km, 322m up, 820m down)

Continue through the campsite and start a moderate ascent to the west of a minor tributary on the Rockwall trail. The trail climbs through sparse trees to Numa Pass (2335, 2.7, C27). The alpine path descends to the north, reaches a long series of switchbacks in trees and then arrives at a large

Tumbling Glacier near Tumbling Pass. A hiker is visible atop the moraine to the left.

Rockwall Pass, seemingly in winter. Except this is late July in 1996.

meadow at the foot of a waterfall (1780, 3.7, c28). A good trail combines bridges and boardwalks to avoid boggy sections before arriving at the Numa Creek campsite (1560, 2.8, c29).

Numa Creek campsite to Tumbling Creek campsite (7.7km, 720m up, 391m down)

Walk 500m through the Numa Creek campsite to the Numa Creek trail junction (read 'Other access'). Turn left and stay on the south side of the tributary. The trail ascends moderately to the west. After a series of switchbacks the route crosses a branch of the tributary in 2.2km and ascends into trees briefly for a steep climb up to alpine meadows and Tumbling Pass (2235, 5.2, c30). Keep to the east above a long mound of recessional moraine and descend into trees. In 2.2km there is a trail junction (again see 'Other access'). Turn left, cross a bridge and in 300m arrive at the Tumbling Creek campsite (1890, 2.5, c31).

Rockwall Pass as it should be, in the summer of 2009. Photo: Cynthia Lane.

Limestone Peak stands at the northern end of the Rockwall trail, near Helmet Falls.

Tumbling Creek campsite to Helmet Falls campsite (11.6km, 585m up, 709m down)

From the Tumbling Creek campsite, continue uphill southwest on good trail and then up steep switchbacks above Tumbling Creek falls. In subalpine meadows the Rockwall trail passes the Wolverine Patrol Cabin trail junction, on the right in 2.4km, and then the Wolverine Pass trail junction, on the left 500m farther. If you turned left (southwest) at Wolverine Pass, you could follow the trail 250m and cross the boundary out of Kootenay National Park. You can random camp anywhere outside that boundary. Staying on the main route, you go straight through the junction and then climb gradually, 600m, to Rockwall Pass (2165, 3.5, c32) under Mount Drysdale. Climb above the pass and then descend to a bridge (1955, 2.7, c33) over the outflow of a small tarn. Winding through piles of moraine, the route descends to a bridge and crosses a smaller creek. Good trail ascends moderately though sparse forest to a saddle (2165, 2.2, c34) on a ridge below Limestone Peak. A moderate descent leads you west to a good view of Helmet Falls, the second-highest waterfall in the Canadian Rockies. Good trail crosses a bridge over Helmet Creek, follows the creek downstream and passes through Helmet Falls campsite (1760, 3.2, c35).

SEGMENT 20 – Helmet Falls campsite to the Field, BC, post office (37.1km)

Moderate climb over a high pass on good trail. Horses prohibited. Bikes allowed up to McArthur campsite on Ottertail River trail.

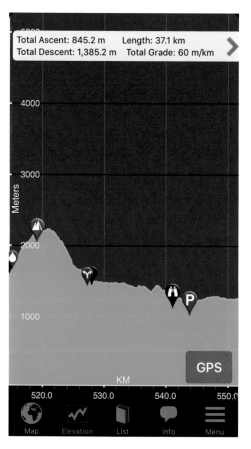

Although most of the segment is below timberline, there are still plenty of views to admire and riverside walking to enjoy. The route is straightforward and easy to navigate, which makes it suitable for novice hikers. The highlights are Helmet Falls and Goodsir Pass. The last 8km of the segment, on Highway 1, is really for thru-hikers going on to the next section.

Maps: 82 N/1 Mount Goodsir, 82 N/8 Lake Louise and 82 N/7 Golden; Gemtrek #4 Lake Louise & Yoho and #10 Kootenay National Park.

Jurisdictions: Kootenay and Yoho national parks.

South access: Via Helmet Creek: drive 19.8km south from the Highway 1 and Highway 93 South

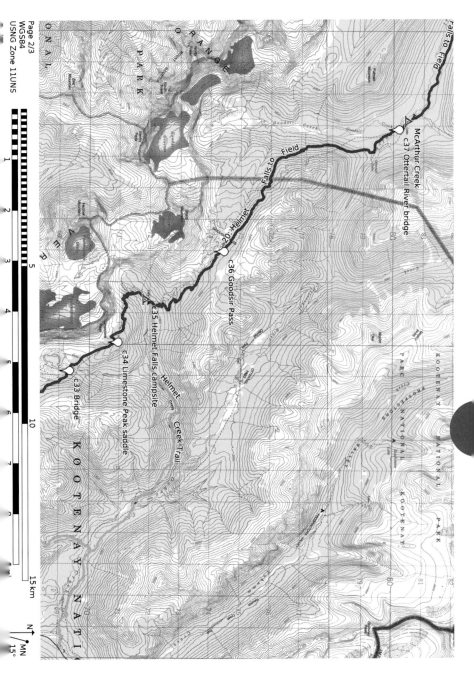

junction to the Paint Pots trailhead parking area (2.6km past the Marble Canyon parking area). Walk the Paint Pots trail over the Vermilion River bridge to join the Helmet Creek trail. Continue along Helmet Creek 2.4km

Helmet Falls, one of the highest waterfalls in the Canadian Rockies, seen from the Helmet Falls backcountry campsite.

to the Tumbling Creek trail junction. If you turned left here, you would reach the GDT in 6.6km. Continue through the junction, up Helmet Creek, and pass the Helmet–Ochre Junction campsite in 2.3km. Continuing through this campsite, you will reach the Helmet Falls campsite (#6) in another 8.0km on the Rockwall trail, at the foot of Helmet Falls.

North access: The Ottertail River trailhead parking area is on the Trans-Canada Highway 8.3km east of Field. The northern terminus of this segment is in the town of Field itself. Unless you are a southbound thru-hiker, you will want to start at the Ottertail River trailhead.

Car campgrounds and accommodations: Kootenay National Park has three campgrounds and the closest one to the GDT is Marble Canyon campground, 17km south from the Highway 1 and Highway 93 South junction. The campground charges $21.50 and has no showers.

The closest campgrounds to the GDT in Yoho National Park are 5km east of Field. Turn north onto Yoho Valley Road from Trans-Canada Highway 1. The Monarch and Kicking Horse campgrounds charge $17.60 and $27.40 respectively. Kicking Horse has showers. For more information

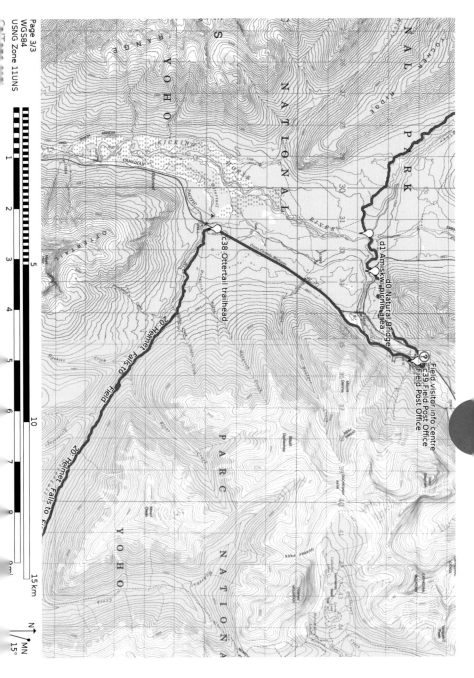

about accommodations in Field, inquire at the Yoho National Park Visitor Information Centre at the turnoff for Field. The Fireweed Hostel is the most affordable place to stay in Field. Rates start at $30 per night for a dorm room. They have free wifi and showers but the coin-op laundry facilities are 100m down the street at Truffle Pigs Lodge, formerly known as Kicking Horse Lodge. The hostel is conveniently located across the street from the post office and not far from the awesome Truffle Pigs restaurant and general store. The town of Field has cell phone service and is a hiker-friendly resupply town because everything is in such close proximity.

Camping: National park campsites at Helmet Falls (#6) and MacArthur Creek (#1).

Information sources: Yoho National Park information centre (at the junction of the Field access road on Highway 1), Kootenay National Park information centre and the Lake Louise information centre.

Resupply station: Field post office. There are a couple of ways to get there by road from the Ottertail River trailhead for NOBO hikers.

1. Head northeast 8.3km on Highway 1 to the main intersection for Field (you can actually cut off a bit sooner and follow a municipal trail beside a ball diamond along the river) and turn right on the Field access road. Go 200m and cross a bridge over the Kicking Horse River. Turn left on E 2nd street. Follow it around to the right 250m and turn right (walking) on the one-way Stephen Avenue. Continue 300m southwest on Stephen Avenue to the post office. As mentioned above, the hostel is across the street.

2. Head northeast 4.9km on Highway 1 and turn right onto a one-way back road for Field, 500m before the highway bridge crosses the Kicking Horse River. The back road continues north 3.4km on the east bank of the river and becomes Stephen Avenue in Field, where the post office and hostel are located. This only works if you are walking or cycling. Cars have to go via description 1.

Special notes: The Kootenay National Park information centre in Radium, BC, doesn't open until May 18th each year. Keep this in mind when planning your trip: book online. Cyclists are permitted along Trans-Canada Highway 1 from Field to the Ottertail River trailhead parking area, of course, and then a further 15km to the McArthur Creek campsite up the Ottertail River trail. Hikers recommend walking beside the road if you plan to hike the 9km between the trailhead and the town of Field. The railway is private property and not wide enough to safely walk beside.

Helmet Falls campsite to Goodsir Pass
(3.9km, 450m up, 0m down)

Continue downstream through the Helmet Falls campsite, reaching a tributary bridge near a patrol cabin in 100m. Cross the small bridge and pass in front of the warden cabin. NOBO hikers, the next 14km can be dry; make sure you collect water here. The Goodsir Pass trail junction is 300m past the cabin. Turn left at this signed junction for Goodsir Pass and climb a preliminary set of switchbacks. As the grade eases, the trail ascends to Goodsir Pass (2205, 3.9, c36).

Goodsir Pass to McArthur Creek campsite (9.6km, 68m up, 775m down)

The Goodsir Pass trail climbs gently to the north, crossing the park boundary from Kootenay into Yoho in 1.6km, and then contours to the north, down into the Goodsir Creek valley. The moderate descent eases lower down. Go straight past a junction with a trail for Ottertail Falls in 7.0km from the boundary. In 600m to the north, the trail reaches a bridge over the Ottertail River (1515, 9.2, c37). From the bridge the trail climbs briefly and travels another 400m to the McArthur Creek campsite and warden cabin. SOBO hikers should consider collecting water here, as the next 14km to Helmet Creek can be dry.

McArthur Creek campsite to the Ottertail River trailhead (15.2km, 192m up, 504m down)

Beyond the campsite, you join the Ottertail River trail, an old fire road. Cross McArthur Creek and pass the McArthur Pass trail junction in 600m. Continue downstream on the Ottertail River trail, staying on the north bank. The condition of the road deteriorates in places where washouts have swept through. The road climbs briefly to a viewpoint in another 11.9km. The access road continues to the Ottertail River trailhead parking area (1200, 15.6, c38) on Trans-Canada Highway 1.

Ottertail River trailhead to the Field, BC, post office (8.3km, 135m up, 106m down)

If you are thru-hiking to the next section, refer to 'Resupply station' in the info block above. The best way to walk to the post office in Field is option 2 in that description – 8.3km one way, only 4.9km of which is on the highway. Accommodations can be tricky to find in Field if you haven't booked in advance. If you don't have a reservation in town, call ahead to Fireweed Hostel as soon as you have cell phone reception in this segment. There is no public campground in Field – refer to 'Car campgrounds and accommodations' for this segment. Field, BC, is waypoint (1260, 8.3, c39).

Section D: *Field to North Saskatchewan River*

Segments 21–23, 105.1 km

Location	Near waypoint	NOBO km	SOBO km
Natural Bridge	d0	557.0	576.2
Amiskwi River junction	d1	558.7	574.5
Amiskwi River ford	d2	575.3	557.9
Amiskwi River ford and campsite	d3	582.1	551.1
Amiskwi River ford	d5	589.7	543.5
Amiskwi Pass and campsite	d6	593.4	539.8
Ensign Creek Road	d7	596.6	536.6
Amiskwi Lodge*	d7	596.6	536.6
Blaeberry Bridge	d8	609.7	523.5
David Thompson trailhead and campsite	d9	616.8	516.4
Lambe Glacier outflow	d10	623.9	509.3
Howse Pass	d11	628.4	504.8
Glacier Lake Trail junction	d14	644.1	489.1
Promontory and campsite	d14	648.2	485.0
Mistaya Canyon	d16	654.1	479.1
RESUPPLY: The Crossing resort*	d17	657.7	475.5

Introduction

This is the shortest leg of the GDT between easily accessible resupply points. Though it is the shortest section, it garners the most complaints from hikers due to its unmaintained and overgrown trails. I would like to remind those hikers that this is an explorer's route. David Thompson, a now celebrated Canadian explorer and fur trader who travelled here 200 years ago, probably faced much worse conditions. With that said, he did choose to travel in winter to avoid the brush.

The real attraction of this leg of the GDT is the solitude of the Amiskwi and Howse rivers and the good chance of observing wildlife. The ability to legally random camp in two national parks below timberline is an enjoyable experience. The licence to sleep outside of official campsites lets you set your own itinerary and rhythm for hiking.

The route takes advantage of three major watercourses: the Amiskwi, Blaeberry, and Howse rivers. You travel through Yoho National Park over Amiskwi Pass, through the Columbia Forest District and back into Banff National Park over Howse Pass. The upper Amiskwi Valley endured a serious forest fire in the recent past and now has brushy trails from all the

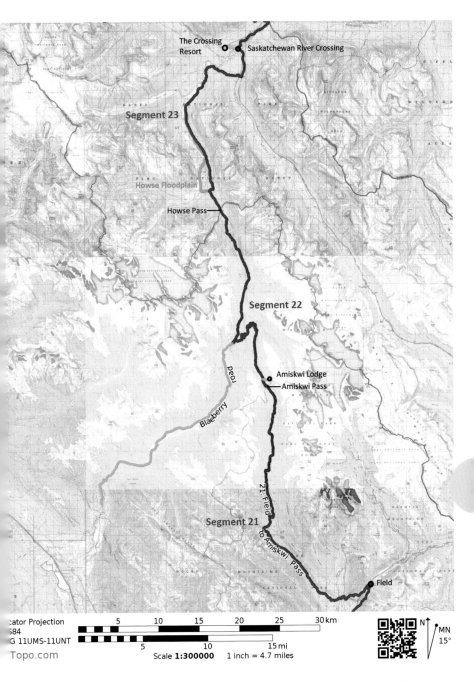

The Crossing Resort

Saskatchewan River Crossing

Segment 23

Howse Floodplain

Howse Pass

Segment 22

Amiskwi Lodge
Amiskwi Pass

Blaeberry road

21: Field to Amiskwi Pass

Segment 21

Field

cator Projection
684
G 11UMS-11UNT
Topo.com

5   10   15   20   25   30 km

5   10   15 mi

Scale **1:300000**   1 inch = 4.7 miles

N↑ MN 15°

regeneration. There are two waist-deep fords of the river. Bikes are technically allowed on the Amiskwi trail, 19km up to Otto creek, but I wouldn't recommend them until the trail is cleared again.

After a very brief cross-country hike over Amiskwi Pass, the route enters the heavily managed Columbia Forest District, which brings logging cut blocks right to the edge of the national parks. The route follows narrow logging roads through most of the Blaeberry Valley until reaching the David Thompson Heritage (DTH) trail. Unfortunately this sporadically maintained trail suffers from washouts and dense brush. It is also missing a bridge over the Lambe Glacier outflow, which makes for a tricky ford. Over Howse Pass the trail is in much the same (poor) condition until it nears the Icefields Parkway. The GDTA had plans in 2017 to assess a bridge replacement and work on the DTH trail.

If you are considering hiking an alternate route to this section, there are options. River Taig and I hiked one of them in 2017. While I thought our route was too difficult to include in this guidebook, River wants others to know of its existence and might even include it in the Atlas Guides app. Another alternate could be a newly proposed bike path beside the Icefields Parkway.

The main range of the Canadian Rockies north of the Trans-Canada Highway is too high and glaciated for reasonable hiking. In fact the main range is so rugged that the GDT only crosses the Continental Divide twice in over 350km, at Amiskwi and Howse passes. Therefore the route north of Howse Pass to Jasper avoids the Divide and even loses sight of it. Divide purists can ski tour the entire distance of the icefields from Field to Mount Robson. You can find a description of this route in Chic Scott's *Summits and Icefields*.

Long valleys easily interconnect with their low passes, providing a natural corridor for travel between Field and Saskatchewan River Crossing. Consequently the trails and roads serve as an artery for wildlife. On my journey I encountered two black bears in this section and followed a fresh set of wolf prints for the length of the DTH.

Amidst the complaints, I have heard praise for this section of the GDT. The hikers that enjoyed this section counsel others to plan on a slower pace for segments 21 and 23. With the efforts of the GDTA and the annual passage of thru-hikers, this route will undoubtedly improve over the next several years.

SEGMENT 21 – Field to Amiskwi Pass (41.0km)

Easy hike on fair trail with only a gradual climb to one pass. Horses prohibited. Bikes permitted – see 'Special notes.'

From the town of Field, BC, the GDT follows the Amiskwi River valley to a low pass on the boundary of Yoho National Park. This remote segment provides the opportunity to random camp in a national park, which

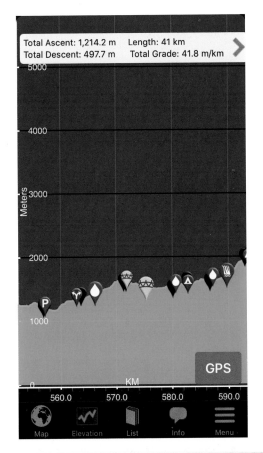

Total Ascent: 1,214.2 m   Length: 41 km
Total Descent: 497.7 m   Total Grade: 41.8 m/km

Meters

5000

4000

3000

2000

1000

0

KM

560.0   570.0   580.0   590.0

GPS

Map   Elevation   List   Info   Menu

The Amiskwi River trail is an important link for the GDT route.

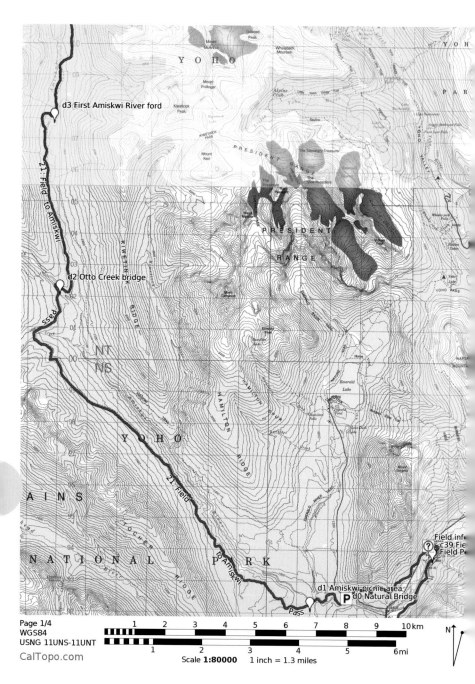

d3 First Amiskwi River ford

21: Field to Amiskwi

d2 Otto Creek bridge

PRESIDENT RANGE

Emerald Lake

21: Field

to Amiskwi

Field inf
C39 Fie
Field P

d1 Amiskwi picnic area
d0 Natural Bridge

Scale **1:80000**   1 inch = 1.3 miles

N↑

may mitigate your experience of the sometimes poor condition of the trail. Remember to call out in brushy areas near creeks especially, to alert nearby bears to your presence and not surprise them.

Maps: 82 N/7 Golden and 82 N/10 Blaeberry River; Gemtrek #4 Lake Louise & Yoho and #3 Bow Lake & Saskatchewan River Crossing.

Jurisdiction: Yoho National Park.

South access: Driving on Trans-Canada Highway 1, turn north onto the Emerald Lake access road 2km west of Field. Park at the gate near the Natural Bridge parking lot. NOBO hikers will start in Field.

North access: From the junction of Highways 1 and 95 at Golden, drive west on Trans-Canada Highway 1 for 11.6km to Moberly Branch Road. Follow this road 1.9km and then turn left on Golden Donald Upper Road. Travel 1km and turn right on Oberg Johnson Road for 2km. Turn left on Moberly School Road and follow it for 0.5km where it curves to the right and becomes the Blaeberry forest service road. In another 6.5km, look for a sign for M Road. Turn left 0.2km past the M Road sign, and cross the Blaeberry River. Follow the Blaeberry road 42km to the Cairnes Creek recreation site. This road was washed out in recent years 3km before the recreation site. Bring chicken wire to fence off the undercarriage of your vehicle from porcupines if you plan to park here.

Car campgrounds and accommodations: The closest campgrounds to the GDT in Yoho National Park are 5km east of Field. Turn north onto the Yoho Valley road from Trans-Canada Highway 1. The Monarch and Kicking Horse campgrounds charge $17.60 and $27.40 respectively. Kicking Horse has showers. For more information about accommodations in Field, inquire at the Yoho National Park visitor information centre at the turn-off for Field. The Fireweed Hostel is the most affordable place to stay in Field. Rates start at $30 per night for a dorm room. They have free wifi and showers but the coin-op laundry facilities are at Truffle Pigs Lodge, formerly known as Kicking Horse Lodge, 100m down the street. The hostel is conveniently located across the street from the post office and not far from the awesome Truffle Pigs restaurant and general store. The town of Field has cell phone service and is a hiker-friendly resupply town because everything is so close.

Camping: Random camping and Amiskwi Lodge (700m off-route). Amiskwi Lodge is a self-guided and self-catered backcountry lodge with access by helicopter. There is a satellite phone, sauna, showers and other amenities. The rates listed on their website are for multiple days and include helicopter transport. It would be best to call in advance to book a night there. Dogs aren't permitted at the lodge.

Information sources: Yoho National Park information centre.

Resupply stations: Field post office.

Special notes: To random camp in the Amiskwi Valley in Yoho National

Park, you must camp at least 5km from the Amiskwi picnic area. This segment starts with waypoint 'd0,' which used to be known as c39 when it was the end of Section C in previous editions of this book. Bikes are permitted from Field to the Otto Creek bridge, d2, 22.9km into this segment.

Field, BC, to the Amiskwi picnic area (6.3km, 61m up, 90m down)

From the post office in Field, go north 300m on Stephen Avenue. Turn left and follow E 2nd Street downhill and around to the left 250m. Turn right on the Field access road and go over the bridge and 200m to the junction with Highway 1. The Yoho National Park visitor centre is at this intersection, on the left. They have public washrooms. Turn left and walk 500m

Julia Lynx compares her hand size to the claw and bite marks left by a bear near the Amiskwi River trailhead.

Roche Lynx walks over the unique bridge near the Amiskwi River trail trailhead.

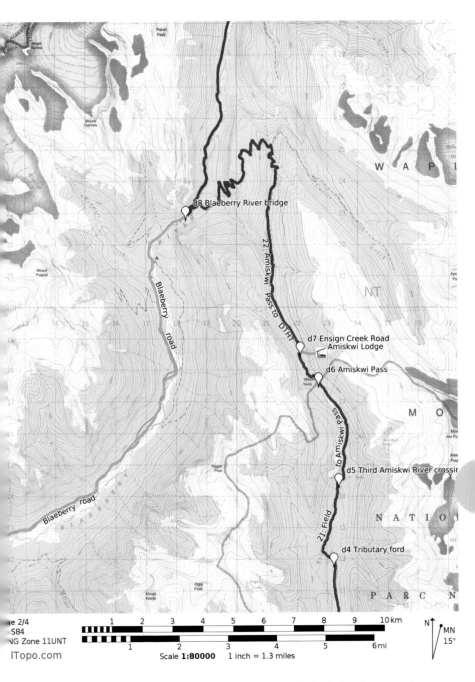

d8 Blaeberry River bridge

22: Amiskwi Pass to DTIHT

d7 Ensign Creek Road
Amiskwi Lodge

d6 Amiskwi Pass

Blaeberry road

Blaeberry road

to Amiskwi Pass

21: Field

d5 Third Amiskwi River crossir

d4 Tributary ford

ITopo.com

Scale **1:80000**   1 inch = 1.3 miles

southwest on Highway 1. Staying on the north side, look for the start of
the Tally Ho trail. Follow that trail over a short rise to a junction in 2.3km.
Keep left at the junction and follow trail down to the Emerald Lake road in

1km. Cross the road to the Natural Bridge parking area and trailhead (1220, 4.6, d0). At the northwestern corner of the parking lot (perhaps hidden behind innumerable tour buses) is a gated road. Pass the gate and walk down the road with occasional and precipitous views of the Kicking Horse River below. Cross over Emerald River at 1.3km and the Amiskwi River in another 200m. Only 100m past that second bridge, you arrive at the Amiskwi picnic area (1170, 1.7, d1) and Otterhead River trail junction. The Amiskwi River trailhead is across the retired parking lot. The picnic area beside the Amiskwi River has little more than outhouses and picnic tables.

Amiskwi picnic area to Otto Creek bridge (16.6km, 543m up, 220m down)

The Amiskwi River trail diverges from the river and gently climbs through forest. Although you are following an old road, the trail is overgrown and requires extra effort to travel in some places. This reclaimed fire access road has corduroy sections of spars laid side by side through muddy areas. In 4.5km go straight through a trail junction, staying on the old road-bed. Cross a creek in 200m more. The route frequently crosses seasonal creeks, many of which have washed out their culverts, but not all drainages have water in them. Cross another stream in 2.8km. The trail reaches a bridge over Fire Creek beneath Burnt Hill, 6.8km farther up the valley. It is possible to make a campsite at this location. Beyond that bridge, the trail emerges into clearings and the stark remains of a burnt forest before reaching the Otto Creek bridge (1500, 16.6, d2).

Otto Creek to Amiskwi Pass (18.1km, 610m up, 188m down)

Descend briefly south for 200m after the bridge. Look for flagging tape. The trail soon angles to the north again. Boggy and brushy conditions abound. Stay on the west bank of Amiskwi River all the way to the first Amiskwi River ford (1540, 6.8, d3). The Amiskwi River is normally an easy ford – perhaps harder if there has been a lot of precipitation. Look for yellow markers indicating where the trail starts again on the eastern bank. If the water is too high, you can stay on the western bank and follow a faint trail north to rejoin the Amiskwi River trail at the next crossing, but I don't recommend it. From the river ford, you climb gently on noticeably better track, and in 1.6km splash through Cross Creek. The trail diverges from the Amiskwi River and comes to another tributary ford (1620, 4.7, d4). Evident trail descends 400m to the second ford of the Amiskwi River and follows the west bank to a third ford of the river (1695, 2.9, d5) in view of Amiskwi Falls. Pick up water here if you plan to camp higher up. The trail (a roadbed) disappears briefly after this final crossing. The trail does pick up again on the east bank of the river and begins a moderate ascent with good views over your shoulder of the Amiskwi valley. Rough trail re-enters forest and brings you to Amiskwi Pass (1975, 3.7, d6) in a small meadow on the boundary of Yoho National Park. A warden cabin is just off-route and to the west. There are flat clearings suitable for camping here.

SEGMENT 22 – Amiskwi Pass to David Thompson Heritage Trail trailhead (23.3km)

Mostly easy walking on gravel roads. Horses and bikes permitted outside Yoho National Park.

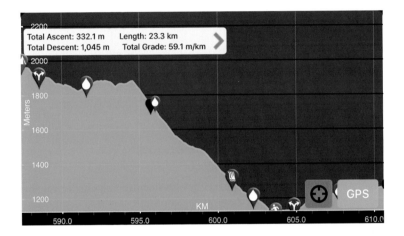

This unique segment of the GDT is nearly all road. Thru-hikers will enjoy walking on this remote road in comparison to the poor trail elsewhere in the section. Below Amiskwi Pass the road edges along the high valley walls of the upper Blaeberry River, affording excellent views of Mummery Glacier, an arm of the Freshfield Icefield that straddles the Divide.

Maps: 82 N/10 Blaeberry River; Gemtrek #3 Bow Lake & Saskatchewan River Crossing.

Jurisdictions: Columbia Forest District (BC) and Yoho National Park.

South and north access: From the junction of Highways 1 and 95 in Golden, drive west on Trans-Canada Highway 1 for 11.6km to Moberly Branch Road. Follow this road 1.9km and then turn left on Golden Donald Upper Road. Travel 1km and turn right on Oberg Johnson Road for 2km. Turn left on Moberly School Road and follow it for 0.5km to where it curves to the right and becomes the Blaeberry forest service road. In another 6.5km, look for a sign for M Road. Turn left 0.2km past the M Road sign and cross the Blaeberry River at the junction. Follow the Blaeberry FSR 12km to where it is closed to non-commercial traffic. It is 22km to the Blaeberry bridge. You should bring chicken wire to protect the undercarriage of your vehicle from porcupines if you plan to park here.

Car campgrounds and accommodations: Driving the Blaeberry River road you will encounter two active BC recreation sites: Thompson Falls and Split Creek. Thompson Falls campground is on M Road just beyond the Blaeberry FSR junction. Split Creek campground is 12km up the Blaeberry FSR from the M Road junction. Split Creek is open to the public and accessible by 2-wheel-drive vehicles and motorhomes. See sitesandtrailsbc.ca.

Camping: Random camping and Amiskwi Lodge (700m off-route). Amiskwi Lodge is a self-guided and self-catered backcountry accommodation with access by helicopter. It has a satellite phone, sauna, showers and other amenities. The rates listed at amiskwi.com are for multiple days and include helicopter transport. It would be best to call in advance to book a night there. Dogs aren't permitted at the lodge.

Information sources: Yoho National Park visitor information centre.

Resupply stations: None.

Amiskwi Pass to Blaeberry River bridge (16.2km, 135m up, 992m down)

Look for flagging tape and a discernible trail continuing north over the pass. Continue on this trail down to Ensign Creek. The trail turns downstream and follows the creek for a kilometre to where it cuts 100m over to the end of the Ensign Creek road (1910, 1.1, d7). Amiskwi Lodge is 800m east of this point and 200m higher in elevation. There used to be a sign proclaiming the Amiskwi Lodge trailhead. If you follow a compass bearing due east, you should find a creek drainage leading steeply uphill. Follow that drainage and find Amiskwi Lodge just above timberline at the edge of an alpine plateau.

The GDT follows the Ensign Creek road northward and contours along cleared slopes toward Collie Creek. Cross a creek culvert in 3km. The icefalls spilling over Mounts Mummery and Cairnes from the Freshfield Icefield are in clear view to the northwest from the road. Nearing Collie Creek the trail starts descending switchbacks on the road. While OHV trails seem to take a more direct route between the switchbacks, the forestry road provides the easiest route. In 4.6km from the creek culvert, you reach a road junction; turn sharply left. Long switchbacks bring you 6km to the Ensign Creek Bridge. Finally, the route comes to the Blaeberry River bridge (1110, 15.1, d8).

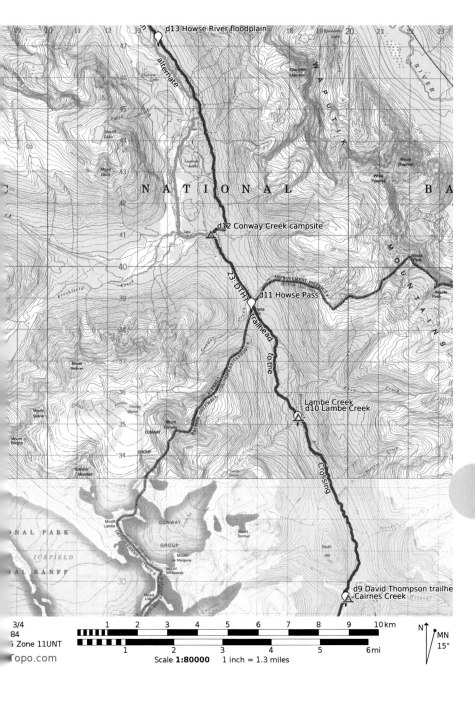

d13 Howse River floodplain

d12 Conway Creek campsite

d11 Howse Pass

Lambe Creek
d10 Lambe Creek

d9 David Thompson trailhe
Cairnes Creek

3/4
84
Zone 11UNT
Topo.com

1 2 3 4 5 6 7 8 9 10km

1 2 3 4 5 6mi

Scale **1:80000**   1 inch = 1.3 miles

N
MN
15°

The author hiking north along the Blaeberry River FSR.

This fresh wolf track near the David Thompson Heritage Trail trailhead is 8–10cm wide.

Blaeberry River bridge to the David Thompson Heritage Trail trailhead (7.1km, 209m up, 53m down)

Cross the bridge and turn right on the Blaeberry forest service road. Follow the narrow track north. A recent washout in 1.2km might make it necessary to take a higher, parallel trail, rejoining the road 1.3km farther north. The Blaeberry FSR continues to the unmarked David Thompson Heritage Trail trailhead (1230, 7.1, d9). North of the intersection by 100m and slightly off-route is the decommissioned Cairnes Creek campground on the western bank of the Blaeberry River near a wrecked bridge. The retired campground still has picnic tables and fire pits.

SEGMENT 23 – David Thompson Heritage Trail trailhead to Saskatchewan River Crossing (40.8km)

Difficult hiking on deteriorating and overgrown trail. Horses permitted. Bikes prohibited in Banff National Park.

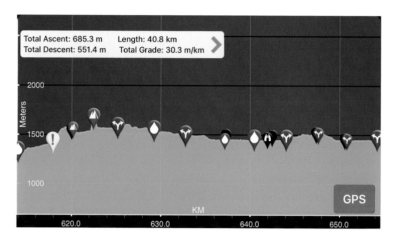

Total Ascent: 685.3 m Length: 40.8 km
Total Descent: 551.4 m Total Grade: 30.3 m/km

2000

Meters

1500

1000

GPS

KM

620.0 630.0 640.0 650.0

Howse Pass is below timberline and is the gateway between the Blaeberry and North Saskatchewan river valleys. Despite the poor hiking trail, this segment is the real gem of the entire section. Wildlife activity adds to the charm of this segment. In some areas I found it difficult to distinguish animal tracks because of their number and variety.

Maps: 82 N/10 Blaeberry River and 82 N/15 Mistaya Lake; Gemtrek #3 Bow Lake & Saskatchewan River Crossing.

Survey Peak hovers in the distance above marsh that surrounds the lower Howse River.

Jurisdictions: Columbia Forest District (BC) and Banff National Park.

South access: From the junction of Highways 1 and 95 in Golden, drive west on Trans-Canada Highway 1 for 11.6km to Moberly Branch Road. Follow this road 1.9km and then turn left on Golden Donald Upper Road. Travel 1km and turn right on Oberg Johnson Road for 2km. Turn left on Moberly School Road and follow it for 0.5km to where it curves to the right and becomes the Blaeberry forest service road. In another 6.5km, look for a sign for M Road. Turn left 0.2km past the M Road sign and cross the Blaeberry River at the junction. Follow Blaeberry FSR 12km to where it is closed to non-commercial traffic. It is 22km to the Blaeberry bridge. You should bring chicken wire to protect the undercarriage of your vehicle from porcupines if you plan to park here.

North access: Park at the Mistaya Canyon turnout on the Icefields Parkway (Highway 93 North) at 5.4km south of Saskatchewan River Crossing – better known as The Crossing. The trailhead is 75km north of Lake Louise and 158km south of Jasper.

Car campgrounds and accommodations: At the HI Lake Louise Alpine Centre in Lake Louise rates start at $50 a night for a dorm room. This hostel is affiliated with the Alpine Club of Canada and has all the amenities, including showers, wifi, restaurant and lounge. The HI Rampart Creek and Mosquito Creek hostels are both closer to the GDT and start at $25 per night. From the Crossing on Highway 93, Rampart Creek Hostel is 11km north and Mosquito Creek Hostel is 53km south. Members of Hosteling International receive a discounted rate. Consult hihostels.ca/en for more information and booking any of these three facilities. The hostels have few amenities beyond a bed and cooking area and they don't allow dogs.

The Crossing Resort has rooms starting at $210 per night. See 'Resupply stations' below for more info.

Car camping is available on the Icefields Parkway. The Rampart Creek campground is 11km north of The Crossing on Highway 93. Waterfowl campground is 20km south of the Crossing. These Banff National Park campgrounds charge $17.60 and $21.50 respectively. Neither has showers, though.

Camping: Random camping.

Information sources: Lake Louise information centre.

Resupply stations: The Crossing Resort. The restaurant in the main tourist building has a store, public washrooms and a restaurant. The restaurant offers a good deal for a breakfast and lunch buffet: $25 for all you can eat. The pub behind the main buildings offers food deals and has a paid wifi service which you can also get in the main lobby of the hotel. There is a gas station and coin-op laundry at the resort. There is no cell phone service here, or anywhere on the Icefields Parkway, except closer to Jasper and Lake Louise.

Special notes: Cairnes and Lambe creeks at the start of this segment are glacier fed and can be very difficult to cross later in the day. Plan to cross both on the same morning. Though horses and bikes are permitted, neither mode of travel is recommended at this time. There are too many blowdowns and bad trail conditions.

David Thompson Heritage Trail trailhead to Howse Pass (11.6km, 520m up, 101m down)

Turn left from the Blaeberry River road 100m south of the decommissioned Cairnes Creek campground at the unsigned David Thompson Heritage Trail trailhead, which resembles a creekbed. NOBO hikers should plan their day to finish at this campground so they can ford Cairnes and Lambe creeks early the next morning. Follow faint trail to the Cairnes Creek ford in 300m. Try looking upstream for a log crossing; otherwise wait until morning (as mentioned) to attempt the ford. From the other side of the ford the David Thompson Heritage Trail cuts northeast over to the western bank of the Blaeberry River. Follow the riverbank northward past the aptly named Doubt Hill to the west. It is a poor trail for the most part, with deeply rutted areas that are usually muddy and full of rocks and protruding roots. The path reaches the Lambe Glacier outflow ford (1405, 7.1, d10) below a three-tiered waterfall. There isn't a lot of room to look for a ford – it all looks bad. You certainly can't cross where the bridge used to be. Hikers have opted to ford the Blaeberry River itself 200m downstream of the Lambe confluence and then cross back over above the confluence. Again, I recommend doing this ford early in the morning when the water flow is at its lowest. It is glacier-fed, so the flow does slow overnight. Be very careful. There is a poor campsite on the other side of the torrent, which could be useful for SOBO hikers planning to wait until morning.

Though the trail is more evident on the other side of the ford, wildlife seems to provide the only trail maintenance for the remainder of the way up to Howse Pass. Walking cross-country is just slightly more difficult than using the DTH trail. Approaching Howse Pass, you hike through boggy meadows and around seasonal lakes. From the ford of the Lambe Glacier outflow, the trail diverges from the Blaeberry River for good. The trail heads uphill to a forested bench in 1.4km at 1570m, which is at a higher elevation than Howse Pass yet still 2km short of the pass. In 1.0km the trail may disappear as it enters a large meadow only to reappear on the other side, requiring a little scouting. Look for flagging tape. After a couple of minor creek fords the faint path reaches a large monument at Howse Pass (1530, 4.5, d11) on the Continental Divide, as you re-enter

The Lambe Glacier outflow on the David Thompson Heritage trail.

Julia Lynx provides a little first aid to her feet near the Howse River.

A right of passage? The Howse Pass trail in Banff National Park is an obstacle course of fallen trees and faint trail. Many hikers divert to the gravel bars of the river below instead of clawing through this mess.

Alberta. North of Howse Pass the GDT does not cross the Divide for the next 272.3km until Centre Pass in Section F.

Howse Pass to Glacier Lake Trail junction (15.6km, 78m up, 337m down)

Go north-northwest and cross a creek in 100m. Good trail continues from the other side of that stream crossing. The trail stays on the east side of a drainage, coming down to a trail junction (1510, 2.7, d12). Turn right and cross a potentially sizeable tributary of Conway Creek. Hikers report that if you turn left instead, the trail takes you to the floodplain but that the hiking from that point is not much better than the trail. Turning to the right at that junction, prepare yourself for a full-body workout. There are hundreds of deadfall trees on the indistinct trail for the next 4.4km, at which point you have the option to easily cut-over 200m west from the trail to the gravel bars of the Saskatchewan River floodplain. You can follow those gravel bars to the next waypoint, paralleling the GDT, and take a break from the next several hundred blowdowns on the trail. The trail does meet the gravel bars of the floodplain (1480, 7.5, d13) at an open area. Not far north you can decide to return to the gravel bars or take your chances on the trail. The trail and parallel gravel bar route converge again at the signed Glacier Lake trail junction (1445, 5.4, d14). I don't recommend

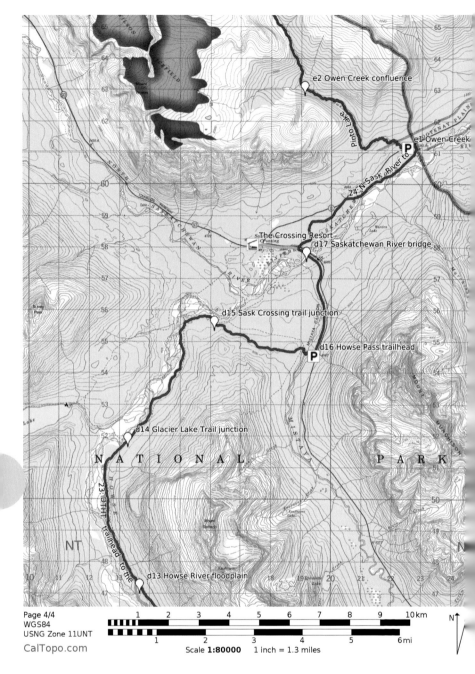

e2 Owen Creek confluence

e1 Owen Creek

24: N Sask River to

The Crossing Resort

d17 Saskatchewan River bridge

d15 Sask Crossing trail junction

d16 Howse Pass trailhead

d14 Glacier Lake Trail junction

N A T I O N A L   P A R K

23: DTH trailhead to the

d13 Howse River floodplain

Page 4/4
WGS84
USNG Zone 11UNT

CalTopo.com

Scale **1:80000**   1 inch = 1.3 miles

trying to cross the river; it has too many braids, some of which are deceptively deep and fast flowing. The river water is generally too opaque to see your footing, making it even more treacherous.

Glacier Lake trail junction to Mistaya Canyon turnout (10.0km, 83m up, 51m down)

The condition of the trail improves as it winds its way along the river's eastern bank. After passing several ponds amidst marshy flats, the trail reaches an obvious junction (1440, 5.9, d15) with a horse trail. That trail continues upriver, fords the Mistaya River, and then reaches the highway – I don't recommend it, because the Mistaya is normally too high to ford safely. Instead, turn right and follow the trail east-southeast for 3.7km to another trail junction. Continue straight through the junction and head over the bridge. Take a moment to gawk at the deep channel of the Mistaya River canyon. Follow a gravel access road 400m uphill to the Mistaya Canyon parking area (1500, 4.1, d16) on the Icefields Parkway, Highway 93 North.

Mistaya Canyon turnout to the North Saskatchewan River (3.6km, 4m up, 62m down)

This road walk is a necessary link for thru-hikers continuing north to the next section of the GDT. Turn left and follow the Highway 93 shoulder north to the bridge over the North Saskatchewan River (1442, 3.6, d17), 500m beyond the Saskatchewan Crossing warden station. The warden station has a tiny office, open on weekdays, with a public telephone mounted outside the door. The Crossing is 1.9km north of the bridge on the Icefields Parkway, Highway 93 North. The trail resumes 400m past the bridge, visibly cutting across an embankment, to the right.

The Crossing resort – a convenient resupply between sections D and E.

SECTION E: *North Saskatchewan River to Jasper*

Segments 24–28, 192.3 km

Location	Near waypoint	NOBO km	SOBO km
Owen Creek trailhead	e1	664.1	469.1
Owen Creek campsite	e2	668.0	465.2
Owen Pass	e3	674.3	458.9
Michele Lakes Pass (highest point on GDT)	e4	677.6	455.6
Pinto Pass	e5	682.2	451.0
Pinto Lake horse camp 1	e5	685.0	448.2
Pinto Lake horse camp 2	e6	688.1	445.1
Pinto Lake campsite	e6	689.9	443.3
Cataract Creek pictographs campsite	e10	695.0	438.2
Cataract Pass campsite	e11	706.2	427.0
Boulder Creek #15 campsite (Jasper NP)	e14	717.8	415.4
Four Point #16 campsite (Jasper NP)	e15	721.2	412.0
Jonas Cutoff #23 campsite (Jasper NP)	e18	739.1	394.1
Waterfalls #25 campsite (Jasper NP)	e19	748.5	384.7
Avalanche #100 campsite (Jasper NP)	e20	757.2	376.0
Maligne Pass – Six Passes alternate junction	e22	762.5	370.7
Mary Vaux #110 campsite (Jasper NP)	e22	766.9	366.3
Old horse camp #110 (Jasper NP)	e22	769.3	363.9
Mary Schaffer #110 campsite (Jasper NP)	e23	777.5	355.7
Trapper Creek #110 campsite (Jasper NP)	e24	788.4	344.8
Evelyn Creek #27 campsite (Jasper NP)	e26	798.9	334.3
Little Shovel #28 campsite (Jasper NP)	e27	801.3	331.9
Snowbowl #29 campsite (Jasper NP)	e27	805.6	327.6
Watchtower #33 campsite (Jasper NP)*	e28	811.8	321.4
Curator #30 campsite(Jasper NP)*	e28	813.6	319.6
Tekarra #31 campsite (Jasper NP)	e30	824.6	308.6
Signal Mountain #32 campsite (Jasper NP)	e31	830.5	302.7
Maligne Canyon Hostel*	e32	838.8	294.4
Whistlers car campground (Jasper NP)*	e34	848.0	285.2
RESUPPLY: Jasper*	e34	850.0	283.2

Introduction

The route between the North Saskatchewan River and Jasper is a joy for anyone who likes trekking above timberline. The Skyline Trail, for instance, in the northern part of this section of the GDT, stays in high meadows and rocky passes for over half of its 50km distance. The highest point

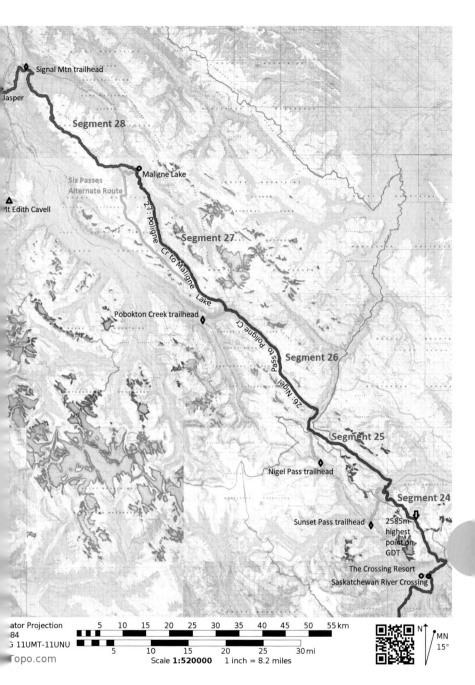

Signal Mtn trailhead

Jasper

Segment 28

Six Passes
Alternate Route

Maligne Lake

Mt Edith Cavell

27: Poligne Cr to Maligne Lake

Segment 27

Pobokton Creek trailhead

26: Nigel Pass to Poligne Cr.

Segment 26

Segment 25

Nigel Pass trailhead

Segment 24

Sunset Pass trailhead

2585m
highest
point on
GDT

The Crossing Resort

Saskatchewan River Crossing

ator Projection
84
11UMT-11UNU

Topo.com

5   10   15   20   25   30   35   40   45   50   55 km

5   10   15   20   25   30 mi

Scale **1:520000**   1 inch = 8.2 miles

N↑

MN
15°

on the GDT is in this section, Michele Lakes Pass, above Michele Lakes, at 2590m.

This is the only section of the GDT that does not cross the Continental

Divide, which is surprising since it reaches so many high elevations. The route stays mostly within frequented areas of Jasper National Park, paralleling the Icefields Parkway. Knowing that the route never gets more than 30 trail kilometres away from a popular highway may ease your anxieties if you are embarking on a long backcountry trip for the first time. However, I would not recommend the section for those with little backpacking experience, for it is long and arduous.

The majority of the first 65km of Section E is above timberline and cross-country. While the route-finding is straightforward and the hiking rewarding, the walk along Owen and Cataract creeks is very difficult. The Owen Creek route is steep, with the trail disappearing amongst the boulders on the creek bank. Cataract Creek has a serious ford and a trail littered with toppled trees to scramble over. However, these route conditions are only a hindrance if you do not allow sufficient time on those segments.

Nowhere else on the GDT will you see a chasm quite like the Owen Creek canyon or the imposing Wilson Icefield set against the skyline. The Michele lakes make for a precious view, their serenity contrasting with the corniced and jagged ramparts that loom to the west. The succession of three very high passes is also unique to this part of the GDT. And even amidst the forest and tangle of fallen trees on the Cataract Creek trail there is the treasure of finding ochre pictographs.

The Cataract–Nigel–Jonas Pass trails and the Skyline trail in Jasper National Park provide an equally fulfilling route. On the maintained and well-marked trails of the national park, you are unencumbered by route-finding decisions and cross-country obstacles. The campgrounds offer several conveniences like food hangs and pit toilets. You will even see other backpackers who aren't expressly hiking the GDT! All the passes are definite highlights. Jonas Shoulder and Maligne Pass are wonderful vantage points. The Skyline Trail has superlative views for almost its entire length. The view from The Notch of brilliant Curator Lake nestled in orange boulder fields is unforgettable.

Regardless whether you are a thru-hiker, section hiker or a hiker with only a weekend to spare, you will find this part of the GDT very fulfilling. The remote and intimidating spots like the Cataract Creek ford will hone your wilderness senses. The climbs over the high passes will stun you with alpine scenery. With any luck, you will start seeing more signs of wildlife than in the south. You now have a chance of seeing mountain caribou, for example. My thrill was seeing a wolverine as an unseen spectator to its hunt. Bounding for its life, a moment ahead of the determined predator, was a deer in full flight.

SEGMENT 24 – North Saskatchewan River to Pinto Lake (31.9km)

Strenuous hiking over three high passes with cross-country travel in the alpine. Horses and bikes prohibited.

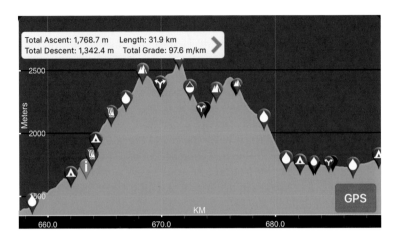

Total Ascent: 1,768.7 m   Length: 31.9 km
Total Descent: 1,342.4 m   Total Grade: 97.6 m/km

This segment offers the hardest won and most rewarding hiking on the GDT. It is a backcountry hiker's paradise. The route up Owen Creek is difficult but instantly gratifying, with a truly astounding canyon that cannot be more than a couple of metres wide in places yet breathtakingly deep. Chockstones wedged along the mouth of the canyon let you peer into its sonorous depths. Farther up the valley, you will see the Wilson Icefield as an icy skyline montage. Near the head of Owen Creek the trail parallels an immense rock wall for 18km, mostly through the alpine. Waterfalls all along this precipice relieve the grand cornices and remnant snow pack of their meltwater well into late summer. You pass beautiful Michele Lakes and surmount the highest pass of the entire GDT. Every cirque holds its own surprise, and it is hard not to feel like an explorer seeing this wondrous land for the first time.

Maps: 82 N/15 Mistaya Lake and 83 C/2 Cline River; Gemtrek #3 Bow Lake & Saskatchewan Crossing.

Jurisdictions: Banff National Park; Kootenay–Cline Provincial Park and White Goat Wilderness Area (Alberta Parks).

South access: The Saskatchewan River Crossing is on the Icefields Parkway (Highway 93 North), 79km north of Lake Louise and 154km south of Jasper. Only thru-hikers will begin this segment at the North Saskatchewan River bridge, 1.9km south of The Crossing on the Parkway. Section hikers would park at The Crossing resort or, better yet, near the Owen Creek bridge on David Thompson Highway 11 at 6.4km east of The Crossing, just beyond the Banff National Park gate. There is a parking area beside Owen Creek, on the east side of the bridge and north side of Highway 11, that can fit a few vehicles.

North access: Drive to the Sunset Pass trailhead parking area on the Icefields Parkway, 136km south of Jasper and 16.4km north of The Crossing. The trailhead is near the Norman Creek bridge. Hike 4.4km to the Norman Lake campsite and then 3.8km farther on the main trail to Sunset Pass. The Pinto Lake trail junction is 5.5km downhill. Alternatively you could descend from Sunset Pass at a point 500m east of the main trail. This route is well used by hikers and saves about 2km, but it descends a very steep scree gully which divides the impressive wall surrounding Pinto Lake. This route splits from the main trail near the end of a long subalpine meadow before reaching the pass. The trail approaches the cliff edge above Pinto Lake and descends to the head of a prominent gully. Look for a fixed rope in the gully. Once you reach the lakeshore, turn left and follow the lakeshore trail north through a few campsites to reach the GDT at the lake outflow in approximately 3km. The gully is visible to the south across the lake from the main campsite at the lake outflow. In total, this access accounts for about 13.7km of hiking to reach the GDT from the Icefields Parkway.

Car campgrounds and accommodations: The HI Lake Louise Alpine Centre in Lake Louise starts at $50 a night for a dorm room. It has all the amenities including showers, wifi, restaurant and lounge. The Rampart Creek and Mosquito Creek hostels are both closer to the GDT and start at $25 per night. From The Crossing on Highway 93, Rampart Creek Hostel is 11km north and Mosquito Creek Hostel is 53km south. Members of Hosteling International receive a discounted rate. Consult hihostels.ca/en for more information and to book any of these three facilities. The hostels have few amenities beyond a bed and cooking area, and they don't allow dogs.

The Crossing resort has rooms starting at $210 per night. See 'Resupply stations' below for more info.

Car camping is available on the Icefields Parkway. The Rampart Creek campground is 11km north of The Crossing on Highway 93, and the Waterfowl campground is 20km south of The Crossing. These Banff National Park campgrounds charge $17.60 and $21.50 respectively. Neither has showers, though.

Camping: Pinto Lake campsite (no fee) and random camping.

Information sources: Lake Louise information centre and White Goat Wilderness Area (albertaparks.ca/white-goat).

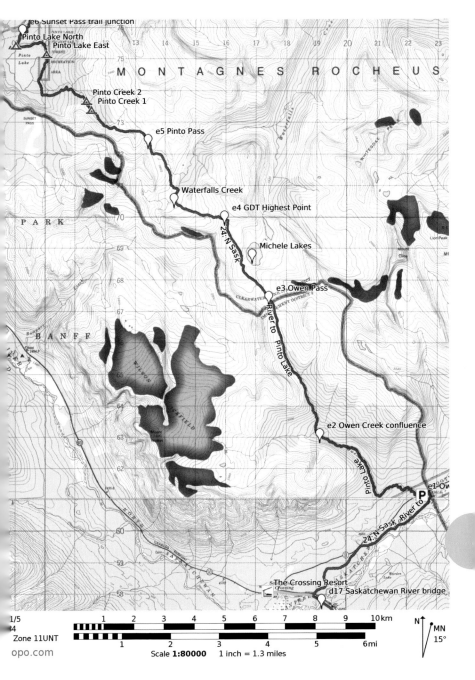

opo.com

Resupply stations: The Crossing resort. The restaurant in the main tourist building has a store, public washrooms and a restaurant. The restaurant offers a good deal for a breakfast and lunch buffet: $25 for all you can eat. The pub behind the main buildings offers food deals and has a paid wifi service which you can also get in the main lobby of the hotel. There is a gas station and coin-op laundry at the resort. There is no cell phone service here, or anywhere on the Icefields Parkway for that matter, except closer to Jasper and Lake Louise.

Special notes: Please practise no-trace camping. The route traverses high alpine meadows that are soggy and easily hold the imprints of those who have hiked before. The rushing water makes the hike up Owen Creek deafening at times. Stay alert for bears for the same reason: they cannot hear you approaching. Do not be surprised to meet day-hikers near Michele Lakes who have arrived by helicopter.

Additional reading: Read *The David Thompson Highway: A Hiking Guide* (2nd ed., 2016), by Jane Ross and Daniel Kyba, to learn more about other hikes in this spectacular area.

North Saskatchewan River to Owen Creek trailhead (6.5km, 34m up, 56m down)

Starting from the Icefields Parkway bridge over the North Saskatchewan River (1442, 0, d17), head north on the shoulder of the road for 400m and turn right on an obvious trail. You can see this trail from the bridge. It affords nice views of the river below and some pleasant hiking. The trail ascends an old roadbed on the north side of the river, gently cutting uphill to the east into the forest. The road is an abandoned access road that goes to the old site of the Crossing in a large meadow, surrounded by debris. Turn right and leave the old access road. Heading northeast, you leave the meadow and follow an abandoned road on a good trail. The trail passes a couple of overlooks above the North Saskatchewan River, generally paralleling the David Thompson Highway. It comes close to the highway in 2.6km. Other than a few fallen trees across the trail, the route is in good shape as you come to a cabin beside Owen Creek, 3.2km farther. This is the abandoned Saskatchewan River warden station and is unlocked but a mess inside. Either follow a trail 400m up the near side of the creek to Highway 11, or cross the creek just upstream of the cabin and continue northeast on a trail 200m to intersect the Banff National Park boundary, which is a narrow dirt road. Turn left and walk 400m north to meet the David Thompson Highway. Turn left again and follow the highway shoulder downhill to the Owen Creek trailhead (1395, 6.5, e1), at the northeast corner of the bridge. There is a small parking area in a meadow beside the creek with a sign about conserving bull trout in the park. The Owen Creek culvert is about 1km east of the Banff National Park gate on the David Thompson Highway and 6.4km from The Crossing by road. There is

Jerry Auld tries to see Owen Creek. Several parts of the impressive gorge are narrow enough that wedged rocks create natural bridges over the chasm.

another route from The Crossing on the north side of the highway, starting at the intersection of the DTH; there is also a gravel access road behind the resort, but it only goes as far as the national park boundary.

Owen Creek trailhead to 'Owen' Pass (10.2km, 1132m up, 26m down)

Look for a narrow trail on the eastern bank of Owen Creek. Make sure your dog is on a leash here. The trail quality quickly improves as you follow it upstream. Shortly it begins a steep ascent up to the rim of a very narrow, deep canyon in 500m – hence the leash reminder. As you follow the rim of this chasm, you can see boulders wedged along the extremely narrow mouth of the canyon. Surprisingly this narrow gorge is quite long.

Upstream of the start of the canyon is a second, miniature one with an obvious underground tributary that feeds into Owen Creek. The area is spectacular. Look for orange painted blazes.

The GDT follows the creek southwest as it bends around the foot of a prominent ridge. Turning north again, the Wilson Icefield comes into view, dominating the skyline to the west. There is a potential campsite in another 3.4km. Continue following the east side of Owen Creek to a major confluence (1675, 5.2, e2), where the two forks of the creek merge at an exposed rocky area. (The trail was maintained to just beyond this point in 2016.) Stay on the east side of the creek and follow the north fork steeply uphill due north, alternately on the creek bank and in the forest. Stay above the steep creek bank and continue looking for orange blazes. Pass a waterfall in 500m (if you see a trail branching off to the right here, avoid

Jerry Auld descends from the highest point on the GDT, an unnamed pass unofficially called the 'Michele Lakes' pass.

it and continue up the creek). There is another potential campsite 400m beyond the waterfall. As the grade eases, you can either stay on the creek bank or parallel the creek through the sparse trees above the eastern bank. Avoid a newly cut trail heading east up the valley wall, away from the creek. In another 1.4km, cross a substantial tributary near timberline in sight of a small waterfall. On the western side of Owen Creek, beside the tributary, is suitably flat ground for camping. The route continues up the eastern side of Owen Creek into the alpine and climbs to the unofficially named 'Owen' Pass (2481, 5.0, e3) on the Banff National Park boundary. Visible to the south are the many towers of Mount Murchison.

'Owen' Pass to the highest pass on the GDT, 'Michele Lakes' Pass (3.3km, 257m up, 114m down)

Reminiscent of the Rockwall trail in Kootenay National Park, the GDT parallels a continuous escarpment for 18km to the Cline River ford. From 'Owen' Pass, you can easily see the cross-country route leading to the next pass. Hikers report that contouring to the next pass is ideal because you get a better view. The main route goes down to the soggy flood plain (above upper Michele Lake, which isn't visible from the pass). The camping around the flood plain and Michele Lakes is poor owing to wet and uneven ground. From there, hike cross-country to the highest pass on the GDT, the unofficially named 'Michele Lakes' Pass (2585, 3.3, e4). A remnant cornice snakes toward the rock wall on one side of the pass, and a very climbable, uniform slope rises to a good viewpoint to the northeast on the other side. Look for a GDTA summit register, in a canister placed in the cairn.

Looking north over Waterfalls Creek from the highest point on the GDT. You can see the unofficially named 'Pinto' Pass in the upper right.

Pinto Lake from the Sunset Pass access route at the end of segment 24.

'Michele Lakes' Pass to 'Pinto Pass'
(4.6km, 312m up, 431m down)

The descent from the pass is steep. Before you leave, though, you should look for an obvious trail across the valley to the northwest. Failing that, look northwest across the valley and spot a tributary that flows down from Pinto Pass – aim for the upper and left (west) side of it. Cross Waterfalls creek about 800m up from the confluence with the tributary. There are more cairns now and there is a trail after crossing Waterfalls Creek. As mentioned, the trail climbs up to and then follows the west side of the tributary drainage and then traverses the steep mountainside above a long scarp. The moderate climb eases as you enter a wide alpine meadow. A brief but steep ascent brings you up to the unofficially named 'Pinto' Pass (2442, 4.6, e5).

'Pinto Pass' to Pinto Lake campsite
(7.3km, 33m up, 715m down)

A well-used, marked horse trail descends from Pinto Pass to join the Cline River trail. It was cleared and blazed in 2016. However, this trail is not that apparent above timberline. Descend cross-country, angling northwest (left) from the pass, staying a few hundred metres above the creek, on the north side of the valley. As you approach timberline, a narrow but unmistakable trail should come into view within 600m. The trail soon drops down to follow the creek and mainly stays in the forest. Pass a couple of horse camps, then ford the creek in 2.2km above a steep gorge. The descent is moderate along the winding trail. Nearing Pinto Lake, the trail refords the creek in 2.0km and meanders north, paralleling the lakeshore but staying well within the forest. There is a campsite in 1.2km where the trail approaches the lakeshore. From here the trail follows the lakeshore, with boardwalks, 1.4km to the Cline River ford (which is the outflow of Pinto Lake). Across the outflow is the Pinto Lake campsite. An evident trail follows the river downstream from here, 300m to the Sunset Pass trail junction (1740, 5.0, e6).

SEGMENT 25 – Pinto Lake campsite to Nigel Pass (25.3km)

Strenuous hiking up poorly maintained trail and over one high pass with some route-finding challenges. Horses and bikes prohibited.

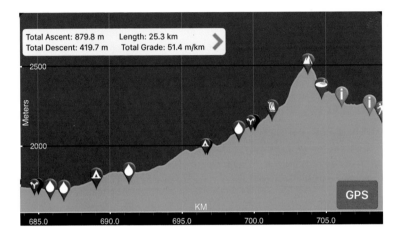

This segment involves a difficult hike in an enchanting area outside the national parks known as the White Goat Wilderness Area. The only mode of travel sanctioned in the wilderness area is by foot and there seems to be only a handful of hikers who travel the length of Cataract Creek each year. The potentially difficult creek fords and rough trail conditions probably deter many potential visitors from travelling in this remote area. The trail up Cataract Creek rewards backpackers with a collection of pictographs and a supreme view from Cataract Pass, one of the highest passes on the GDT. One hiker described it as on par with his experience of Mount Assiniboine! I had the pleasure of watching a grizzly bear near this pass flip over large rocks and lick up the insects.

Maps: 83 C/2 Cline River and 83 C/3 Columbia Icefield; Gemtrek #2 Columbia Icefield (partial coverage of Nigel and Cataract passes only).

Jurisdictions: White Goat Wilderness Area (Alberta Parks) and Jasper National Park.

South access: Drive to the Sunset Pass trailhead parking area on the Icefields Parkway (Highway 93 North), 136km south of Jasper and 16.4km north of The Crossing. The trailhead is near the Norman Creek bridge. Hike 4.4km to the Norman Lake campsite and then 3.8km farther on the main trail to Sunset Pass. The Pinto Lake trail junction is 5.5km downhill. Alternatively you could descend from Sunset Pass at a point 500m east of the main trail. This route is well used by hikers but it descends a very steep scree gully that divides the impressive wall surrounding Pinto Lake, saving about 2km. This route splits from the main trail near the end of a long subalpine meadow before reaching the pass. The trail approaches the cliff edge above Pinto Lake and descends to the head of a prominent gully. Look for a long fixed rope in the gully. Once you reach the lakeshore, turn left and follow the lakeshore trail north through a few campsites to reach the GDT at the lake outflow in approximately 3km. The gully is visible to the south across the lake from the main campsite at the outflow. In total this access accounts for about 13.7km of hiking to reach the GDT from the Icefields Parkway.

North access: The Nigel Pass trailhead is in Banff National Park on the Icefields Parkway (Highway 93 North), 114km north of Lake Louise (37km north of The Crossing resort) and 116km south of Jasper. Hike 7km up Nigel Creek to meet the GDT over Nigel Pass, just across the Brazeau River.

Car campgrounds and accommodations: The HI Lake Louise Alpine Centre starts at $50 a night for a dorm room. It has all the amenities, including showers, wifi, restaurant and lounge. The Rampart Creek and Mosquito Creek hostels are both closer to the GDT and start at $30 per night. From The Crossing on Highway 93, Rampart Creek Hostel is 11km north and Mosquito Creek Hostel is 53km south. Members of Hosteling International receive a discounted rate. Consult hihostels.ca/en for more information and to book any of these three accommodations. These hostels have few amenities beyond a bed and cooking area, and they don't allow dogs.

The Crossing Resort has rooms starting at $210 per night. See 'Resupply stations' below for more info.

Car camping is available on the Icefields Parkway. The Rampart Creek campground is 11km north of The Crossing on Highway 93. The Waterfowl campground is 20km south of The Crossing. These Banff National Park campgrounds charge $17.60 and $21.50 respectively. Neither has showers, though.

Camping: Pinto Lake campsite and random camping.

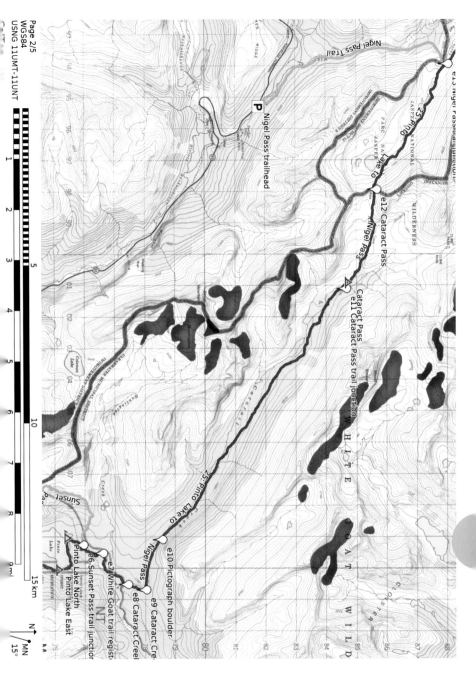

Information sources: Lake Louise information centre, the seasonal Parks Canada information desk at the Icefield Centre (open 10am–5pm daily,

780-852-6288), the Parks Canada trail office at the Jasper townsite information centre, and White Goat Wilderness Area (albertaparks.ca/white-goat).

Resupply stations: None.

Special notes: While there is a horse trail on the east side of the Cline
River that is in much better condition than the main route, the problem
with following this trail is the formidable river ford you face downstream in
order to hike up the Cataract Creek trail. The hiker's trail is in poor shape
but navigable. Fishing is permitted at Pinto Lake.

Additional reading: *The David Thompson Highway: A Hiking Guide* (2nd
ed., 2016), by Jane Ross and Daniel Kyba, describes some trails in the
White Goat Wilderness Area.

Pinto Lake campsite to Cataract Creek ford (3.2km, 6m up, 27m down)

The Pinto Lake campsite is well used with several areas suitable for even
the largest of tents. The camp has fire pits, a toilet, and a cabled food
hang. From the campsite, follow the trail downstream along the west
side of the lake outflow, the Cline River, 300m to the Sunset Pass trail
junction (1740, 5.0, e6). The hiking route follows the north bank of the
Cline, while a horse trail follows the south. Keep right at the junction
and continue downstream, staying on the west side of the river. There
are frequent tree blazes, which become scarcer as the path becomes more

Ochre picto-
graphs on the
Cataract Creek
trail. Several
panels appear
below an over-
hang on a dis-
tinctive boulder.

Julia Lynx stopping to rest on the way to Cataract Pass.

obscure. The rough trail reaches the White Goat Wilderness Area boundary (1730, 1.2, e7) at a sign and an active trail register box beside the river. Descend to the base of the waterfall and pick up the path again. A muddy trail continues along the western bank of the Cline River, fords the silty Huntington Creek in 700m at its confluence, and then passes through an old campsite before reaching the Cataract Creek ford (1720, 1.7, e8) 300m upstream from its confluence with the Cline River.

Cataract Creek ford to Cataract Pass (17.0km, 841m up, 56m down)

Look for cairns on the other side of the ford. Follow a faint trail upstream on the east side of Cataract Creek to a junction (1750, 0.7, e9). Turn left and follow the creek upstream. Look for new blazes marking the way. The trail improves as it follows the creek around a right-angle bend. The route now heads northwest, still on the same (north) side of the creek. The fair trail continues through forest, tracing the bottom of a large slide path, with occasional deadfall. Soon you will encounter a large boulder (1795, 1.5, e10) sitting between the trail and a 15m precipice above the creek. There is enough flat ground here to pitch a tent but the water is difficult to access. This gigantic trailside boulder is unmistakable and offers a well-preserved record of ochre pictographs below its overhanging southern flank. The deadfall continues. Cross a tributary creek in 2.3km and another in 1.0km farther. Pass a small campsite in another 5.5km – not near water. Reach timberline in another 500m at an elevation of 2000m. In subalpine, 2.6km farther, there used to be an easy-to-miss trail junction (2125, 10.9, e11) that is now completely missing – it was with a trail that leads north, up to Cline Pass. Keep left at the junction and keep following Cataract Creek's eastern bank on gravel bars for 300m to a major confluence. There

Many hikers describe Cataract Pass as one of their highlights of the entire GDT.

The headwaters of the Brazeau River, north of Cataract Pass (which appears near the centre of this photo).

is a good spot to camp here. Ford the large tributary above the confluence and continue following Cataract Creek upstream on a narrow trail. In 1km you ford the creek again near a waterfall. A faint path leads west-northwest up the colourful moraine and becomes more distinct as it approaches the pass, with cairns marking the way. The trail cuts across scree nearly on a level with Cataract Pass (2513, 3.9, e12) for the final 300m. The route enters Jasper National Park and leaves the White Goat Wilderness Area as indicated by a sign and a trail register box. This is not the Divide but it is a remarkable viewpoint.

Cataract Pass to Nigel Pass trail junction (5.1km, 33m up, 337m down)

An evident trail descends to the northwest into the valley. You might see cairns that lead up from the pass, but ignore those. Angle down and to the right. A steep descent on shale slopes brings you to the eastern bank of the Brazeau River (the lake outflow) in 900m. Cairns mark the way. Take

Julia Lynx stands below the site of a massive (and ancient) landslide that filled the valley between Nigel and Cataract passes with immense boulders. It can be a challenging trail.

your time here; the route is like a maze. You shouldn't have to rock climb over any boulders – there is a trail. If you find yourself cut off, retrace your steps and try a different way. Continue along the northern bank of the river through heaps of avalanche debris and great boulders to Nigel Pass trail junction (2155, 5.1, e13), in the alpine.

SEGMENT 26 – Nigel Pass to Poligne Creek (39.1km)

Moderate hiking on excellent trail with a steep climb over Jonas Shoulder. Horses permitted. Bikes and dogs prohibited. See 'Special notes.'

The hiking on this segment is excellent and there are plenty of campsites. Abundant alpine scenery and a very good vista on Jonas Shoulder, a prominent ridge crest, combine to make this segment special. In comparison with the previous two segments, this is a popular and well-travelled trail where the feeling of remoteness might slip away but the grandeur of the area still pervades.

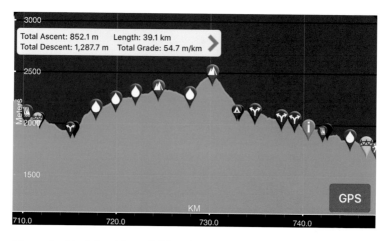

Total Ascent: 852.1 m   **Length:** 39.1 km
Total Descent: 1,287.7 m   **Total Grade:** 54.7 m/km

Maps: 83 C/3 Columbia Icefield and 83 C/6 Sunwapta Peak; Gemtrek #2 Columbia Icefield (partial coverage from Nigel Pass to Jonas Shoulder).

Jurisdictions: Banff and Jasper national parks.

South access: The Nigel Pass trailhead is in Banff National Park on the Icefields Parkway (Highway 93 North), 114km north of Lake Louise (37km north of The Crossing resort) and 116km south of Jasper. Hike 7km up Nigel Creek to meet the GDT over Nigel Pass, just across the Brazeau River.

North access: The Poboktan Creek trailhead is on the Icefields Parkway (Highway 93 North), 158km north of Lake Louise and 72km south of Jasper. From the trailhead, hike 6km to the Maligne Pass trail junction near the Poligne Creek bridge.

Car campgrounds and accommodations: The Wilcox Creek campground is 10km north of the Nigel Pass trailhead on Highway 93, and the Columbia Icefield campground is 1km farther. These campgrounds are both in Jasper National Park and charge $15.70 each. The Jonas Creek campground is 5km south of the Poboktan Creek trailhead and charges $15.70 a night. All three of these campgrounds are 'primitive,' meaning no showers. They do have water and cooking shelters, though.

The Hilda Creek Hostel is 4km north of the Nigel Pass trailhead and 9km south of the Icefields Discovery Centre. The Beauty Creek hostel is 14km south of the Poboktan Creek trailhead and 24km north of the Glacier Discovery Centre on Highway 93. The hostels charge approximately $30 per night and have no shower facilities. Dogs aren't permitted. Prepare to spend $200 per night if you want to stay at the Glacier View Inn (brewster.ca/hotels/glacier-view-inn).

A hoary marmot at Nigel Pass.

Camping: National park campsites: Boulder Creek (15), Four Point (16), Jonas Cutoff (23), Waterfalls (25) and Poboktan (26).

Information sources: Lake Louise information centre, the seasonal Parks Canada information desk at the Icefield Centre (open 10am–5pm daily, 780-852-6288), and the Parks Canada trail office at the Jasper townsite information centre.

Resupply stations: None.

Special notes: All trails are marked with national-park signage. Junctions have signs that indicate trail distances. Dogs are prohibited from Nigel Pass to Jasper due to sensitive mountain caribou habitat. Horses are permitted through most of this segment except over Jonas Shoulder. Equestrians could follow an alternate route from Nigel to Brazeau Lake and then west over Poboktan Pass to join the GDT again.

Nigel Pass to Boulder Creek campsite (2.9km, 30m up, 198m down)

Continuing on the eastern bank of the Brazeau River, you walk past the Nigel Pass trail junction. The excellent trail climbs steeply and then contours to the start of a switchback descent. Descend past a series of waterfalls to the Brazeau River bridge (2035, 2.9, e14) and the Boulder Creek campsite just past the bridge.

Boulder Creek campsite to Four Point Creek campsite (3.4km, 11m up, 127m down)

From the campsite, descend 900m to a unique bridge over Boulder Creek and then climb through sparse forest. Drop down to the western bank of the Brazeau River and follow it to the Four Point Creek campsite (1915, 3.4, e15). Here you will find an active trail register in the centre of the campsite.

e18 Poboktan Pass trail junction
Jonas Cutoff

26. Nigel Pass to

e17 Jonas Shoulder

Jonas
Shoulder

Poligne Cr

e16 Jonas Pass

Poligne Cr

e15 Four Po

26. Nigel Pass to

Boulder
e14 Brazeau River bridge

e13 Nigel Pass tra

I T A I N S

C H E U S E

N A L   J A S P E R

B R A Z E A U

MU
MT

Scale **1:80000**   1 inch = 1.3 miles

1 2 3 4 5 6 7 8 9 10 km

1 2 3 4 5 6 mi

N

Four Point Creek campsite to Jonas Shoulder
(15.0km, 677m up, 108m down)

Hike past the campsite and quickly reach the Brazeau Lake trail junction. Turn left and head uphill. After a brief climb through forest, the trail comes within sight of the creek and follows its southwestern bank. The trail crosses a number of small tributaries and has occasional muddy sections on the way to Jonas Pass (2325, 9.2, e16) in the alpine. The route descends to a spring that flows from the margin of avalanche debris, and then angles uphill for a steep ascent. The grade becomes more moderate as the trail traverses open slopes and attains the rocky Jonas Shoulder (2477, 5.8, e17) on a ridge crest.

Jonas Shoulder to Jonas Cutoff campsite
(2.9km, 0m up, 350m down)

The trail descends on long switchbacks to a rock hop across a tributary and enters meadows. Trending north, the route enters sparse forest and switchbacks down to the south entrance of the Jonas Cutoff campsite (2120, 2.9, e18). Turn left and proceed to the north entrance of the campsite, 100m ahead. Do not turn off for the signed Poboktan Pass trail.

Jonas Cutoff campsite to Waterfalls campsite
(9.4km, 97m up, 309m down)

The GDT stays on the northeastern side of Poboktan Creek. A horse trail diverges from the hiking trail and rejoins it at various points at signed junctions – stay on the hiking trail unless you are on a horse or want to ford the creek many times. Pass the McCready horse camp in 1.5km and the Waterfalls warden cabin in another 5.9km. Waterfalls campsite is about 1.8km past the cabin. In 100m past the campsite, the trail crosses a bridged tributary to arrive at a gate (1875, 9.4, e19). There is an excellent view of the waterfall from this point.

Waterfalls campsite to Poligne Creek
(5.5km, 37m up, 196m down)

The trail undulates and passes the Poboktan campsite in 4.2km at a bridge. The excellent trail continues through forest and crosses the Poligne Creek bridge to meet the Maligne Pass trail (1740, 5.5, e20). A sign marks the trail junction and distances.

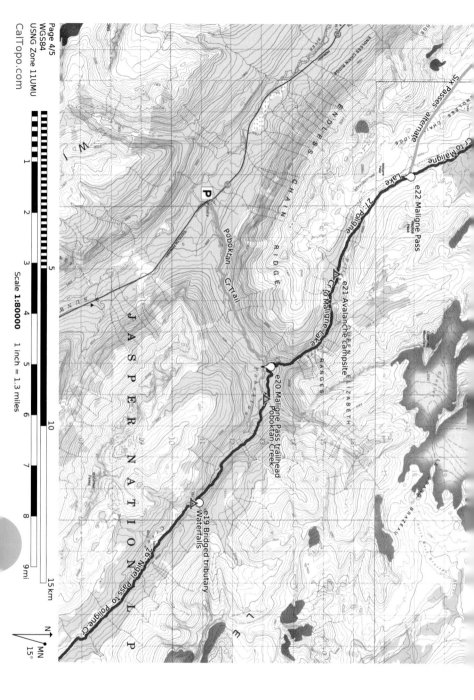

Segment 27 – Poligne Creek to Maligne Lake (40.1km)

Moderate hiking on good trail. Horses permitted. Bikes and dogs prohibited.

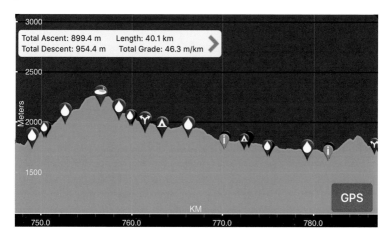

This splendid high valley hike briefly touches the alpine over Maligne Pass. Beyond the pass, much of the route is below timberline. You do get views of the Maligne and Queen Elizabeth mountain ranges through subalpine meadows but the majority of the hike is riverside, in forest. Parks Canada decommissioned the Maligne River trail in 2012. Since then, campsites, bridges, and the trail itself have deteriorated. Wear long pants, in other words! The trail was still passable at the time of writing but the future of this important link is uncertain. For that reason, I have decided to include an alternate high traverse known affectionately as the Six Passes route from Maligne Pass to Maligne Lake. This is a cross-country hike devoid of trail but it is easy to navigate, and in my opinion the hiking is a sublime experience and not to be missed.

Maps: 83 C/6 Sunwapta Peak, 83 C/11 Southesk Lake and 83 C/12 Athabasca Falls; Gemtrek #1 Jasper & Maligne Lake (mostly covers the segment except for the important junction at waypoint e20).

Jurisdiction: Jasper National Park.

South access: The Poboktan Creek trailhead is on the Icefields Parkway (Highway 93 North), 158km north of Lake Louise and 72km south of Jasper. From the trailhead, hike 6km to the Maligne Pass trail junction near the Poligne Creek bridge. Horses are permitted on this trail.

North access: Drive 5km east from Jasper to the Maligne Lake road. Follow it for 47km to the lake. Park at the Maligne Lake parking area. The Skyline trailhead kiosk is across the Maligne Lake road from the parking lot, while the Maligne Pass trailhead is 300m up the adjacent gravel road.

Car campgrounds and accommodations: The Jonas Creek campground is 5km south of the Poboktan Creek trailhead and charges $12 a night. The Beauty Creek Hostel is 14km south of the Poboktan Creek trailhead and 24km north of the Glacier Discovery Centre on Highway 93. The hostel has no showers and charges $30 per night. Dogs are not permitted. Prepare to spend $175 if you want to stay at the Glacier View Inn near the Columbia Icefield (banffjaspercollection.com/hotels/glacier-view-inn). Maligne Canyon Hostel is near the start of the Maligne Lake road and charges $30 a night for non-members. This is a rustic facility with no showers.

Camping: *National park campsites*: Avalanche (site 100) and five decommissioned campsites – Mary Vaux, Mary Schäffer, Trapper Creek, and two horse camps – that are all under the heading of Maligne Pass North (site 110), online. Parks Canada limits backcountry usage in this segment to one group on each side of Maligne Pass per day for the summer to protect important grizzly bear habitat. You must stay in one of the designated (though decommissioned) campsites. When you make your itinerary and book online (or call the Jasper trail office), it is important to realize that if you want to stay one night at Mary Vaux and another at Trapper Creek, you will book site 110 "Maligne Pass North" for two nights. According to JNP backcountry rules, two nights is the maximum stay for a wildland area. This means you can't stay three nights at "Maligne Pass North – site 110" despite the fact that you are in a physically different campsite for each of those nights. This is unlike any other backcountry rule or booking restriction in any of the parks, so I hope I haven't added to the confusion in my attempt to explain it.

If you are interested in hiking the Six Passes alternate route, you will have to contact the Jasper trail office to reserve a backcountry permit for random camping on the route – it can't be booked online.

Information source: Parks Canada trail office at the Jasper townsite information centre

Resupply stations: None.

Special notes: Equestrians can travel the main route in this segment but must get a backcountry permit and grazing permit. The main route is unmaintained, so all campsites except Avalanche are returning to nature. Facilities such as bear hangs are still in place but their wires may be missing the clips to attach your bags. I'm not sure what will happen with

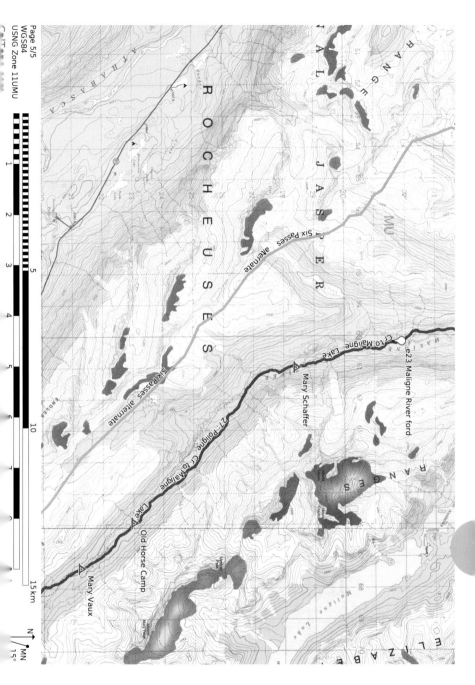

the plastic pit toilets at these locations – they will likely be removed in time. You must have a bear-proof container for this segment.

The first pass of the Six Passes alternate route is in the centre, above this small lake in Maligne Pass.

Poligne Creek to Avalanche campsite
(3.2km, 212m up, 5m down)

Shortly after crossing Poligne Creek you reach the Maligne Pass trail junction. Turn right and walk 200m to another bridge over Poligne Creek. The trail ascends steeply to start with. Cross Poligne Creek in another 1.0km. The grade eases before you reach a tributary crossing 1.6km farther. The trail continues to the Avalanche campsite (1965, 3.2, e21) near timberline.

Avalanche campsite to Maligne Pass
(5.3km, 294m up, 2m down)

Cross Poligne Creek in 1.4km. The condition of the path is poor through wet areas as you follow the creek up a long meadow, but it does improve. Climb to a traverse line just above the meadows on the northern side of the valley. A few springs are encountered before reaching a shallow lake on Maligne Pass (2260, 5.3, e22) in the alpine. Just past the lake, the Six Passes alternate route goes cross-country to the high pass 2.5km directly northwest.

SIX PASSES ALTERNATE ROUTE –
36.9KM INSTEAD OF 31.6KM. HIKERS ONLY.

This is one of my favourite hikes of the entire GDT, a real gem. I've hiked it and skied it. I loved it both times and I highly recommend it. I did not include this alternate in previous editions of the guidebook because of the maintained trail and facilities in the valley. When the decommissioned Maligne River trail becomes impassable, however, this alternate will be the only viable link for the GDT route through Jasper National Park. It does

Miro Rak and friend negotiate the short scramble to the summit near the northern end of the Six Passes alternate route.

involve some easy scrambling but nothing like the Barnaby Ridge alternate in Section A or the Coral Pass alternate in Section C. The route-finding is easy and the hiking is unparalleled for cross-country travel. There is plenty of water en route between each of the passes. Don't attempt it too early in the season, though, due to snow and caribou calving. Late July to late September is the optimal period. The caribou rutting season begins in late September. Parks Canada advises visitors not to travel from then until late October. They won't issue a random camping permit for the route during periods that are sensitive for the caribou.

The key to the alternate route is to visually line up all six passes and keep an eye on them as you descend through the subalpine valleys. This route follows the base of the unbroken and impressive escarpment of Endless Chain Ridge. There are lakes, waterfalls, alpine meadows, and continual vantage points. It is a strenuous route, with a total 2057m elevation gain and 2597m loss. The route is suitable for running or fastpacking but the footing gets technical in the lower meadows between the passes, where tussocks (small, grassy mounds) form.

From waypoint e22 at the shallow lake on Maligne Pass, hike cross-country 2.5km up to Pass #1 at 2492m elevation. From there, look northwest and sight the next pass in the chain. Descend into the long meadow to a low point of 2023m at km 9.5. Climb steeply up to Pass #2, 2225m, at km 10.4. Still following the rock wall northwest, descend to a low point of 2065m at km 12.1. Then ascend to 2315m for Pass #3 at km 13.2.

From Pass #3 the route goes slightly more northward, descending to a low point of 1922m at km 15.9. It angles up to Pass #4, east of Sympathy Peak, at km 17.8 and 2228m. Descend to a marshy low point of 2084m at km 19.0 Ascend past two alpine lakes to 2335m Pass #5 at km 20.0 Finally,

Miro Rak regards the last two passes on a SOBO hike of the Six Passes alternate route.

Miro Rak with the author at a viewpoint at the end of the Bald Hills trail on the Six Passes alternate route.

descend to 1985m at km 21.9 before climbing up to Pass #6 at 2260m and km 24.9.

Instead of dropping down over this pass as you have become accustomed to doing, angle up to the barren ridge crest to the north. Follow this ridge crest right up to the cairn on the impressive summit at 2568m. The route follows the ridge that goes directly east from the summit down through some steep terrain. Be careful not to dislodge a rock if you are following someone else. It is a brief but easy scramble down. Two novice scramblers joined me when I hiked the route years ago. They had no difficulty with the scrambling except being winded from the steep ascent (SOBO).

The author fords
the Maligne River
just north of
Maligne Pass.

The angle of the descent lessens as the ridge broadens. The now easy ridge walk curves to the north. Stay to the right on the ridge crest, clambering over a couple of minor rock steps, eventually joining the Bald Hills trail at km 29.6 at a cairn on a 2374m ridgeline summit. Good, signed trail brings you down the remaining 7km along the ridge and then down through forest to rejoin the main route at the Bald Hills trail junction, 200m from the trailhead kiosk at the Maligne Lake parking lot. There is a trail junction 2.5km before reaching parking – perhaps 750m down from the lookout, in forest, as shown in the Atlas Guides app. The condition of the retired path is likely poor, since it's not marked as an official trail. If you turn left you will reach the Evelyn Creek campsite on the Skyline trail in 2.7km and bypass the busy trailhead at Maligne Lake. If navigable, this shortcut shaves 7.3km off the main route, nearly making up for the extra distance of the entire alternate route.

End of Six Passes alternate route

Maligne Pass to Mary Vaux campsite
(4.4km, 14m up, 273m down)

From the shallow lake on Maligne Pass, descend 2.0km to a brisk, ankle-deep ford of the Maligne River near its source. A steep descent brings the trail 1.5km to another ford of the Maligne River and reaches the Mary Vaux campsite in another 900m.

Mary Vaux campsite to Mary Schäffer campsite
(10.6km, 91m up, 291m down)

Continue descending the Maligne River valley on the northeastern bank. The trail is in good condition and most of the tributaries have bridges. In 2.4km, the trail passes Old Horse Camp, its only facilities being a fire ring and some tables. There are some blowdowns. The trail reaches a creek crossing 2.9km farther and then starts to deteriorate, becoming brushy. The trail is in terrible shape for the next 4.6km – hikers suggest getting out your GPS or app to stay on the trail through this stretch – at which point you should reach a bridged creek crossing. Find the Mary Schäffer campsite 700m beyond the bridge.

Mary Schäffer campsite to Trapper Creek campsite
(10.9km, 115m up, 202m down)

The route crosses a log bridge in 1.2km below Mount Unwin. The trail winds through meadows 2.5km to the Maligne River ford (1770, 18.7, e23). After the ford it is easy to lose the trail in the dense brush. Angle northwest 600m to the treeline. The trail improves as it enters forest. Staying on the west side of the creek you should reach a small campsite in 3.5km, and in another 3.1km the Trapper Creek campsite (1720, 7.2, e24).

Trapper Creek campsite to the Maligne Lake trailhead
parking area (5.7km, 173m up, 181m down)

Beyond the campsite, the quality of the route improves as it crosses a bridge and climbs 130m over a broad ridge. After descending off the ridge, you reach the Moose Lake Loop trail junction in 4.4km. Turn left. The condition of the trail improves vastly. You soon reach the Bald Hills trail junction in 1.0km, where the Six Passes alternate route rejoins the main GDT route. In another 200m, find the Maligne Pass trailhead (1705, 5.7, e25) on a gravel access road at a covered trailhead kiosk. There is a pay telephone here. Across the large parking lot, toward the lake, are the outhouses.

Follow the Maligne Lake road downhill to the Skyline trailhead, which you will find on the left-hand side. Trapper Creek is the closest campsite

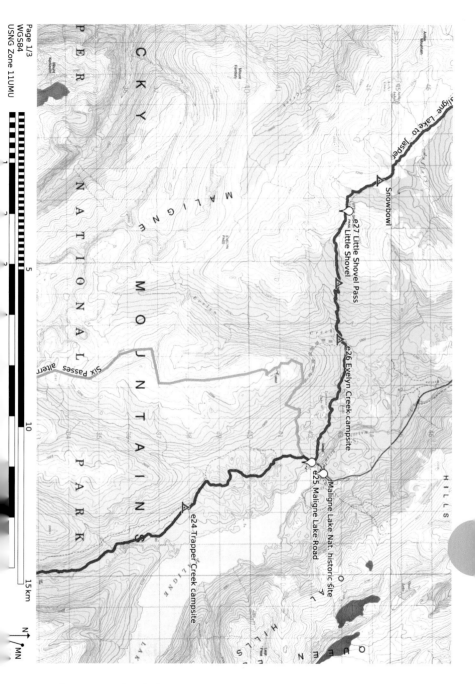

to the start of the Skyline trail if you can't reserve a spot at the Evelyn Creek or Little Shovel campsites in the next segment.

SEGMENT 28 – Maligne Lake to Jasper (55.9km)

Strenuous climbing on excellent hiking trail. Horses and bikes not permitted. Dogs prohibited.

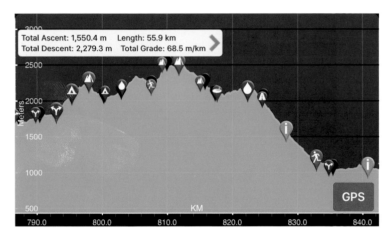

The Skyline trail takes advantage of as much of the alpine terrain as possible between Maligne Lake and Jasper. The strenuous climbs over high passes will make you sweat – a trade-off for some of the best views of the GDT. The only drawback is the popularity of the segment, which inevitably leads to fully booked campsites. The trail is so good, however, that you can hike the entire Skyline Trail in a long day if needed. After segment 27, it is such a relief to be able to look around while you hike and not have to watch every step.

Maps: 83 C/12 Athabasca Falls, 83 C/13 Medicine Lake and 83 D/16 Jasper; Gemtrek #1 Jasper & Maligne Lake.

Jurisdiction: Jasper National Park.

South access: Drive east from Jasper 5km to the Maligne Lake road. Follow it for 47km to the lake. Park at the Maligne Lake parking area. The Skyline trailhead kiosk is across the Maligne Lake road from the parking lot, while the Maligne Pass trailhead is 300m up the adjacent gravel road.

Other access: Drive the Icefields Parkway (Highway 93 North) to the Wabasso Lake trailhead, 15km south of Jasper and 89km north of the Glacier Discovery Centre. Hike past Wabasso Lake, meet the Old Fort Point trail junction in 4.2km, and turn right for the way up to the Skyline trail. You pass Curator campsite (site 30) in another 10.0km and intersect the GDT 800m farther on the Skyline at a point 1.9km beyond Big Shovel Pass.

Follow Maligne Lake Road 18km from Yellowhead Highway 16, to the

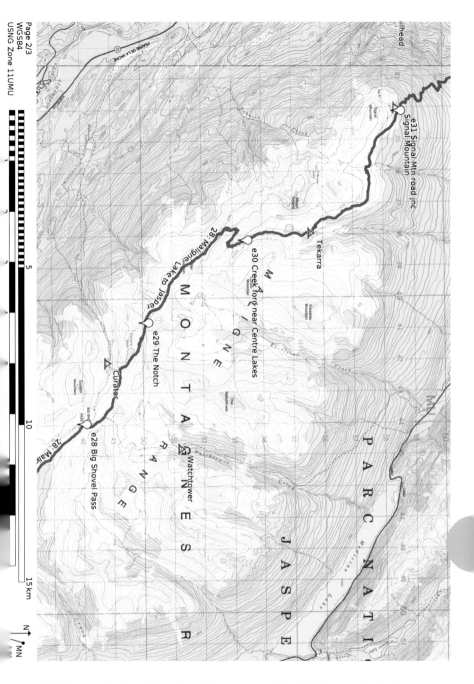

Watchtower Basin trailhead. In 9.8km you pass the Watchtower campsite (site 33) and intersect the GDT in another 3.4km, on the Skyline trail at Big Shovel Pass.

North access: Segment hikers drive 4km south on the Maligne Lake road to the Signal Mountain trailhead parking area. This is the northern end of the Skyline trail, where it meets with local trail #7 that goes into Jasper. Thru-hikers start right in Jasper, at the intersection of Connaught Drive with Highway 93A (as mentioned in the trail description).

Car campgrounds and accommodations: HI Maligne Canyon Hostel is on the Maligne Lake road near the Signal Mountain trailhead and only 1km by trail #7 from the GDT. The hostel charges $30 a night for non-members. This is a rustic facility with no showers, and dogs are not permitted. For the myriad of accommodations in Jasper, you should inquire at the information centre near the post office. The Whistlers campground is 3km from Jasper on the Icefields Parkway (Highway 93 North). You can also get there by following Highway 93A southward from the Old Fort Point turnoff mentioned in the route description. The campground's fee is $27.40 per night, including hot showers. Parks Canada staff keep walk-in sites open for hikers and cyclists, while the rest of the massive campground usually fills up.

Recently hikers have been recommending the Jasper Downtown Hostel, which is near the post office and major stores. Rates start at $40 per night for a bunk. Amenities include a kitchen and lounge, laundry facilities, privacy curtains and cozy comforters. Private rooms are also available. Book in advance. Visit the North Face Pizza restaurant for a quick and deeply filling meal at a great price, northfacepizza.com. This is my go-to poutine place for post-adventure carb-loading.

Camping: National park campsites: Evelyn Creek (site 27); Little Shovel (28); Snowbowl (29); Watchtower (33) – 3.4km off route; Curator (30) – off route by 800m; Tekarra (31); and Signal (32). No random camping.

Information sources: Parks Canada trail office at the Jasper townsite information centre

Resupply stations: Jasper post office.

Special notes: Reserve your campsites on the Skyline trail as soon as you can – hopefully as soon as the online backcountry reservations system opens up for the year in January. You can also contact the Jasper trail office to make the reservations (only three months in advance, however) and to learn about trail conditions. Check the trailhead kiosk for special bulletins such as campsite closures.

Maligne Lake to Evelyn Creek campsite
(4.8km, 144m up, 30m down)

From the Skyline trailhead on the Maligne Lake road, follow an excellent trail west. Hike through forest past the Lorraine Lake trail junction in 1.9km and the Mona Lake junction 400m farther. In another 2.4km you encounter a trail junction for the Atlas Guides Bald Hills shortcut where the Six Passes route rejoins the GDT. The Evelyn Creek campsite (1760, 4.8, e26) is just past the creek bridge. (Segment hikers, if you plan to arrive at Maligne Lake late in the day, this is a good campsite to reserve, because the hike in is very quick.)

Evelyn Creek campsite to Little Shovel campsite (2.4km, 256m up, 0m down)

After crossing the Evelyn Creek bridge, the trail ascends steeply to the west on switchbacks. The grade eases and you pass Little Shovel campsite in 2.4km below timberline. The roomy campsite perches on a hillside.

Little Shovel campsite to Snowbowl campsite (4.3km, 195m up, 168m down)

The Skyline trail gently ascends into the alpine in another 2.6km, reaching Little Shovel Pass (2240, 5.0, e27). For the next 28km you travel predominantly above the treeline. A gradual descent to a creek ford, followed by a meadow traverse, takes you 1.7km to Snowbowl campsite.

Snowbowl campsite to Curator campsite trail junction (8.0km, 310m up, 195m down)

After leaving the campsite, the trail crosses a bridge in 1.0km and then traverses the vast meadows of Snowbowl. Gradually, in 4.4km, the path ascends to Big Shovel Pass (2310, 7.1, e28) below Curator Mountain. The Skyline trail contours 800m across shale slopes to the Watchtower trail junction (read 'Other access' above). Continue straight ahead and descend

Just north of Big Shovel Pass, Julia Lynx admires the view of Mount Edith Cavell across the Athabasca River valley.

Curator Lake on the Skyline trail in Jasper National Park.

another 1.8km to the Curator campsite trail junction. Turn left and walk a steep 800m downhill if you are staying at the Curator campsite. That trail continues 14.2km past the campsite to Highway 93 (read 'Other access'). Continue straight through the junction to stay on the Skyline trail.

Dustin and Julia Lynx hike toward The Notch beyond Curator Lake.

The author crosses a remnant snowfield toward The Notch on the Skyline trail.

Dustin and Julia Lynx on the final steep ascent to The Notch. A broken cornice is in the background.

Julia Lynx near the summit of Amber Mountain.

Curator campsite trail junction to The Notch
(2.0km, 266m up, 6m down)

Continue through the junction and in 500m walk beside Curator Lake through a colourful boulder field. NOBO hikers, pick up water at Curator Lake; the next 7km is normally dry, unless you want to melt snow. Climb moderately above the northeast side of Curator Lake. The grade becomes steeper as you ascend abrupt switchbacks 1.5km to get to The Notch (2505, 4.6, e29). Remnant snow usually clings to The Notch throughout the summer.

The Notch to Tekarra campsite
(9.0km, 80m up, 499m down)

Leave the view of Curator Lake and traverse the shale slopes of two minor summits to the northwest. The trail leaves the open mountainside for the crest of Amber Mountain. Follow the windswept ridge crest. In 4.3km, exit the ridge to the north. Switchbacks bring the Skyline trail 2.2km down to a creek crossing (2205, 6.5, e30) below Centre Lakes. SOBO hikers should pick up water here, as the next 7km can be dry. Pass Tekarra Lake in 1.7km and reach Tekarra campsite in another 800m down the trail.

Tekarra campsite to Signal campsite
(5.9km, 171m up, 252m down)

The trail stays just above timberline as it contours north and then west around the northern flank of Mount Tekarra. The Skyline trail reaches the Signal Mountain road junction (2000, 8.3, e31). Continue to the right, downhill. Signal campsite is just down the road, 100m past the junction.

Signal campsite to Signal Mountain trailhead
(8.3km, 0m up, 866m down)

The GDT follows the fire road down moderate switchbacks to the Signal Mountain trailhead (1160, 8.4, e32) on Maligne Lake Road. Hikers report that you will find several maintained mountain bike trails that criss-cross the gravel road and make for better walking. At the trailhead you should see a sign that declares "Northern Terminal Great Divide Trail." Turn left and follow the River–Canyon #7 loop trail. Look for #7 markings. If you turn right, you can walk to Maligne Canyon Hostel in less than a kilometre on the #7 trail. See 'Campgrounds and accommodations.' Across the road from the hostel is the Maligne Canyon resort, with a café and telephone. The famous Maligne Canyon is only a short walk from the hostel. Some hikers prefer to visit the canyon and then walk the more direct Maligne Lake Road into Jasper. It can be gratifying to follow the Maligne Canyon trail instead of the main route, when you consider that you have followed the Maligne River all the way from its source at Maligne Pass to its confluence with the Athabasca River.

Signal Mountain trailhead to Jasper
(11.2km, 128m up, 263m down)

The #7 loop trail parallels the busy Maligne Lake road downhill and comes to a trail junction at Soggy Dog Lake (1095, 2.3, e33). Turn left, away from the paved road that goes to Edith and Annette lakes. Now heading south, enter forest on the marked #7 trail. Go straight through another junction in 1.3km. The path stays on the eastern perimeter of the Fairmont Jasper Park Lodge and golf course. In 5.4km come to another junction and turn left onto trail #7B. This trail goes 200m to the Old Fort Point trailhead (1055, 6.9, e34).

Cross the bridge and look for the start of trail #1B in 300m on the right of the Old Fort Point road. Follow this trail 1.0km past the south side of a small lake to Highway 93A. Where the 'Red Squirrel' trail 1B ends, the GDT goes to the right on Highway 93A and continues northwest into Jasper. (Whistlers campground is 3km distant from this point if you turned left instead, and left again on Highway 93 North, the Icefields Parkway.)

Follow Highway 93A 600m to the intersection with Connaught Drive. End of Section E.

If you need to pick up a package at the post office, continue 100m to Patricia Street and turn right. The post office is 300m down Patricia Street, across from the Parks Canada trail office at the Jasper townsite information centre.

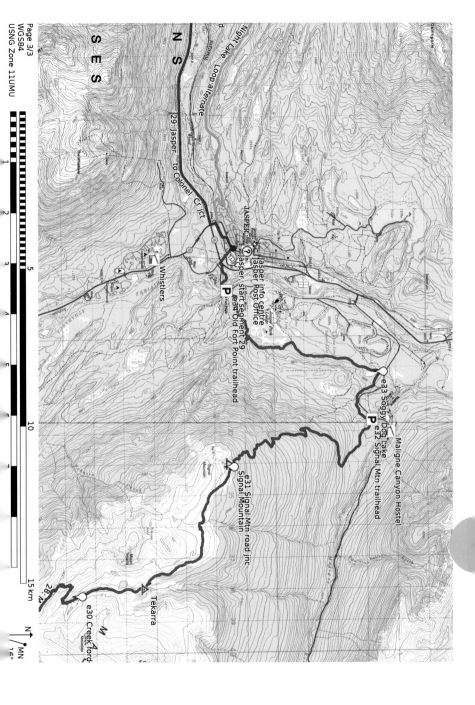

N S
N
S
E
S

Night Lake Loop alternate

29: Jasper to Colonel Cr jct

Whistlers

JASPER

Jasper info centre
Jasper Post Office
Jasper, start segment 29
e34 Old Fort Point trailhead

e33 Soggy Dog Lake
e32 Signal Mtn trailhead

Maligne Canyon Hostel

e31 Signal Mtn road jnc
Signal Mountain

Tekarra

e30 Creek ford

5

10

15 km

N
MN
1.6°

SECTION F: *Jasper to Mount Robson*

Segments 29–30, 130.0 km

Location	Near waypoint	NOBO km	SOBO km
Jasper townsite	e34	850.0	283.2
Miette River campsite	f3	886.8	246.4
Miette Lake campsite	f5	898.4	234.8
Colonel Pass campsite	f9	912.1	221.1
Horse Camp (Trio)	f11	921.1	212.1
Steppe Creek campsite	f13	932.7	200.5
Horse Camp (Slide)	f14	938.1	195.1
Moose Pass	f15	942.8	190.4
Smoky River ford	f16	950.6	182.6
Adolphus campsite (Jasper NP)	f16	953.2	180.0
Robson Pass campsite (BC Parks) [see note below]	f16	955.8	177.4
Rearguard campsite (BC Parks) [see note below]	f16	956.8	176.4
Berg Lake campsite (BC Parks) [see note below]	f16	957.8	175.4
Marmot campsite (BC Parks) [see note below]	f16	959.8	173.4
Emperor Falls campsite (BC Parks) [see note below]	f16	962.6	170.6
Whitehorn campsite (BC Parks) [see note below]	f16	967.0	166.2
Kinney Lake campsite (BC Parks) [see note below]	f16	970.4	162.8
RESUPPLY: Mount Robson Visitor Centre	f16	979.0	154.2

NOTE: Mount Robson PP requires that you reserve permits for these campsites.

Introduction

Starting with this edition of the guidebook, I am splitting up the northernmost section of my description of the GDT route. The consensus among hikers and the GDTA is that most thru-hikers plan to start or end their journey at Mount Robson. Not only is Robson the original northern terminus of the Great Divide Trail, it is also an inspirational symbol as the tallest peak in the Canadian Rockies. Logistically, this means that the seventh section, G, starts in the middle of nowhere, with the Berg Lake trail listed as the southern access. But it works, in my opinion. At 130.0km including the Berg Lake trail, Section F now rivals Section D as the shortest.

Section F now has three alternate routes that avoid the substantial 22km road walk out of Jasper. I strongly recommend you consider taking the Saturday Night Lake Loop trail alternate route, so you can reserve a spot at the Minnow Lake campsite, 8.5km out of town. This well-maintained path is popular with locals for its proximity and beautiful montane environment, with trembling aspen, grassy meadows, and numerous

Mercator Projection
WGS84
USNG 11ULU-11UMV

lakeshores. It is a multi-use trail, shared with mountain bikers, and nestles between long ridges that are invisible from the busy highway.

The Elysium Pass alternate route is new for this edition. It follows good trail into alpine northwest of Jasper and stays above timberline until it re-joins the main route at Miette Pass (or Colonel Pass). The route is ideal for advanced hikers looking for a challenge and untrammelled high-alpine travel.

The third alternate route, proposed in 2016 by a Jasper local, Rogier Gruys, is a historic tote road used to construct the railway a century ago. This alternate links the Saturday Night loop to the Decoigne warden station and manages to avoid the highway. The description of all three of these alternate routes follows in segment 29.

Parks Canada classified the upper Miette River as 'wildland' in 2012 and decommissioned the trail. Fortunately, local outfitters in the area still maintain the trail for guided horse trips. They like to keep it open because of the enormous alpine meadow east of Mount Mahood called Miette and Centre Pass and the outstanding scenery there.

The route negotiates Grant and Colonel passes before descending to the Moose River in Mount Robson Provincial Park in BC. The GDT briefly re-enters the national park before reaching the famed Berg Lake trail that wraps around Mount Robson and brings you through an old-growth cedar forest back to Highway 16 at the Mount Robson visitor centre.

SEGMENT 29 – Jasper to the Moose River (68.7km)

Moderate climbs over three remote passes on poor but scenic trail. Horses permitted. Bikes prohibited.

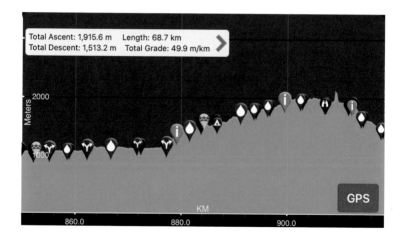

Total Ascent: 1,915.6 m Length: 68.7 km
Total Descent: 1,513.2 m Total Grade: 49.9 m/km

Thru-hikers are the only folks who would start this segment from the town of Jasper. Section-hikers can drive to the Miette River trailhead described as the south access and remove 24km of road walking from this

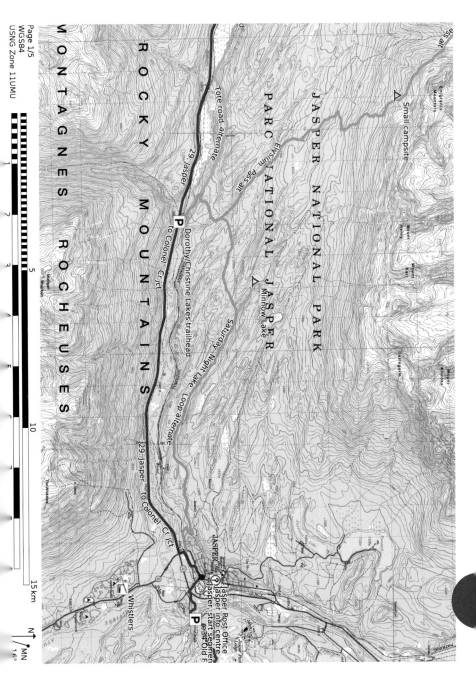

already long and challenging segment. Miette/Centre Pass at the head of the Miette River is an absolute wonder, a dream destination for any backpacker. This pass on the Divide is easily five square kilometres of open,

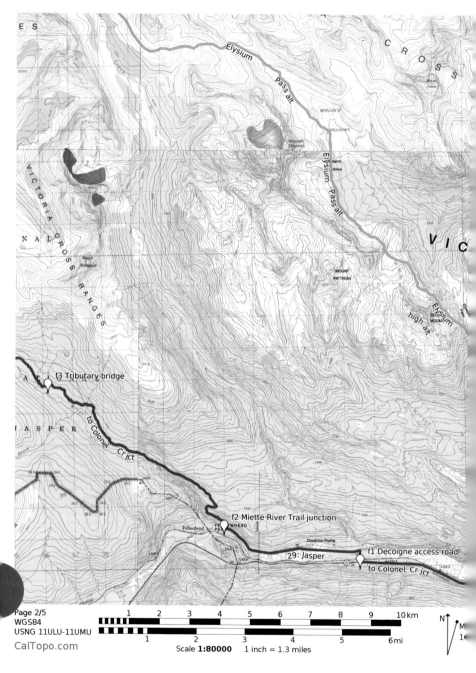

f3 Tributary bridge

to Colonel Cr jct

JASPER

f2 Miette River Trail junction

29: Jasper

f1 Decoigne access road
to Colonel Cr jct

Scale **1:80000**   1 inch = 1.3 miles

Elysium

Elysium pass alt

Elysium pass alt

Elysium high alt

rolling meadows tethered to limestone towers and icefalls at its fringes.
You will find several such special places in this segment.

Maps: 83 D/16 Jasper, 83 D/15 Lucerne, 83 E/1 Snaring River (Elysium

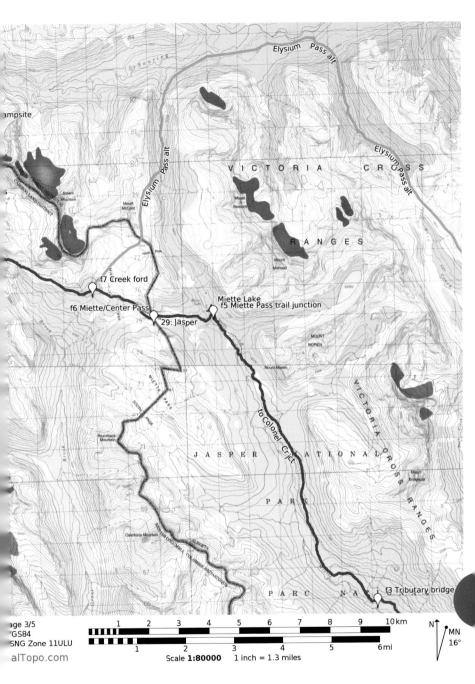

Elysium Pass alt

VICTORIA CROSS RANGES

Elysium Pass alt

f7 Creek ford

f6 Miette/Center Pass

29: Jasper

Miette Lake
f5 Miette Pass trail junction

to Colonel Crjct

VICTORIA CROSS RANGES

JASPER NATIONAL PARK

PARC NAT

f3 Tributary bridge

PARC

age 3/5
GS84
SNG Zone 11ULU
alTopo.com

Scale **1:80000**   1 inch = 1.3 miles

N MN 16°

alternate only) and 83 E/2 Resplendent Creek; Gemtrek #1 Jasper & Maligne Lake (partial coverage only, to Elysium Pass alternate and partway to the Miette River trailhead).

Jurisdictions: Jasper National Park and Mount Robson Provincial Park (BC Parks).

South access: Park at the Miette River trailhead for the main route. From the Yellowhead Highway 16 junction with the Icefields Parkway (Highway 93 North), drive 20.7km west on Highway 16 to an intersection with a gravel access road 200m east of the Jasper National Park west gate (tollbooth). Follow the gravel road over a bridge and railway tracks and turn left at a T-intersection. The parking area is at the end of the gravel road, near the Decoigne warden station.

If you plan to hike the Elysium Pass or tote road alternate routes, follow Highway 16 11.1km west from the Icefields Parkway junction, to the Dorothy–Christine Lake trailhead parking area.

North access: Drive Yellowhead Highway 16 to a gravel access road 29km west of the Jasper National Park west gate and 3km east of the Moose Lake boat launch. Turn north onto the gravel road and drive a short distance to the end. Walk across the railway tracks and follow the road to the right. Soon you meet the Moose River trail and turn left. From here it is 22km to meet the GDT at waypoint f11.

Car campgrounds and accommodations: The Lucerne campground, the closest one to the Miette River trailhead, is in Mount Robson Provincial Park, 10km west of the provincial boundary on Highway 16 at Yellowhead Lake or 50km east of the Mount Robson visitor centre. There are no showers at the campground but you will find a beach suitable for swimming. The fee at Lucerne campground is $28. The Whistlers campground is 3km from Jasper on the Icefields Parkway. You can also get there by following Highway 93A southward from the Old Fort Point turnoff mentioned in the route description. The campground's fee is $27.40 per night, which includes hot showers. Parks Canada staff keep walk-in sites open for hikers and cyclists, while the rest of the massive campground usually fills up.

Recently hikers have been recommending the Jasper Downtown Hostel, which is near the post office and major stores. Rates start at $40 per night for a bunk. Amenities include a kitchen and lounge, laundry facilities, privacy curtains and cozy comforters. Private rooms are available.

Camping: Jasper National Park backcountry campsite at Minnow Lake (site 40). Random camping. The campsites mentioned in this segment are simply level areas big enough to accommodate a couple of tents. These sites show signs of previous use, with obvious tent clearings and fire rings. You can still reserve the Miette Lake campsite for your backcountry permit if you like.

Information sources: Jasper trail office, Jasper information centre; Mount Robson visitor centre.

Resupply station: Jasper post office.

Special notes: Parks Canada states that visitors to wildland areas must have a bearproof container to store their food.

I am repeating this verbatim from the 'Safety' section earlier in this book: Yellowhead Highway 16 is an extremely busy road, full of distracted drivers during the summer months. It only takes a second of inattention while gawking at the scenery for a driver to swerve slightly onto the shoulder and injure or kill a pedestrian or cyclist. In fact, your presence on the side of the road is another distraction. For this reason, there are three alternate routes listed in particular for the GDT out of Jasper, at the start of Section F. I strongly urge you to arrange for a shuttle out of Jasper if you aren't interested in hiking one of the alternate routes.

Additional reading: Pick up the free "Day Hiker's Guide to Jasper National Park" at the Jasper information centre. This pamphlet has a good road and trail map for the Jasper townsite. (Also available online.)

Jasper to Miette River trailhead
(22.9km, 285m up, 218m down)

From the intersection of Highway 93 and Connaught Drive in Jasper, look for a trail going southwest that stays in the sparsely forested corridor between the railway tracks and Connaught Drive. Follow this trail 1.1km to where the railway crosses over Highway 93. Turn left and walk 200m to the intersection with Highway 16 (also known as the Yellowhead Highway).

Follow Highway 16 west to the Decoigne warden station access road (1120, 23.9, f1) just 200m east of the Jasper National Park west gate (toll-booth) on Highway 16. Turn right and follow the gravel road over the Miette River bridge 350m to a T-intersection and turn left. In just over 500m the gravel road passes the warden station and reaches a vehicle gate and parking area at the Miette River trailhead.

SATURDAY NIGHT LAKE LOOP TRAIL ALTERNATE ROUTE – 14.6KM INSTEAD OF 12.6KM

I do recommend walking the southern half of the Saturday Night Lake circuit trail out of Jasper. There is a short bit of difficult cross-country to join up with the Dorothy–Christine Lake trail, but in my opinion it is worth it. By taking this route you can find a Parks Canada backcountry campsite within a half day's walk and minimize the amount of road walking.

From the intersection of Connaught Drive at the start of this segment, look for a trail going southwest that stays in the sparsely forested corridor between the railway tracks and Connaught Drive. Follow this trail 1.1km to where the railway crosses over Highway 93. Go under the bridge and cross the road at a safe place and then resume following the path

The trailhead for Dorothy, Christine, and Virl lakes, a pivotal trailhead in segment 29 for three alternate routes: Saturday Night Lakes, Elysium Pass, and Tote Road.

southwestward, staying on the north side of the tracks. The municipal trail curves to the north, skirting a residential subdivision, and meets the Saturday Night Lake loop trail in 800m. Turn left.

Follow the southern portion of the circuit trail toward Marjorie and Caledonia lakes. Don't turn off for those lakes; continue straight, past the trail #3A junction farther along. In 8.2km reach the Minnow Lake trail junction. To the left is the Minnow Lake campsite in 300m and to the right the circuit trail continues. It's up to you where you want to cut off and go cross-country to get around Dorothy Lake to the southwest. I recommend going due south over a forested ridge to the eastern shore of the lake and then following the shoreline around to the trail. You might decide to go west and follow the ridge for a bit before dropping down to the western edge of Dorothy Lake. It's up to you – either way, it's about 2km. Take your time. Hikers describe it as 'nasty' but short. The maintained trail is between Dorothy and Christine lakes.

It is 1.5km from Dorothy Lake to the signed Elysium Pass trail junction. It is another 3.0km to the Dorothy–Christine lakes trailhead on Highway 16 just west of the Meadow Creek bridge. Continue another 11km to the Miette River trailhead along Highway 16 westward. However, if you had no problem with the bit of cross-country and would still like to avoid the highway walking, there is another alternate route to consider. Read on.

End Saturday Night Lake Loop Trail alternate route

TOTE ROAD ALTERNATE ROUTE –
SLIGHTLY LONGER THAN THE ROAD WALK

Trail description by Rogier Gruys, included here with his permission.
Coordinates are in UTM.

In Jasper National Park there is a missing section in the Great Divide

Trail: hikers have to walk 21 km along Highway 16 west from the town of Jasper to the start of the Miette trail at Decoigne near the BC boundary. In his book *Hiking Canada's Great Divide Trail*, Dustin Lynx suggests an alternative route via Minnow Lake and a cross-country section to the Virl/Dorothy lakes trail. From there hikers still have to walk 11.5km along Highway 16. However, dedicated through hikers with good route-finding skills can avoid Highway 16 altogether by hiking for about 4km along a historic wagon road between the Dorothy Lake and Golden Lake trails. This trail was built during the construction of the railroad in the early 1900s to move supplies among workers' camps. It has not been maintained since then, but it is still in good shape for most of the way. From the Golden Lake trailhead, you follow the old railbed all the way to the start of the Miette Valley trail. When coming from Virl/Dorothy lake, descend the well-maintained trail (Trail 60 on hiking maps) towards Highway 16 until the last switchback, where the trail turns to the southeast. The old wagon road starts about 10m past the turn at 414929E, 5858969N, at a sharp right angle. There is a new blaze on a tree beside the trail. The old trail is faint here, and there is quite a bit of blowdown, but it easy to follow until 414731E, 5859020N. In this clearing, look for the trail ahead and uphill. If you lose the trail, bushwhack through relatively easy forest to 414221E, 5859322N. You should be back on the trail again. From here, the trail contours along the mountainside at approximately 1200m. Hike west along the trail to a creekbed and fire guard. If you lose the trail before you get to the creek, on the west side the trail starts at 413488E, 5859726N. From here the trail is easy to follow until another open area where you may lose it. Going westwards, it reappears at 413142E, 5859586N. It should now be easy to follow until you join the old but excellent trail to Golden Lake at 411955E, 5859779N. Continue westwards and follow the trail down the hill to an old, grown-in parking lot at 5859586E, 5859472N. You emerge onto an old, wide roadbed. About a kilometre west this becomes the old railbed. Follow this beautiful railbed west, past the Decoigne station, all the way to the Miette trailhead, at 401958E, 5861318N, just before the railbed dead-ends at the Miette River. Aside from a bit of bushwhacking and route-finding, this is a very pleasant route and a great, historic alternative to walking along the highway! (Author's note: please visit the GDTA website for a downloadable track for this alternate route.)

End Tote Road alternate route

ELYSIUM PASS ALTERNATE ROUTE – 50KM INSTEAD OF 40.8KM

This alternate route is for experienced thru-hikers who crave high-alpine cross-country travel and remote wilderness. Dogs are permitted here, as well as horses. Elysium Pass is a horse trail but I can only see equestrians

Jerry Auld and Tenaya Lynx descending to Elysium Pass. Mount Monarch is in the centre, Elysium Mountain to the left. It is possible to hike over Elysium and rejoin the alternate route.

Tenaya Lynx watches her footing on the snow-covered descent from the narrow col north of Mount Monarch on the Elysium Pass alternate route.

travelling as far as the 'notch' mentioned in this description. If you commit to this route, expect 6km of slow bushwhacking into and out of the Snaring River valley.

I originally became interested in this alternate after reading Rick Bombaci's trip report documenting his 2008 thru-hike. Instead of proceeding north over the broad pass at the head of the Derr Creek valley, he chose to go south and follow Derr Creek almost back to the start of the Miette River trail. In 2016, I hiked a large loop through the area with my daughter Tenaya and good friend Jerry Auld looking for a more direct passage to Miette Lake on the GDT. Coincidentally, during the same year, GDT hiker Zdenek Sychrava hiked this alternate and described his experience on his blog (fordingriver.wordpress.com/great-divide-trail-2016/section -7-jasper-to-mt-robson). Reading his account will likely help you decide if this alternate is something that interests you or not.

The Elysium Pass alternate route starts at the Dorothy and Christine lakes trailhead on the Yellowhead Highway, 12.2km from the start of

Section F, in Jasper. The trailhead is well marked and it has a large gravel parking area. The route follows a gravel road for 200m and crosses the railway tracks and then a bridge over the Miette River. From the Elysium Pass trail junction at km 3.0 on the Dorothy Lake–Christine Lake trail, turn left and follow good trail uphill. Watch for tree blazes and diamond-shaped tin markers along the way. There is little water on this trail for the next 8.2km to a spring. Only 100m past the spring, tucked under some large Douglas fir trees next to a very wet subalpine meadow, is a small campsite suitable for two tents, at km 11.3.

The route continues, following good trail through subalpine meadows to an incredible viewpoint at km 13.0 at 2123m elevation. From here you can look northwest and see Elysium Pass and Elysium Mountain. To the right (north) of Elysium Mountain is Mount Monarch, hulking in the distance. Monarch will be your companion for the next day as you walk around its eastern bulwarks and cut around a hidden lake cradled on its northern flank.

Descend on fair trail to Elysium Pass in 900m. Here the trail disappears in some knee-high willows around the small creek. It is now up to you to find your own way, cross-country.

The best route is northwest. Aim for the upper edge of the subalpine forest on the northeastern ridge of Elysium Mountain, where the rock and shale slopes meet the subalpine, 1.8km away. You will find some remnant trail through short stretches of forest, notably on the left side of a cascade. Keep travelling northwest along the base of Elysium Mountain, climbing over lightly forested ridges and aiming for the pass on the eastern side of Mount Monarch. (If you have a clear day, you can hike over the summit of Elysium Mountain instead and then follow its ridge crest due north and back down to rejoin the lower route, described here.) In 6.1km you reach the edge of a prominent boulder field in Monarch Meadows. While cutting through the boulders is kind of fun, the faster route is to skirt around them to the east, through the wet meadows. The route continues northwest for 4.4km up to a narrow alpine pass on the eastern side of Mount Monarch at km 26.2.

Continue over the pass to the northwest for 700m. As you walk you will see a continuous cliff band about 150m tall between you and Mount Monarch to the west. Follow the base of this rock wall and watch for a break where a steep scree slope angles up to a notch. Don't go beyond the 700m mark. If you do, you will begin a steep descent to the northwest into forest. Instead, turn southwest and follow the steep scree up to the notch in the cliff band. The notch is 90m above this point and only 400m hiking (11 U 0402432m E 5876414m N, or 53.029367, –118.458533).

From the notch at 2207m elevation, descend west, aiming for the

Tenaya Lynx and Jerry Auld look toward the notch in the centre of the photo, above an unnamed lake on the northern flank of Mount Monarch on the Elysium Pass alternate route.

northern shore of a lovely round lake that you reach in 1.1km. Start angling up to the west from the lakeshore through the alpine and in 1.6km reach a 2108m highpoint on a ridge. Contour around the ridge to the north into the Derr Creek valley. Don't drop down to the creek. Keep above treeline and aim for the obvious pass at the head of Derr Creek valley. Rock-hop a creek in 1.2km at 2052m. Continue northwest for another 2.0km to the broad alpine pass at 2030m at km 33.2. From here, I use only approximate distances and a summary of the route as described in Zdenek Sychrava's trip report.

Continue north-northwest over the pass and follow the drainage down to a couple of small lakes within 5km. The route steepens as it continues following the creek 2km to the Snaring River below. The real bushwhack starts as the elevation loss diminishes and you near the river. There is no need to go all the way to the river, though. Turn left (west) and go up-valley. You will cross a creek in 500m and then another in 2km.

Within 1.5km beyond the second creek crossing, you reach the valley that leads up to Miette Lake and lies between Mount Beaupré to the east and the steep walls of Mount McCord to the west. Turn south and follow the creek up this narrow valley to reach a cluster of lakes within 3km. At the largest lake, take the opportunity for a clear view from its shoreline to look for a drainage below Mount McCord that leads up into the alpine. Not far from the lake – only 500m – the drainage starts angling steeply uphill to the southwest. This is the preferred route. If you were to continue directly up to Miette Lake, you would reach a waterfall and impassable cliffs.

Leave the bushwhacking and progress slowly up the steep drainage for 1km. Once you reach the alpine the angle of ascent eases and the route opens up. Contour through the alpine for 2km to the closest pass directly below Mount McCord, not the one marked as North Pass on the NTS maps. From the pass follow the drainage southwest 2km down to the GDT at waypoint f7.

End Elysium Pass alternate route

Miette River trailhead to old Miette warden cabin site (13.9km, 588m up, 170m down)

From the Miette River trailhead, the gravel road continues west beyond the vehicle gate. Follow it for 4.3km to a point 100m before crossing the Miette River. Look for a poor trail with a yellow marker that goes north. This is the Miette River trail junction (1152, 5.2, f2). Turn right and ascend the moderate grade through bushy sections of trail up a long, curving switchback. Notice the diamond-shaped tin markers nailed to trees at head height. The path comes to the first boardwalk in 1.9km – I'm not sure how much longer these will last now that the trail is officially unmaintained. The first good water source is a spring in another 2.4km. Past a bridge 2.3km farther, the condition of the trail worsens, becoming muddy and brushy. Cross another stream in 900m. Continue 1.8km farther to a bridged tributary (1532, 9.3, f3) 300m before the foundation of the old Miette warden cabin. There is a campsite on the right, just before the bridged tributary.

Old Miette warden cabin site to Miette/Centre Pass (14.0km, 513m up, 66m down)

The condition of the path becomes worse as it follows a bend in the river due west, nearly approaching it in 1.9km before resuming a northwest heading. There is more mud and overgrown trail over the next 2.4km, on your way to a creek crossing (1730, 4.6, f4). The trail quality improves for a ways after this crossing as it continues north. In 3.1km, cross a larger creek just as riverside meadows start to appear. On the other side of this wet crossing there is a small campsite. The path disappears in bogs beyond here but does reappear before reaching an easy ford of the Miette River in 2.6km to the west side. The route passes through meadows below Mount Moren, then refords the river to the east side in 1.2km. From here there is a stunning view of the symmetrical ridges of Mount Mahood. (In 2016 I tried linking the Elysium Pass alternate with the high col beyond the unnamed lake cradled between those ridges, without success. It would be a class 4 alpine climb on the other side.) The path ascends 400m to a knoll above the Miette River where there is a signed Miette/Centre Pass trail junction (1880, 7.3, f5). The pretty Miette Lake campsite is 200m beyond. There are no amenities save for a good tent site. From the junction, go southwest, ford the river again, and ascend steeply through trees. The

Miette Pass and Centre Pass sit in the same extensive alpine meadow.

The Miette River trail south of Miette Pass in segment 29.

route angles west to a soggy meadow where the trail quickly disappears. To stay on the route, look west for a medium-sized boulder in the meadow. It is 1km from the signed junction. Continue on a gradual ascent directly west from the boulder 1.4km to the provincial boundary marker number 1-T (1970, 2.4, f6), on Centre Pass. Remarkably, this is the first time the GDT route crosses the Continental Divide since Howse Pass, 272.3km to the south.

Miette/Centre Pass to Colonel Pass campsite
(11.3km, 423m up, 501m down)

From the boundary marker the route goes cross-country through the meadows to the west-northwest. You'll want to follow the top of the tree-line south of Mount McCord and not sacrifice any elevation. Find the trail again at a creek crossing (1950, 2.1, f7) or a little beyond, where the trail enters trees again below talus. This trail was marked with tree blazes in 2011. The Elysium Pass alternate joins the trail after descending from North Pass. Once on the trail, ascend through sparse trees and boulders, past seasonal lakes, to a traverse along talus below the southern ridge of Salient Mountain. The now well-defined trail encounters a few tributary fords at the foot of ribbon-like waterfalls and then ascends gently to narrow Grant Pass (1945, 6.0, f8) on the Divide. Below the hanging glaciers of Mount Machray, the trail descends through heaps of moraine. The trail disappears for about 400m through meadows but continues north. Blazed trail enters forest to arrive at the outflow of a lake rimmed by small crags and the Colonel Pass campsite (1840, 3.2, f9).

Colonel Pass campsite to Colonel Creek trail junction
(6.6km, 136m up, 552m down)

The route goes west 500m over the pass completely under forest cover, crossing the provincial boundary back into BC and Mount Robson Provincial Park. The descent quickly steepens and has a switchback. It stays on the south side of Colonel Creek, crossing several tributaries. In 2.4km from the pass you reach an area burned by a 1998 forest fire. Fireweed grows in abundance here, as in other burned areas. Recent trail maintenance has improved the route but it is still easy to lose and slow going. Continue down the moderate descent to the Colonel Creek ford (1600, 3.4, f10). The GDT follows the north bank of the creek and is still in rough shape. If you lose the trail, return to the creek bank to find it again. In 3km the trail veers to the north, away from Colonel Creek, and in 200m more meets the Colonel Creek trail junction (1415, 3.2, f11). There is a single, burnt sign at the junction. The old route continues northwest to a ford of the Moose River: Trio campsite is 1.5km farther.

SEGMENT 30 – Colonel Creek trail junction to Mount Robson visitor information centre (61.3km)

Difficult hiking on poor trail and cross-country with several serious river fords. Horses permitted. Bikes prohibited. Dogs not permitted overnight on Berg Lake Trail.

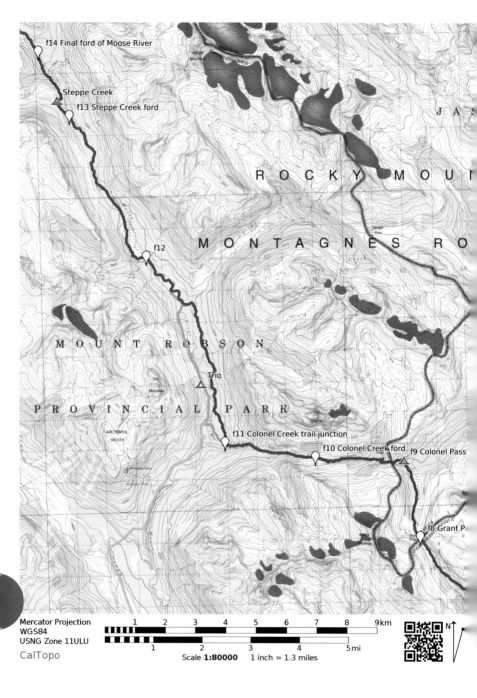

f14 Final ford of Moose River

Steppe Creek
f13 Steppe Creek ford

f12

R O C K Y   M O U

J A S

M O N T A G N E S   R O

M O U N T   R O B S O N

Trio

P R O V I N C I A L   P A R K

ARCTOMYS
VALLEY

f11 Colonel Creek trail junction

f10 Colonel Creek ford   f9 Colonel Pass

f8 Grant P

Mercator Projection
WGS84
USNG Zone 11ULU
CalTopo

| 1 | 2 | 3 | 4 | 5 | 6 | 7 | 8 | 9 km |

| 1 | 2 | 3 | 4 | 5 mi |

Scale **1:80000**   1 inch = 1.3 miles

N↑

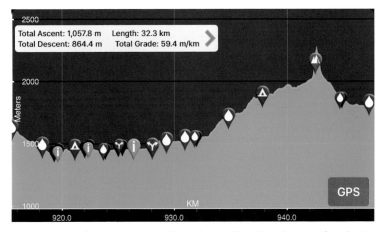

Total Ascent: 1,057.8 m   Length: 32.3 km
Total Descent: 864.4 m   Total Grade: 59.4 m/km

The elevation profile is up to the North Boundary Trail junction , the start of Section G.

Prepare to get wet. Several waist-deep fords characterize the hiking along the upper Moose Valley. You should definitely save the Moose River and Steppe Creek fords for later in the season when much of the runoff has already dissipated. When the circulation in your extremities resumes a few kilometres beyond the last ford, you will experience the climb over stunning Moose Pass that makes the whole segment so worthwhile. The pass is famous for its abundance of wildflowers and terrific views.

Maps: 83 E/2 Resplendent Creek and 83 E/3 Mount Robson.

Jurisdictions: Mount Robson Provincial Park (BC Parks) and Jasper National Park.

South access: Drive the Yellowhead Highway 16 to a gravel access road 29km west of the Jasper National Park west gate and 3km east of the Moose Lake boat launch. Turn north onto the gravel road and drive a short distance to the end. Walk across the railway tracks and follow the road to the right. Soon you arrive at the Moose River trail and turn left. From here it is 22km to the GDT at waypoint f11.

North access: Drive to the Kinney Lake Road intersection near the Mount Robson visitor centre, 80km west of Jasper and 20km east of Tête Jaune Cache, on Yellowhead Highway 16. Turn north and drive to the Berg Lake trailhead at the end of the short road.

Car campgrounds and accommodations: Robson Meadows campground is closest to the visitor centre (just across the highway), and Robson River campground is down an access road, west of the visitor centre by 1km. Both campgrounds are open from May 15 to September 15, have all facilities, and cost $28 per night.

You will need to ford the Moose River up to five times through segment 30.

Camping: *In Jasper National Park on the NBT*: Adolphus (site 81) and Adolphus horse camp (82). Despite the NBT being classified as wildland, you do have to stay in the official, though decommissioned, campsites in this area.

In Mount Robson Provincial Park: Robson Pass, Rearguard, Berg Lake, Marmot, Emperor Falls, Whitehorn, and Kinney Lake. Unlike other provincial parks, you do need to reserve campsites on the popular Berg Lake trail, obtainable at the Mount Robson visitor centre or at discovercamping.ca. Learn more at www.env.gov.bc.ca/bcparks/reserve/reserveBerg.html. Random camping is allowed south of the Smoky River.

Information sources: Jasper trail office, Jasper information centre; Mount Robson visitor centre.

Resupply stations: Mount Robson visitor centre.

Special notes: There used to be a bridge upstream on the Coleman Glacier outflow, but it got washed out in 2014 and there apparently are no plans to replace it. As with glacier-fed streams elsewhere en route, it is best to wait until morning to attempt crossing the Smoky River. Though the ford is marked, it is important to remember that conditions change from year to year. The best place might be upstream or downstream when you attempt it. If you have advice for other hikers, post it as a comment in the Atlas Guides GDT app or send it to the GDTA to post online.

Colonel Creek trail junction to Steppe Creek campsite (14.0km, 267m up, 131m down)

From the Colonel Creek trail junction, still 1.0km away from reaching the Moose River, turn right (north) and follow a restored trail on the east side of the Moose River. The trail crosses a tributary in 3.2km and then enters

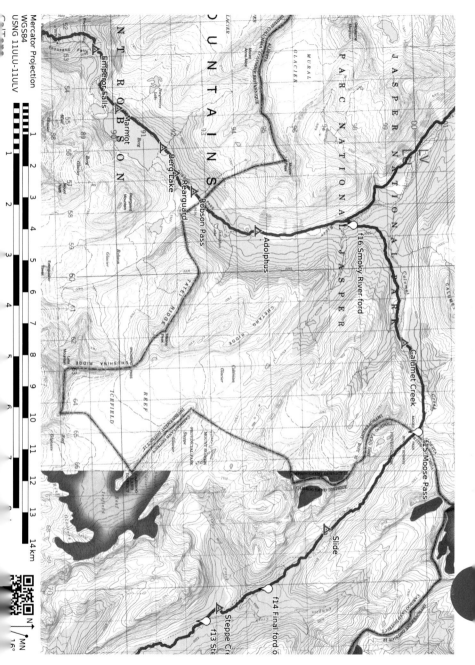

burnt forest, staying at least 200m above the east bank of the river. The trail continues through the burn 2.0km to the Upright Creek ford. From the north bank, the trail turns left and follows the creekbank 300m down to the Moose River but doesn't cross it. Instead, turn north and follow the riverbank 300m farther north to the first ford of the Moose.

Follow the river's west bank through marsh around several bends for 2.0km to the second Moose River ford (1450, 7.8, f12). Follow the horse trail through bog or take the gravel bars next to the river (whichever is easiest). When in doubt, follow the horses, hikers advise. Follow the northern bank as the river briefly turns west. Continue north 1.9km up the east side of the river to the third ford. From here the trail improves on the west side of the river as it enters forest and diverges from the river. In 1.2km you will find the fourth ford, at a sharp bend in the Moose River. The trail follows the east bank for 1.7km to the fifth ford.

Continue 1.1km up the western side of the river, following a path to the first Steppe Creek ford (1545, 5.9, f13). Almost as soon as you emerge from the first ford, the route goes only 300m to the next ford. On the other side is the first Steppe Creek campsite (stay at the next one in 500m instead).

Looking south at the headwaters of the Moose River from Moose Pass.

Moose Pass is vast and well known for its flowers at the height of the season.

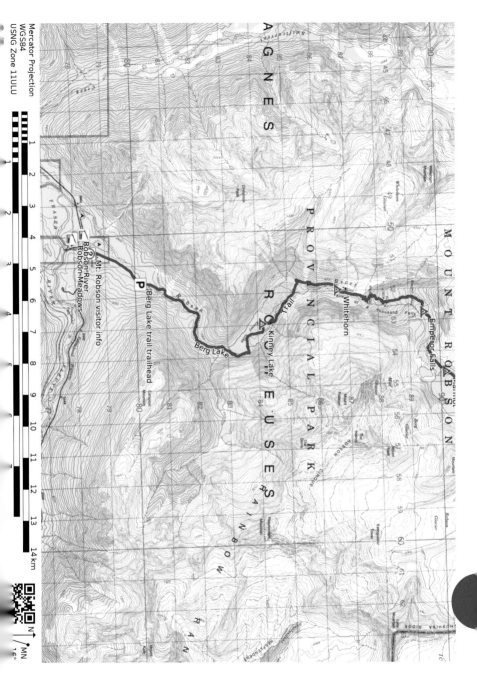

Steppe Creek campsite to Moose Pass
(10.1km, 762m up, 64m down)

After the trail fords Steppe Creek for the third and final time, in another 500m you reach the Steppe Creek campsite, well used by equestrians and in better condition than the lower one. The trail is in better shape from here to the pass. The route ascends steeply through forest over a ridge and then approaches the Moose River again in 1.9km and comes to the final ford (1680, 2.7, f14) of the river. Fair trail brings you to the Slide campsite in 3.0km, near timberline. A horse camp sits at 1870m near the eastern end of a lake that can be accessed by way of a spur trail. Good trail brings you up what appears to be a false pass from the NOBO hiker's perspective. The route reaches Moose Pass (2140, 7.7, f15) in a wide meadow on the Great Divide that separates BC from Alberta and Mount Robson Provincial Park from Jasper National Park.

Moose Pass to North Boundary/Mount Robson trail junction
(8.2, 29m up, 653m down)

Moose Pass sits astride a gigantic alpine meadow well known for its abundance of wildflowers. The trail is in good condition over the pass. It descends to the west-southwest and touches Calumet Creek in 2.4km. The trail stays on the south side of a huge gravel wash at first and then cuts down through the middle of it, likely disappearing until you reach the line of trees downstream – look for reflective yellow diamonds as you near the trees. After fording a substantial tributary in 2.1km more, the trail enters the forest (at the line of trees already mentioned). The faint path diverges from Calumet Creek, contours to the south through forest, and descends to a point near the Smoky River flood plain where you leave the good trail (1615, 7.8, f16). Turn right and walk southwest over the gravel bars to choose the best place to ford. There used to be a bridge 400m upstream at Yates Torrent, over the Coleman Glacier outflow, but it washed away in 2014 and isn't scheduled to be replaced. BC Parks Mount Robson is looking for funding to replace this bridge but it would be very expensive for an engineered solution. Walking up there to see if the bridge is back in place probably isn't worth the effort – you certainly can't ford there. Check the GDTA website or the Jasper trail office in advance for updates.

The Smoky River ford is best in the early morning when the glacial water subsides to its lowest point – it does subside overnight. Be careful and aim southwest, across the gravel flats. Yellow blazes mark the best ford. On the other side of the ford, look for a short trail that leads up to a junction with North Boundary Trail (NBT). All told, this junction is only 400m from waypoint f16, on the other side of the Smoky River.

North Boundary trail junction to Mount Robson visitor information centre (29.0, 550m up, 1347m down)

The Berg Lake trail is not only worth the substantial side trip for those picking up a resupply, but also a very fitting northern terminus for those completing their journeys here. Turn left at the NBT junction and follow good trail 3.2km to the decommissioned Adolphus #81 campsite and horse camp #82, still in Jasper National Park. Go another 2.0km to the park boundary and final crossing of the Great Divide (for many hikers). The Robson Pass campsite is 600m past the boundary, nearly at the toe of an enormous glacier that

The author gets lucky and crosses the Smoky River on a sturdy log at the end of segment 30. This can be a very challenging ford.

Mounts Rearguard and Robson above Adolphus Lake.

Mount Robson busy generating its own weather over Berg Lake.

wraps its way down from Mount Robson. Rearguard campsite, described as a quiet camp with only five sites, is 1.0km farther, near the glacial out-flow. The Berg Lake campsite is another 1.0km along the trail, on the edge of the colourful lake. It is likely the busiest of all seven of the campsites on the Berg Lake trail. Continuing along the northern lakeshore, you arrive at Marmot campsite in 2.0km, near the lake's outflow – also described as quiet. The trail follows the head of the Robson River around a gravel wash to the Emperor Falls campsite at 1635m in 2.8km. From there the trail plunges into the valley below. It passes Emperor Falls on switchbacks, reaching Whitehorn campsite at 1135m in 4.4km. In another 1.8km the trail comes to an immense gravel wash and continues 1.6km to Kinney Lake campsite at 980m elevation. The trail continues 6.4km through an old-growth cedar forest to the Berg Lake trailhead after crossing a bridge over the Robson River. From there it is 2.2km to the Mount Robson visitor information centre, just off the Yellowhead Highway 16.

Section G: *Mount Robson trail junction to the Kakwa Lake trailhead*

Segments 31–34, 182.2 km

Location	Near waypoint	NOBO km	SOBO km
Smoky River ford	f16	953.2	180.0
Adolphus #81 campsite (Jasper NP)*	f16	953.2	180.0
Adolphus horse camp #82 (Jasper NP)*	f16	953.2	180.0
Wolverine North #80 campsite (Jasper NP)	g1	959.3	173.9
Timothy Slides horse camp #79 (Jasper NP)	g2	968.7	164.5
Chown Creek #77 campsite (Jasper NP)	g2	972.4	160.8
Chown Creek horse camp #78 (Jasper NP)*	g2	972.4	160.8
Bess Pass	g3	979.1	154.1
Jackpine Pass campsite	g5	984.3	148.9
Blueberry Lake campsite	g6	996.6	136.6
Jackpine River trail junction	g8	1003.1	130.1
Jackpine alternate N junction	g9	1020.8	112.4
Pauline Creek campsite	g12	1031.3	101.9
Morkill campsite	g15	1048.2	85.0
Casket Creek campsite	g19	1067.9	65.3
Sheep Creek campsite	g21	1074.3	58.9
Kakwa Lake campsite	g28	1104.4	28.8
Buchanan Creek campsite	g29	1121.6	11.6
Bastille Creek trailhead for Kakwa PP	g29	1133.2	0.0

Introduction:

This northernmost section of the Great Divide Trail offers a superlative wilderness experience. It is remote, relatively untravelled and a challenge to navigate. You will brush shoulders with hanging glaciers, waterfalls, and the magnificent peaks that these forces carve. The subtle hiking trail may fade out, forcing you to use your navigational equipment. You may choose to forge your own way on the lengthy alternate route. Presented with the opportunity to test your resolve, endurance, and wilderness skills, you will undoubtedly experience the pinnacle of backcountry travel in Section G.

This section starts on the North Boundary trail at a point two thirds of the way through Section F. It departs at the Mount Robson trail junction and stays in Jasper National Park. It then leaves the park over Bess Pass for the Willmore Wilderness at the head of the Jackpine River. After this narrow valley and its moose-filled wetlands, the trail makes a remarkable

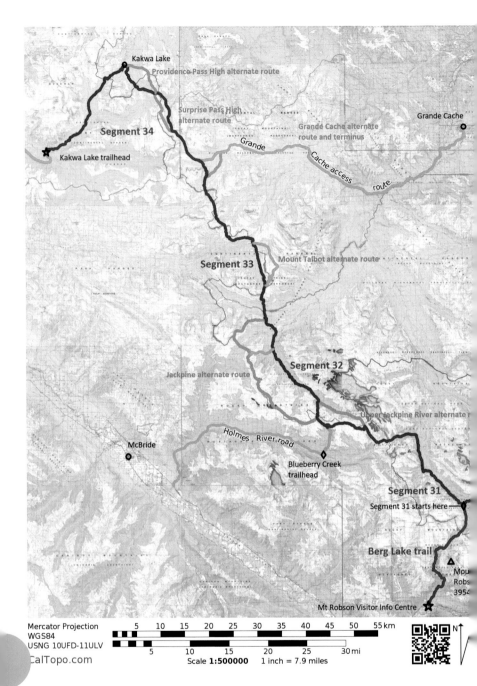

Kakwa Lake

Providence Pass High alternate route

Surprise Pass High
alternate route

Grande Cache alternate
route and terminus

Grande Cache

Segment 34

Grande

Kakwa Lake trailhead

Cache access

route

Mount Talbot alternate route

Segment 33

Jackpine alternate route

Segment 32

Upper Jackpine River alternate r

Holmes River road

McBride

Blueberry Creek
trailhead

Segment 31

Segment 31 starts here

Berg Lake trail

Mou
Robs
395

Mt Robson Visitor Info Centre

Mercator Projection
WGS84
USNG 10UFD-11ULV
CalTopo.com

5   10   15   20   25   30   35   40   45   50   55 km

5   10   15   20   25   30 mi

Scale **1:500000**   1 inch = 7.9 miles

N

high-level traverse that criss-crosses the Divide numerous times before reaching Kakwa Lake Provincial Park in BC. The aptly named Providence Pass will deliver you to Kakwa Lake.

The Great Divide Trail ends in Kakwa Provincial Park, not because the Continental Divide suddenly drops into oblivion or the trail ends, but because Kakwa Lake, as difficult an access as it is, is the last access for the next 200km northwest to Monkman Provincial Park. Adventurous navigators who want to go to the Monkman will face even greater route-finding challenges. The trail only goes as far as Moonias Pass, north of Jarvis Lakes. From there you are on your own. Beyond the Monkman, the Canadian Rockies take a siesta, with lower intervening passes and fewer glaciers past the Peace Reach of Williston Reservoir. The northern Rockies in the Muskwa–Kechika region would be the eventual destination of such a route, ending at the Liard River, where the Canadian Rocky Mountain range ends. My explorations in that park showed me a wilderness that looks much like the GDT would have looked two centuries ago, with herds of bison, a thriving grizzly bear population, and caribou.

Strongly consider taking the Jackpine alternate. This route stays in the alpine and avoids all the swampy terrain that the lower route goes through. Another alternate stays in the alpine from Surprise Pass to Providence Pass and beyond to Kakwa Lake with the same advantage of avoiding the muddy horse trail below. These alternate routes are largely cross-country. They require more effort but they deserve your consideration when planning your itinerary. If you decide to take advantage of these alternates, you will need more time, owing to the extra distance and elevation gain and loss involved.

Expansive meadows and gentle ridges characterize the Willmore Wilderness. You will find an ease of travel here like nowhere else on the GDT. While you could never hike the Continental Divide through the main ranges of Banff and Jasper national parks, you can walk the Divide nearly all the way through Willmore Wilderness Park. The timberline being 300m lower at this latitude than near the southern terminus of the GDT is a further boon to foot travel.

I caution SOBO thru-hikers against beginning their journey too early in the season. They could face immeasurable difficulties owing to remnant snow and high levels of meltwater. The best time to hike this section is in August and September after the first frosts start killing off the hungry bug populations and slowing the glacier-fed streams. While August is a safe month for backcountry travel in the Rockies, September is even better if summer conditions prevail for an extra month. Hikers should keep in mind, though, that snowfall can white out the alpine and cover the trail at any time. When I walked over Jackpine Pass on August 6, a storm had deposited up to 10cm of new snow, making the higher alternate unfeasible and the lower route a quagmire.

Equestrians maintain much of the trail in this section, and horse trail is not always hiker friendly. The five fords of the Moose River in Section F are a good example of that. In more than one place, equestrians have forged the most expedient trail, which follows the creekbed. It is easy to lose track of the less used portions of the trail, especially through soggy meadows. Good route-finding skills are necessary – not just orienteering, but snooping around for where the path continues!

The remote and special places of this section provide an excellent opportunity to encounter wildlife. Bears, wolves, wolverines, caribou, and moose exist in greater populations in these vast protected areas than in the southern Canadian Rockies.

Including the Berg Lake trail access, Section G is still the longest section and the soul of the Great Divide Trail. From Mount Robson to Kakwa Lake, you will not cross one road, seismic line, power line, reservoir, or permanent settlement. Human artifacts largely disappear. Wildlife probably accounts for the majority of trail usage.

In this edition of the guidebook, I include the 29km road walk from Kakwa Lake down to the trailhead. In all likelihood, unless you have made prior arrangements, you will have to walk much of the 73.5km Walker Creek FSR to reach Yellowhead Highway 16, because there is little traffic on this remote gravel road. Still, the extended northern terminus is worth the extra effort.

SEGMENT 31 – North Boundary trail junction to Bess Pass (28.1km)

Easy walking on excellent trail with an easy cross-country hike but potentially difficult ford. Horses permitted. No bikes.

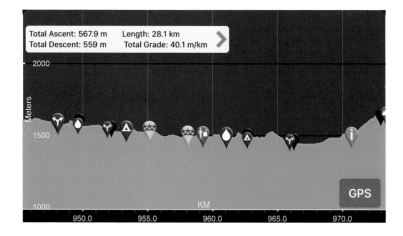

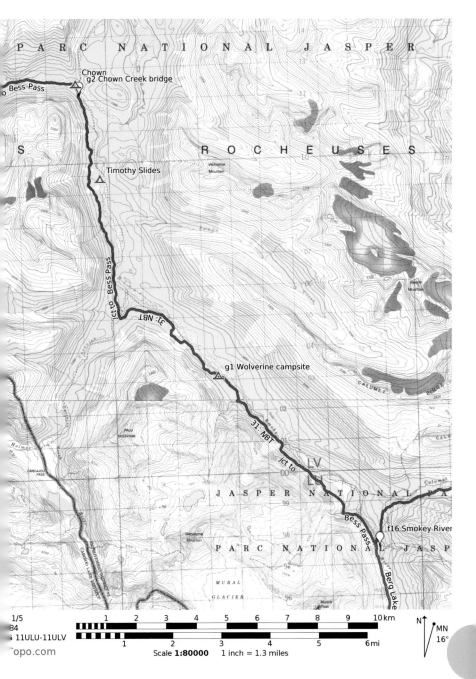

1/5
84
11ULU-11ULV
opo.com

Scale **1:80000**   1 inch = 1.3 miles

N↑ MN 16°

This remote corner of Jasper National Park sees few backcountry travellers despite the good condition of the trail and campsites. The GDT follows over 20km of the now decommissioned North Boundary Trail (NBT) that spans 170km across northern Jasper National Park. I hope enough people will travel this route to keep it passable. The NBT used to be a favoured backcountry destination for backpackers.

Maps: 83 E/3 Mount Robson and 83 E/6 Twintree Lake.

Jurisdiction: Jasper National Park.

South access: Drive to the Kinney Lake Road intersection near the Mount Robson visitor centre, 80km west of Jasper and 20km east of Tête Jaune Cache, on Yellowhead Highway 16. Turn north and drive to the Berg Lake trailhead at the end of the short road.

North access: Turn north on the Holmes River forest service road on Yellowhead Highway 16, 10km south of McBride, just east of where the highway crosses the Holmes River, and 40km north of Tête Jaune Cache. Drive 43.3km up this gravel road, staying alongside the river. Hike 7km on the Blueberry trail to Blueberry Lake, on the GDT, 17.5km north of Bess Pass. The road is suitable for most vehicles, including RVs, but you should check with the Mount Robson visitor centre or the McBride Community Forest Corporation (which maintains the campgrounds on the Holmes River) before planning to drive so far up this road. There is a porcupine advisory for this access: you should bring enough chicken wire to surround the undercarriage of your vehicle if you plan to leave it there for more than a day.

Car campgrounds and accommodations: Robson Meadows campground is closest to the visitor centre (just across the highway), and Robson River campground is down an access road, 1km west of the visitor centre. Both campgrounds are open from May 15 to September 15, have all facilities, and cost $28 per night. There are two campgrounds near the start of the Holmes River road.

Camping: *In Jasper National Park on the NBT*: Adolphus (site 81), Adolphus horse camp (82), Wolverine North (80), Timothy Slides horse camp (79), and Chown Creek (77). Despite the NBT being classified as wildland, you do have to stay in the official, though decommissioned, campsites.

In Mount Robson Provincial Park: Robson Pass, Rearguard, Berg Lake, Marmot, Emperor Falls, Whitehorn, and Kinney Lake. Unlike other provincial parks, you do need to reserve campsites on the popular Berg Lake trail, obtainable at the Mount Robson visitor centre or online at discovercamping.ca. Learn more at www.env.gov.bc.ca/bcparks/reserve/reserveBerg.html.

Information sources: Jasper trail office, Jasper information centre; Mount Robson visitor centre.

Resupply stations: None.

Special notes: In previous editions of this guidebook, I indicated an access trail at the end of the Holmes River road up to Bess Pass. It is no longer viable.

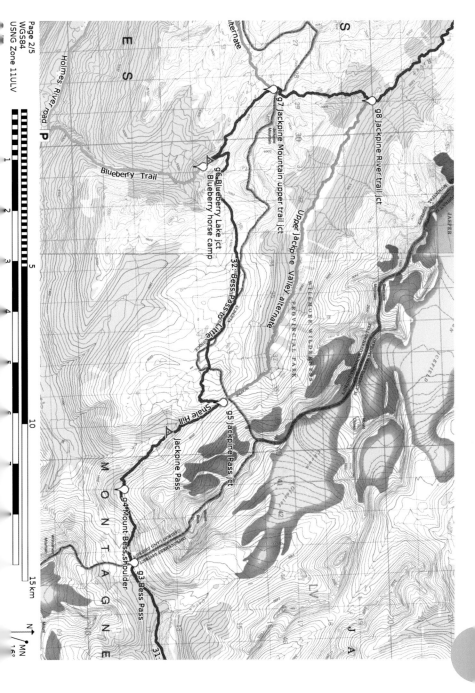

Mount Bess and ice-covered Mount Chown from the gravel wash beside Chown Creek.

Drying out after an unintended swim in the very, very cold Chown Creek.

North Boundary Trail junction to Wolverine campsite (8.3km, 130m up, 229m down)

Thru-hikers who desire a view of Mount Robson can turn left at the North Boundary Trail (NBT) junction, hike to the Adolphus Lake campsite in 2.2km and to Robson Pass in another 3km. The GDT turns right at the North Boundary/Mount Robson trail junction. Staying on the western side of the Smoky River, the trail follows the well-maintained NBT downstream to a horse trail junction. Hikers keep to the left, on the hiking trail. In 2.0km the horse trail rejoins the hiking one. The horse trail breaks off again in another 2.0km, just before a bridged tributary crossing. Hikers keep left and go over the bridge. In 1.4km more, you reach the decommissioned Wolverine campsite (1525, 8.7, g1).

Wolverine campsite to Chown Creek bridge (12.9km, 209m up, 288m down)

Continue down the Smoky River bank, passing a collapsed bridge over a tributary in 1.8km. The trail diverges from the river to ford Carcajou Creek in 2.9km more. Find the Wolverine warden cabin 1.2km afterwards. The trail continues due north 1.8km to a creek ford and another 1.7km to the Timothy Slides horse campsite. After the hiking trail diverges once more from the horse trail you arrive in 3.5km to the Chown Creek bridge (1440, 12.9, g2). To get to the Chown Creek campsite, turn right at the junction across the bridge and walk 200m more. If you continued walking along North Boundary Trail straight across the bridge, you would reach the Lower Smoky warden cabin in 3.5km.

Chown Creek bridge to Bess Pass (6.9km, 229m up, 42m down)

From the bridge, the GDT leaves North Boundary Trail for Bess Pass to the west. If the creek is low enough to ford near the bridge, then the best route is across the bridge and to the left. Walk up the gravel flats on the north side of Chown Creek. At 2km there is a bottleneck in the valley where it is necessary to enter the forest briefly on steep banks. After another 2km of hiking up the gravel flood plain, ford Chown Creek above a major confluence with a glacier-fed tributary. Follow the tributary bank upstream, where the evident trail with an orange metal marker diverges from the gravel wash and climbs into thickening forest. If you chose not to cross the bridge and instead followed the route along the south side of Chown Creek, aim for the same trail with the yellow marker, where the main route enters the trees.

The rough trail ascends southwest through forest, generally following the north bank of the tributary. You will frequently encounter bushy areas on the trail until a final steep climb reaches a subalpine meadow on signed Bess Pass (1625, 6.9, g3). The pass is on the Divide between Jasper National Park and BC's Headwaters Forest District. A little-used campsite sits on the edge of the meadow.

SEGMENT 32 – Bess Pass to Little Shale Hill (50.0km)

Very difficult hiking with cross-country travel and route-finding challenges. Horses permitted. Bikes permitted but not practical.

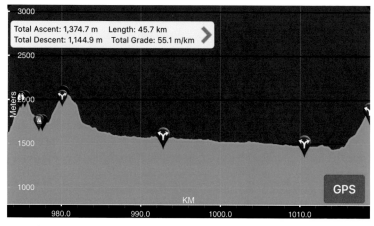

Total Ascent: 1,374.7 m   Length: 45.7 km
Total Descent: 1,144.9 m   Total Grade: 55.1 m/km

Note: this elevation profile is the main route combined with the Upper Jackpine River alternate.

Without a doubt, this is the most adventurous stretch of the GDT. Nestled between dubious access points far from anywhere, the route follows the Jackpine River through the recesses of the Willmore Wilderness. Largely a cross-country hike, this segment is straightforward enough to navigate but challenges your endurance. There are plenty of opportunities to enjoy the excellent views of the surrounding peaks. Bess, Barricade, Lucifer, Saurian, and Draco peaks are substantial mountains, girdled by hanging glaciers and waterfalls. With a lengthy alternate route tracing the Divide, you can choose to see these and other peaks at eye-level. This lengthy crest hike depends on your route-finding skills and requires greater effort but rewards bountifully.

Maps: 83 E/6 Twintree Lake, 83 E/5 Chalco Mountain and 83 E/12 Pauline Creek.

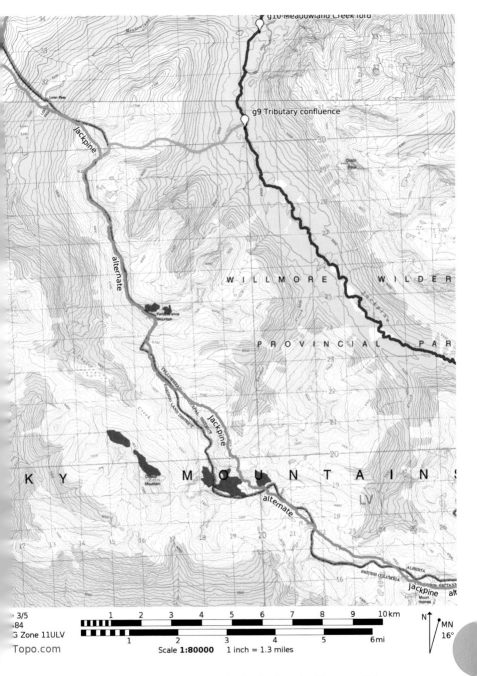

Jurisdictions: Headwaters Forest District (BC) and Willmore Wilderness Park (Alberta Parks).

Other access: Turn north on the Holmes River forest service road from

Yellowhead Highway 16, 10km south of McBride, just east of where the highway crosses the Holmes River, and 40km north of Tête Jaune Cache. Drive 43.3km to the Blueberry Creek trailhead. Hike 7km uphill to Blueberry Lake and campsite, which is 17.5km north of Bess Pass, on the main route of the GDT. The road is suitable for most vehicles, including RVs but you should check with the Mount Robson visitor centre or the McBride Community Forest Corporation (which maintains the campgrounds on this FSR) before planning to drive so far up this road.

North access: Drive 12km west on the Holmes River FSR and turn left (north) on the Chalco Creek road. Continue another 15km to as close to the end of the gravel road as possible. Continue hiking up the logging road to the east 4km and then follow it north 5km up Chalco Creek to Loren Pass at the head of Meadowland Creek to join the Jackpine alternate route north of Loren Lake on the Divide. You need a high-clearance vehicle to make it all the way up this road.

Car campgrounds and accommodations: The Beaver River Falls and Beaver River campgrounds are just off Highway 16, on the Holmes forest service road. From McBride proceed east on Highway 16 for 10km. Turn north on Holmes FSR, just east of the Holmes River, and proceed 500m and 1km to find these sites, on the left. The second one is past a gate. There are no fees.

Camping: Random camping. The campsites en route have flat areas for a fire ring and pitching a tent, nothing more.

Information sources: Mount Robson visitor centre.

Resupply stations: None.

Special notes: This is one of the most remote segments of the GDT. You face at the very least a three-day hike to the nearest travelled road if something goes wrong. Carefully consider your backpacking experience and be sure of your skills before attempting to hike this segment. There is a porcupine advisory for either access: you should bring enough chicken wire to surround the undercarriage of your vehicle if you plan to leave it there for more than a day.

Bess Pass to Jackpine Pass trail junction (7.3km, 699m up, 287m down)

Over Bess Pass there is a trail that curves around to the northwest, descends briefly, and then climbs to a waterfall in 700m. The path becomes very steep and brushy as it continues uphill 400m beside a drainage. The ascent eases, and in 900m you reach a highpoint (1735, 2.0, g4) on the southern ridge of enormous Mount Bess, above timberline. Cairns mark the way.

There is a great view from here of the upper Holmes River valley. A brief, steep descent takes you down to the west and then contours northwest to a creek crossing below another waterfall in 2.3km, below the hanging glaciers of Mount Bess. The trail goes through sparse forest, levels out through subalpine clearings, and in 800m reaches the Jackpine Pass campsite. Walk through the Jackpine Pass campsite to a trail that starts climbing east of the creek. A moderate ascent brings you 2.2km into the alpine and soon reaches the Jackpine Pass trail junction (2025, 5.3, g5) marked with a cairn. From here the main

A waterfall below Mount Bess, between Bess Pass and Jackpine Pass.

Holmes River headwaters.

Majestic Jackpine Pass and the start of the Upper Jackpine River alternate route as seen from the main route.

The upper Jackpine River valley as seen from the main route.

Looking over the meadows east of Jackpine Mountain toward Mount Bess.

route turns left. A rocky trail continues up to Jackpine Pass on the Great Divide and is worth the 600m side trip to see it if you aren't taking the Upper Jackpine River alternate route.

UPPER JACKPINE RIVER ALTERNATE ROUTE – 12.4KM INSTEAD OF 16.6KM (103M UP, 553M DOWN)

The only reason to use this alternate route is if the weather is beyond terrible and you don't want to expose yourself to lightning or whiteouts on the higher main route. This alternate route climbs over the incredibly scenic Jackpine Pass and descends on trail below timberline to the northwest. The route stays on the east side of a tributary until it emerges onto gravel bars of the Jackpine River in 1.8km. The already faint trail disappears. As a horse trail, the route down the Jackpine is the riverbed and surrounding gravel bars. Hikers should follow the southern riverbank to avoid a difficult ford many kilometres downstream. The gravel bars permit efficient walking for only a short distance before the river enters a gorge. Unless the river is low enough to permit walking downstream, you face a thick 1km bushwhack above the southern riverbank. As the river emerges from the gorge, the gravel bars disappear and are replaced with boggy terrain. Again the best hiking route is a faint trail that follows the consolidated southern riverbank. The route reaches waypoint g7 at the confluence south of Mount Lucifer and directly north of Jackpine Mountain, on the main route.

End Upper Jackpine River alternate route

Jackpine Pass trail junction to the Jackpine River trail junction (16.7km)

From the trail junction 300m before Jackpine Pass, look for a faint trail going southwest. Turn left and follow this path 700m up and over a broad meadow. Contour around the southern flank of the unnamed peak to the west of Jackpine Pass. Follow the Divide west-northwest, passing above a shallow lake in 2.3km. In another 2.4km the path angles to the west and then southwest, staying south of the next unnamed peak on the Divide. In 4.8km more the route reaches the Blueberry Lake campsite (1950, 10.2, g6) after a long switchback. See 'Other access' at the start of this segment.

A faint trail descends through sparse forest northwest into the valley below Jackpine Mountain and follows the drainage uphill to an important trail junction (2005, 3.0, g7). The Jackpine alternate route goes left (see the description below) and the main route turns right. The GDT main route leaves the drainage, heading north, and continues 400m uphill to the unnamed pass directly northwest of Jackpine Mountain. It crosses the Divide and then descends through the subalpine to the north another 3.1km, following the creek to where it flows into the Jackpine River (1560, 3.5, g8). This is where the Upper Jackpine River alternate rejoins the main route.

Jackpine Mountain and Blueberry Lake as seen from the start of the lengthy but worthwhile Jackpine alternate route.

JACKPINE ALTERNATE ROUTE – 41.6KM INSTEAD OF 30.7KM

Turn left at the trail junction and head 1.7km southwest, cross-country, to a 2205m highpoint. The route goes down and angles to the west, paralleling the Divide toward Mount Holmes. The trail then climbs to a pass at 2290m in another 1.8km, crossing the Divide. The route descends west-northwest, crossing the Divide, to a point between two lakes north of Mount Holmes. From here go northwest, gently at first and then steeply into the headwaters of Castor Creek, crossing the Divide into Alberta and reaching a low point of 1910m. The route continues west-northwest and ascends to a ridge crest (0320225 E, 5918954 N) at 2439m in 7.1km.

From this highpoint, descend northwest into the headwaters of Spider Creek in the Willmore Wilderness. On the descent, you will pass the north side of a large tarn and then pick your way down steep talus between cliff bands. In 3.0km you reach a low point of 1910m between feeder streams of Spider Creek, still in the alpine. The route goes northwest and steeply uphill to reach the Divide (0317714 E, 5921971 N) in 1.9km at an elevation of 2190m. From here the route-finding is less difficult because you can walk on the crest of the Great Divide north over several summits.

Follow the ridge crest toward the next summit. Instead of climbing over the sharp peak, however, drop off the ridge to the east in 2.1km and contour around its eastern side to a saddle in 700m. Once again on the Divide, at the saddle, follow the line of least resistance north-northeast to the 2370m summit of Mount Perseverance in 1.0km.

Follow the crest northward for 7.0km more over seven peaks. (Between summits 3 and 4, which are very close together, aim for the narrow notch on summit 4 and easily scramble up and over the peak.) At the seventh peak you are still on the Divide, far above Loren Pass. There is no need to go over the final two summits on the Divide, separated by a col. Instead, either commit to Loren Pass by turning left, or to the unnamed creek drainage that leads 5.2km east down to the Jackpine River, by turning to the right. Hikers describe the rest of the Jackpine alternate route to Little Shale Hill as being difficult at best. The scramble over Adventist Peak is doable but dangerous, in the words of others. In the Atlas Guides app, River Taig suggests turning right and descending cross-country to the Jackpine River to rejoin the main route.

To stay on the Jackpine alternate, descend to the 1540m Loren Pass in 3.0km by first going down into a bowl to the north. Cross the drainage and then contour northwest to regain the Divide on the western ridge of a prominent summit. Follow the Divide downhill through gathering forest to Loren Pass. A collapsed cabin is at the northern end of Loren Lake and still makes for a convenient campsite. The Jackpine alternate route continues northwest, following the Divide up the opposite side of the valley.

Aim for the ridgeline summit on the Divide at 2200m, 3.0km from Loren Pass. It is a steep climb and cross-country. Follow the ridge crest northeast over the next summit. Be careful: there is a 200m-wide unstable boulder field on the other side of Adventist Peak until you reach a cliff band. Look for a break in the cliff and continue down the remaining, easy ridge crest to rejoin the GDT on Little Shale Hill in 9.2km at waypoint g11.

End Jackpine alternate route

Jackpine River trail junction to a tributary confluence and junction (17.7km, 112m up, 209m down)

At the confluence, ford the Jackpine River to the east side and continue 100m to the treeline. Turn left and follow the treeline downstream to the north. Cross a major tributary in 1.6km, still on the northeast side of the Jackpine River. (Maps for this area show an equestrian trail that stays in treeline on the northeast side of the river all the way to a ford below the confluence with Meadowland Creek, but I never found it.) Ford the river three times over the next 2.0km, ending up on the southwest bank. The route leaves the open marsh and enters forest in 1.6km more. Cross Castor Creek in 2.0km just above its confluence with the river. Staying on the southeast bank, the route crosses Spider Creek 4.1km farther on. Keep following the same side of the Jackpine River downstream, occasionally shortcutting through forest where the river follows a large bend to the east. In another 6.3km you reach a tributary confluence (1460, 17.7, g9). If you were to turn left here and follow the tributary upstream to the southwest, you would reach the Jackpine alternate route in 5.2km, southeast of Loren Lake. (River Taig recommends that SOBO hikers follow the tributary stream from here for 5.2km to start the Jackpine alternate route in order to avoid the dangerous scramble over Adventist Peak and the Loren Pass bushwhack. NOBO hikers would rejoin the main route at this point if they heeded this advice.)

A decaying trapper's cabin on the Jackpine River where the GDT diverges from the river at last.

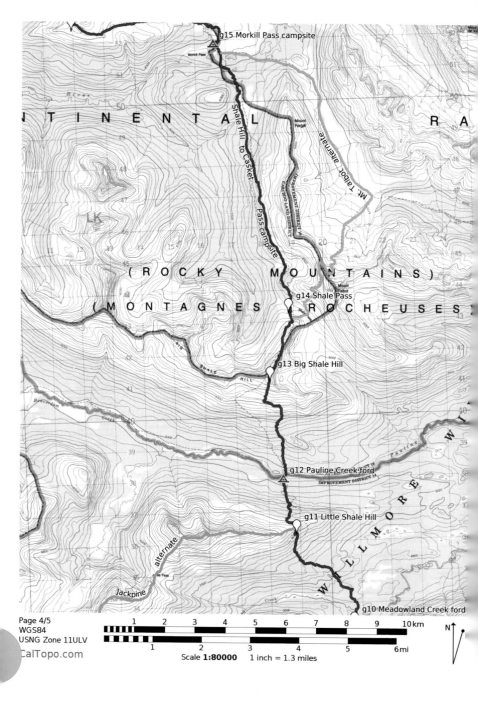

g15 Morkill Pass campsite

Morkill Pass

INTINENTAL RA

Mount Forget

Mt. Talbot alternate

(R O C K Y   M O U N T A I N S)

(M O N T A G N E S   R O C H E U S E S)

g14 Shale Pass

g13 Big Shale Hill

g12 Pauline Creek ford

g11 Little Shale Hill

g10 Meadowland Creek ford

Jackpine

alternate

W
E
L
L
M
O
R
E

Shale Hill to Casket Pass campsite

| 1 | 2 | 3 | 4 | 5 | 6 | 7 | 8 | 9 | 10km |

| 1 | 2 | 3 | 4 | 5 | 6mi |

Scale **1:80000**   1 inch = 1.3 miles

N

Tributary confluence and junction to Little Shale Hill (8.3km, 499m up, 96m down)

Follow the western riverbank downstream for another 1.9km to a clearing and old equestrian campsite. This spot is 100m upstream of a prominent cutbank on the Jackpine River. Look for the trail, take a sharp left turn (north), and follow it past a decaying cabin into forest. Tree blazes mark the way through the woods, but it is still easy to lose. Work your way 2.1km over the low ridge to the Meadowland Creek ford (1420, 4.0, g10).

Poor trail disappears through the swamp on the other side of the ford. The route goes northward to the base of a ridge, where trail reappears on drier ground. Although there are some bushy sections, the trail remains in fair shape as it climbs steeply to the ridge crest of Little Shale Hill (1845, 4.3, g11), which is a long ridge of Adventist Peak to the west. The Jackpine alternate route rejoins the main route at this point. (River Taig recommends that SOBO hikers don't attempt going over Adventist Peak, due to the dangerous scramble, but instead continue 9.5km to a tributary confluence, where they can follow that stream 5.2km up to the alternate route.)

SEGMENT 33 – Little Shale Hill to Casket Pass campsite (38.8km)

Difficult hiking on trail over several summits and high passes with some minor route-finding challenges. Horses permitted. Bikes permitted but not practical.

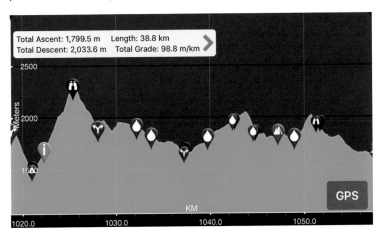

The main attraction of this segment is the high traverse along the Divide over Big Shale Hill and around Morkill Mountain. There is some good trail. All the passes are boggy but beautiful, with incredible views. There is ample opportunity to spot wildlife, and I've talked to more than one hiker who spotted a wolverine along this segment.

Maps: 83 E/12 Pauline Creek and 83 E/13 Dry Canyon.

Jurisdiction: Willmore Wilderness Park (Alberta Parks).

South access: Drive about 12km west on the Holmes River FSR and turn left (north) on the Chalco Creek road. Continue another 15km to as close to the end of the gravel road as possible. Continue hiking up the logging road to the east 4km and then follow it north 5km up Chalco Creek to Loren Pass at the head of Meadowland Creek to join the Jackpine alternate route north of Loren Lake on the Divide. You need a high-clearance vehicle to make it all the way up this road.

North access: I don't recommend using this route as an access to the GDT, because of its length, but it is a well-travelled equestrian route. Drive to Grande Cache on paved Highway 40, 100km north of Hinton, which is on Yellowhead Highway 16. Go 10km north of Grande Cache on Highway 40 and turn left on the Sulphur Gate road. Drive to the end of the road along the Smoky River. Where the road ends, start hiking upstream on the Smoky River horse trail. You ford the Muddywater River and then follow it upstream. The trail refords the river and crosses a subalpine pass to join Sheep Creek. At the creek, you take the Sheep Creek trail up to Casket Pass. This access involves about 60km of hiking but you may prefer finishing your hike here instead of on the Walker Creek FSR.

Car campgrounds and accommodations: Beaver River Falls and the Beaver River campgrounds are just off Highway 16, on the Holmes forest service road. From McBride proceed east on Highway 16 for 10km. Turn north on Holmes FSR, just east of the Holmes River, and proceed 500m and 1km to find these sites, on the left. The second one is past a gate. There are no fees.

Grande Cache is a small town with several campgrounds and B&BS. Inquire locally at the Grande Cache Tourism & Interpretive Centre, 1-780-827-3300 or 1-888-827-3790, grandecache.ca/p/grande-cache-tourism-interpretive-centre.

Camping: Random camping. The campsites en route have flat areas for a fire ring and pitching a tent, nothing more.

Information sources: Mount Robson visitor centre, Switzer Park visitor centre (780-865-5600), albertaparks.ca/willmore, and Grande Cache Tourism & Interpretive Centre.

Resupply stations: None.

Special notes: This is one of the most remote segments of the GDT.

From the crest of Little Shale Hill, the author points toward Big Shale Hill across Pauline Creek below.

The author on the summit of Big Shale Hill, in Willmore Wilderness Park.

A moose antler near Casket Pass welcomes travellers to Alberta's Willmore Wilderness Park.

You face at the very least a three-day hike to the nearest travelled road if something goes wrong. Carefully consider your backpacking experience and be sure of your skills before attempting to hike this section.

Little Shale Hill to Big Shale Hill
(6.6km, 783m up, 392m down)

From Little Shale Hill, you can look north across Pauline Creek and easily see the summit of Big Shale Hill. That's where you are going to next! Steep, tight switchbacks bring the trail down from Little Shale Hill to the Pauline Creek ford (1490, 2.2, g12). The Pauline Creek campsite is on the northern bank, across the ford.

The trail continues due north but is hard to find until you make it about 700m uphill. When in doubt, the trail follows the Divide up to the summit of Big Shale Hill for the first half before jogging to the west. The trail resumes its course toward the peak and then, above treeline, does a long switchback to the west again. A steep ascent brings you to the summit (2270, 4.4, g13) of Big Shale Hill.

Big Shale Hill to Morkill Pass campsite
(12.5km, 267m up, 879m down)

Trail is evident to the north, downslope to the west from the ridge. Traverse the crest line, then descend steeply to Shale Pass (1865, 2.6, f29) and into British Columbia.

MOUNT TALBOT ALTERNATE ROUTE –
14.2KM INSTEAD OF 9.5KM

A GDTA alternate route leaves from Shale Pass and follows switchbacks northwestward up to the northern ridge of Mount Talbot. The route does not go over the summit, but bypasses it by following a ramp up the northeast side of the mountain. Once over the 2190m highpoint on the northeast ridge, the route cuts back, descending steeply to the southeast toward the Mount Talbot summit. After losing elevation, the route resumes a northeast track in the direction of distant Mount de Veber, staying in the alpine as it reaches the pass in 6.5km, directly north of Mount Talbot. From here, if you turned right (south-southeast), it is 7.5km down to the Jackpine River horse trail and another 35km to Grande Cache.

From the pass the route turns north-northwest and follows a drainage downhill through the alpine. At a point about 2km north of Mount Forget, the alternate abruptly turns west at the end of Mount Forget's northern ridge. The route traverses through subalpine for 7.7km over the ridgeline to rejoin the main route 400m before waypoint g15 on Morkill Pass.

End Mount Talbot alternate route

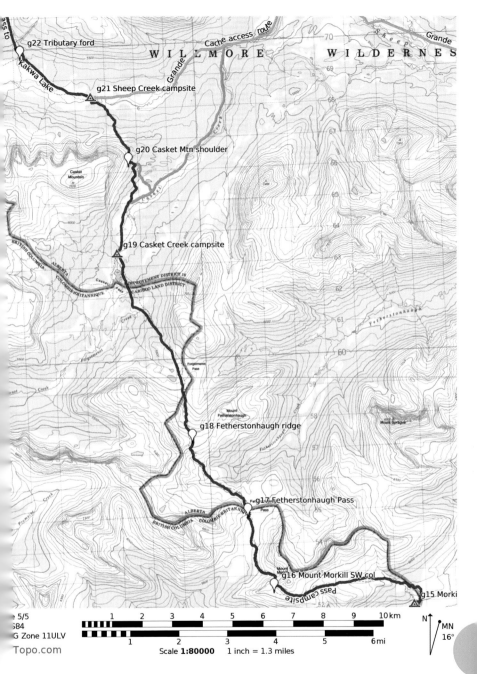

some wet ground. Deep horse prints serve as a good indication of where the route goes. After a brief jaunt into Alberta you reach the Morkill Pass campsite (1660, 9.9, g15). The Mount Talbot alternate route rejoins the main route 400m before this point at a spur trail that goes east to the largest of the several lakes on the pass.

Morkill Pass campsite to Featherstonhaugh Pass (9.3km, 448m up, 282m down)

Good trail starts east of the campsite and follows a minor creek upstream. Within 100m veer north and ford the creek repeatedly as you gradually ascend to an expansive alpine meadow on the Divide. After crossing the meadow westward, follow a drainage steeply at first through subalpine. The ascent eases as you reach timberline. Cross at least two streams before arriving at a col (2020, 6.1, g16) on the southwestern side of Mount Morkill. The trail descends and crosses a creek in 800m. Contour around the west side of Mount Morkill through subalpine patches of forest. The trail turns to the north and gains the western extremity of Featherstonhaugh Pass (1820, 3.2, g17), on the Divide beside a wide meadow.

Featherstonhaugh Pass to Casket Pass campsite (10.4km, 302m up, 481m down)

The trail turns to the northwest, contouring 1.7km to cross Featherstonhaugh Creek at timberline. The trail ascends steeply another 1.8km up to the Mount Featherstonhaugh ridge crest (2050, 3.5, g18). Descend through a wide alpine bowl to the north and ford two creeks. Gently descending to the northwest, you cross the provincial boundary into Alberta and come close to Forgetmenot Pass. The descent, now in sparse forest, levels out as you approach Casket Creek (1640, 6.9, g19) just north of the boggy lake on Casket Pass. The Casket Pass campsite is across the creek. There is another – and by some reports, better – campsite upstream as well.

SEGMENT 34 – Casket Pass to Kakwa Lake trailhead (65.3km)

Difficult hiking over two high passes on often wet trail with minor route-finding challenges. Horses and bikes permitted.

The pleasant hike over Surprise and Providence passes is the cream of the Great Divide Trail. Much of the segment is in the open, either in alpine or subalpine meadows. The trail is in relatively good shape and the scenery splendorous. The shoulder of Casket Mountain spills wildflowers down its slopes in midsummer and you may see caribou feeding on lichens up

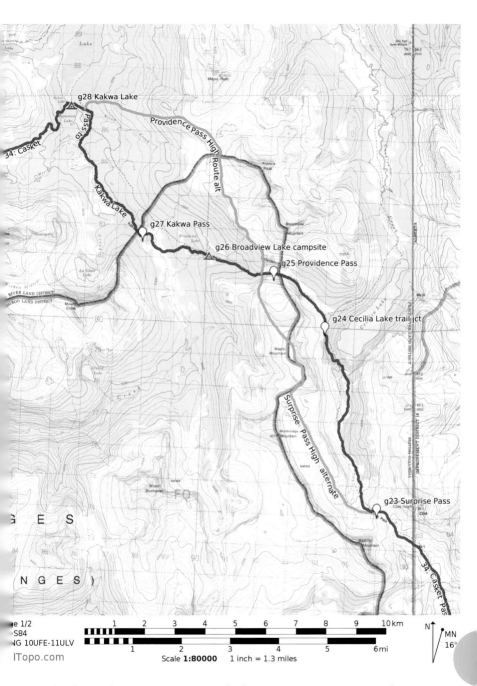

the slopes of Mount Côté. There is a high cross-country traverse to Kakwa
Lake that lets you straddle the Divide for one last time before reaching

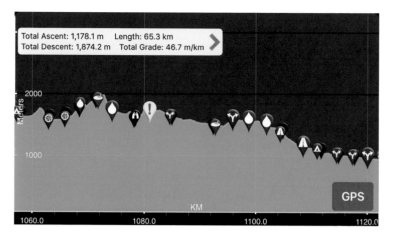

Total Ascent: 1,178.1 m   Length: 65.3 km
Total Descent: 1,874.2 m   Total Grade: 46.7 m/km

the spellbinding lake and the extended northern terminus of the Great Divide Trail.

> *Somehow I didn't know about the cabin open for public use at Kakwa Lake. To discover an immaculate, unlocked cabin, complete with wood stove and dry firewood, and to arrive there after a horrendous day just as the rain began falling again, was the best surprise I could have had, and turned my worst final day into my best final night. As the rain beat down all night, I don't know if it ever got below 70 degrees F with the fire roaring inside the dry, cozy cabin. Wow.*

> —Li Brannfors, in an email describing his 2012 thru-hike.

Maps: 83 E/13 Dry Canyon, 93 H/16 Mount Sir Alexander and 93 I/1 Jarvis Lakes.

Jurisdictions: Willmore Wilderness Park (Alberta Parks) and Kakwa Provincial Park (BC Parks).

South access: Drive 5.8km north on Highway 40 from Grande Cache. Turn left just past the bridge onto Sulphur Gates Road. Pass the signed trailhead for Mount Stearn in 3.5km, across from a gravel pit parking area. Continue another 2.2km to the end of the road, where there is a trailhead parking area. From here the trail follows the northern bank of the Smoky River west-southwest to its confluence with the Muddywater River. Cross the Muddywater above the confluence and follow the south side of the river northwest, crossing it again and cutting through Dry Canyon to Sheep Creek. Turn west after crossing Sheep Creek and continue upstream to reach the GDT at Casket Pass campsite or the Sheep Creek campsite. This

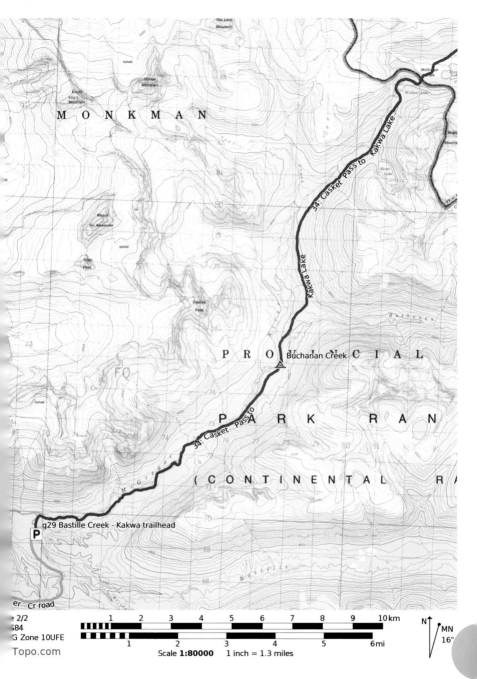

route is 63km of maintained horse trail. If the Smoky River is low enough to ford, you can cross it at the end of Sulphur Gates Road and follow a more direct line into town.

Drive to Grande Cache on paved Highway 40, 100km north of Hinton, which is on Yellowhead Highway 16. Go 10km north of Grande Cache on Highway 40 and turn left on Sulphur Gates Road. Drive to the end of the road along the Smoky River. Where the road ends, start hiking upstream on the Smoky River horse trail. Ford the Muddywater River and then follow it upstream. The trail refords the river and crosses a subalpine pass to join Sheep Creek. At the creek, take the Sheep Creek trail up to Casket Pass. This access involves about 60km of hiking but you may prefer finishing your hike here instead of on the Walker Creek FSR.

North access: To get to Kakwa Lake, follow Yellowhead Highway 16 to 70km north of McBride, BC. Turn east onto the Walker Creek forest service road and follow it 73.5km to the Kakwa Provincial Park trailhead at a gate. The intersection with the highway is well marked and has a typical trail-head information kiosk which describes the conditions of the gravel road. Road conditions vary from year to year, so you should contact the Mount Robson visitor centre or the McBride Community Forest Corporation to see if the road is passable (also check the GDTA website). Currently it is suitable for most vehicles up to km 33.5, but the remaining 40km is rated for high clearance 4-wheel drive only. There is a porcupine advisory for the parking area: you should bring enough chicken wire to surround the undercarriage of your vehicle if you plan to leave it there for more than a day.

Yellowhead Helicopters Inc. services this area from a base in McBride. It wouldn't be cheap but it might work if a group of hikers charter a flight together. See under Contacts, at page 342.

Car campgrounds and accommodations: Grande Cache is a small town with several campgrounds and B&Bs. Inquire locally at the Grande Cache Tourism & Interpretive Centre, 1-780-827-3300 or 1-888-827-3790, grandecache.ca/p/grande-cache-tourism-interpretive-centre.

There are several places to camp on the Walker Creek FSR, including at the Kakwa Provincial Park trailhead.

Camping: Random camping. The campsites en route have flat areas for a fire ring and pitching a tent, nothing more. In 2007 two new cabins replaced the old ones at the southern end of Kakwa Lake. One is for public use and is open to all park users year round, first-come first-served. The cabin has a woodstove, table and bench, accommodations for approximately 10 people with sleeping platforms, and a loft. Please dump grey water into the pit toilet near the cabin.

Information sources: Mount Robson visitor centre, Willmore Wilderness Foundation, and BC Parks (www.env.gov.bc.ca/bcparks/explore/parkpgs/kakwa).

The GDT route is on the right, heading toward Surprise Pass. Bastille Mountain is on the left.

Resupply stations: None.

Special notes: This is one of the most remote segments of the GDT. You face at the very least a three-day hike to the nearest travelled road if something goes wrong. Carefully consider your backpacking experience and be sure of your skills before attempting to hike this section.

Casket Pass campsite to Surprise Pass (14.7km, 557m up, 266m down)

The trail goes through Casket Pass campsite and follows the western bank of Casket Creek downstream through interesting rolling meadows. In 2.0km you encounter a trail junction. NOBO hikers going to Grande Cache would turn right at this point (see the Grande Cache alternate route description below). To stay on the main route, turn left and follow the trail north past a boggy lake. Leaving Casket Creek below, the trail leads 1.7km up a moderate grade to timberline on a northeast ridge of Casket Mountain (1760, 3.7, g20). Of interest, at Intersection Mountain west of Casket Mountain, the provincial boundary stops following the Continental Divide and goes due north. (If you can't find the trail over Casket Ridge, don't panic. You can follow Casket Creek downstream to its confluence with Sheep Creek, turn left and follow Sheep Creek upstream to get back on route.)

The trail descends north-northwest to a long meadow, where it crosses Sheep Creek (1560, 2.5, g21). Very large tree blazes at the edge of the sparse forest mark where the trail resumes. The route enters a large horse campsite on the northern side of the crossing – look for a bench and many cut trees. There is also a junction here, with the Sheep Creek trail on the northern bank of the creek. If you turned right on the Sheep Creek trail, you would travel in the direction of Grande Cache (see the Grande Cache alternate route description below). Turn left on Sheep Creek trail and follow the northern side of Sheep Creek upstream, near the treeline that borders the northern side of the long meadow. The trail frequently disappears as it heads northwest and diverges from Sheep Creek. Cross a clear creek (1630, 3.1, g22) and then head north-northwest. The route ascends through subalpine meadows in the direction of Bastille Mountain. Cross a couple of streams as you gain elevation over 2.1km to an 1810m highpoint on a ridge crest. Contour alpine slopes to the east and uphill of a lake. Over the next 3.3km the route crosses the Divide and then arrives at Surprise Pass (1990, 5.4, g23). The Surprise Pass high alternate route begins here (see below).

GRANDE CACHE ALTERNATE ROUTE – 74.3KM TO AN ALTERNATE NORTHERN TERMINUS. HORSES AND BIKES PERMITTED.

Due to the inaccessibility of the Kakwa Provincial Park trailhead and the potential 74.3km road walk out to Yellowhead Highway 16, some choose to end their journey on the GDT in the small town of Grande Cache, Alberta. From Casket Pass campsite and the Sheep Creek campsite, you can go downstream and follow 72.8km of horse trail and road to reach the town. I describe the route in the 'South access' for this segment. Also see under 'Access and transportation', at page 30, for more information about getting into or out of Grande Cache.

End Grande Cache alternate route.

SURPRISE PASS HIGH ALTERNATE ROUTE – 10.5KM INSTEAD OF 10.8KM. HORSES AND BIKES PERMITTED.

To stay in the alpine you can follow a high traverse from Surprise Pass and avoid all the boggy terrain below around Cecilia Lake. Don't try this alternate in foul or wet weather, though. From the pass, hike cross-country over moraine and fossil beds below the Wallbridge Glacier north-northwest 6.0km to Gravel Pass. Hike to the northeast up from the pass, and join the Wapiti Mountain ridge crest. Follow the ridge crest northward 1.9km to a point just 200m north of the summit proper of Wapiti Mountain. From here, angle downwards to the northwest. Follow a ridge crest steeply down loose talus, and through some steep brush lower down, to Providence Pass on the main route at waypoint g25.

End Surprise Pass high alternate route.

Surprise Pass to Providence Pass
(10.8km, 336m up, 537m down)

The main route follows a faint trail descending gradually across open slopes north of Surprise Pass. The route passes below a waterfall in 700m, where the condition of the path improves. Follow the drainage downhill

Bastille Mountain in Willmore Wilderness Park, segment 34.

Providence Pass between Broadview and Cecilia lakes.

through alpine meadows and cross a creek in 1.2km more. The trail enters the subalpine and skirts around the western edge of the treeline. In an additional 3.7km you pass a good overlook above Cecilia Lake. Boggy terrain continues along the eastern side of Cecilia Creek. Through trees the wet path reaches a creek crossing in another 800m, above Cecilia Lake. A moderate ascent brings the trail 1.2km out of very muddy terrain to a highpoint where there used to be a trail junction (1705, 7.6, g24) for Cecilia Lake. Turn left and ascend northwest through a large subalpine meadow. The path reaches Providence Pass (1715, 3.2, g25) at a junction of two alternate routes. The Surprise Pass high alternate route merges just west of this pass, and the Providence Pass high alternate route begins here for NOBO hikers.

PROVIDENCE PASS HIGH ALTERNATE ROUTE – 9.2KM INSTEAD OF 11.0KM. HORSES AND BIKES PERMITTED; BIKES NOT PRACTICAL.

This cross-country route continues from where the Surprise Pass high alternate meets the main route just west of Providence Pass. If you want to avoid the soaking main route, you can easily regain the alpine north of the pass and start a traverse to the northwest just above timberline. There is no trail, but route-finding is straightforward. After contouring as best as possible across a steep ridge southwest of Francis Peak, you enter a vast alpine haven. Hike toward Mount Ruth to the north, reaching the first of two large, shallow lakes. Climb 70m over the timbered ridge to the north of the first lake and drop down toward the second lake. Angle northwest and then west, joining the crest of the southwestern ridge of Mount Ruth. Look for a marked trail that descends below timberline. The Mount Ruth trail is in fair shape and is steep at times as it descends to Kakwa Lake to the west. In boggy, flat terrain at the base of Mount Ruth, you encounter a three-way trail junction; keep right. Continue through wet, grassy fields, rejoining the main route and following it to the south end of Kakwa Lake. (If you plan to stay at Kakwa Lake for a while, consider doing the easy scramble to the summit of Mount Ruth for the awesome view. Mount Ian Monroe is another good scramble and overlook.)

End Providence Pass high alternate route.

Providence Pass to Kakwa Lake cabins
(11.2km, 61m up, 284m down)

A gentle descent through muddy areas leads to Broadview Lake (1630, 1.9, g26) at the lake's outflow. The trail is obscure in all the marshy areas beyond the outflow until it arrives at the indiscernible Kakwa Pass (1585, 3.3, f42). Look for flagging tape marking the way. The route is level through this wet subalpine terrain. Boggy meadows do afford some views of the area.

The trail lies just in the treeline along the south side of the pass. It descends to Wapumun Lake and skirts meadows on its eastern side. At the Kakwa Lake outflow is Camp #2, or Horse Camp for equestrians, beside the southern tip of Kakwa Lake (1475, 5.8, g27). At this point, the higher, alternate route from Mount Ruth rejoins the main route. Ford the shallow outflow to Camp #1, South Camp for hikers. The trail continues through the campsite and parallels the shoreline for 200m to BC Parks cabins. There is an active trail register at the staff cabin. Park rangers stay at the facility infrequently during the summer, as do park hosts. The other cabin is open for the public to use and in my opinion is preferable to the campsite (see 'Car campgrounds and accommodations' for this segment). For those who want to cross the 54th parallel, follow the lakeshore trail 300m past the cabins.

Kakwa Lake to Kakwa Lake trailhead
(28.6km, 234m up, 787m down)

The Kakwa Provincial Park trailhead is at the end of a 28.6km restricted access road that has been impassable to vehicles in recent years. A narrow road heads southwest from the cabins and meets a tote road in 1.5km. Turn left and follow this larger road past Mariel and Wishaw lakes and over McGregor Pass. Gradually descend along the eastern side of the McGregor River, following the road. Mount Sir Alexander and Obelisk Peak, wrapped in icefalls, come into view. In 15.5km more, the road comes to the Buchanan Creek ford, which normally is not an issue unless it is early in the season. On the other side of the ford is a good campsite. The Kakwa

Lake trailhead is at a gate across the Bastille Creek bridge in another 11.6km, at the end of the Walker Creek FSR (950, 28.8, g29), which continues 73.5km to Yellowhead Highway 16. Hikers describe a depressing scene at the trailhead due to an old trailer and junk that has gathered there. I wouldn't plan to spend the night there. The road passes the confluence of the Bastille and McGregor 700m before reaching the trailhead – that might be a better place to camp.

A female moose trots through the shallow waters of southern Kakwa Lake.

Dan Hunter of Strider Adventures leads llama pack trips into Kakwa Provincial Park. Here, he and some clients pose near the Kakwa Lake BC Parks cabins.

Julia Lynx watches the sun set over Kakwa Lake, the extended northern terminus of the GDT.

APPENDIXES

Appendix 1: *Selected hikes on the GDT*

While you might not have the time or resources to spend weeks on the GDT, the thought of setting foot on at least part of the route can still be appealing. Countless hikes reach either the GDT or the Divide itself in the Canadian Rockies. The following list is a distilled version of shorter variations of the GDT and its alternate routes. The criterion for this list is that the trail must travel some distance on the GDT itself and not just reach the route or the Great Divide. These hikes also have easy access.

For your convenience the descriptions of these shorter routes include information about distances, use restrictions, permits, vehicle access, elevation change and a cross reference to the main body of route descriptions, including which map pages to use. The order of the hikes goes from Waterton Lakes in the south to Jasper National Park in the north and is broken into three sections depending on how long they are.

The ideal routes described here are microcosms of the GDT. Most of the shorter trails are return trips that double back on the same route. The weekend hikes all present a thru-hike that includes a variety of terrain throughout their drastic elevation changes. These hikes access some of the more remote places on the GDT, offering a spell of seclusion and an increased chance of encountering wildlife.

Day hikes

1. Lakeshore Trail, Waterton Lakes National Park

Distance: 12.6km return.

Permits: National park entry pass; horses and bikes not permitted.

Trail description: Refer to segment 1.

Vehicle access: Refer to segment 1, South access for the Lakeshore trailhead.

This superbly maintained trail follows the western shore of Upper Waterton Lake. As the route meanders over the lower reaches of Mount Bertha and Mount Richards, it holds excellent vistas of the lake. At monument 276 on the USA border is the meeting place of the 1133km-long GDT and the 5300km-long Continental Divide Trail that travels all the way to

Mexico. You can choose to stay overnight at either the Boundary Bay or Bertha Bay campsite if you obtain a backcountry permit at the visitor information centre in Waterton.

2. Carthew–Alderson Trail

Distance: 20.1km one way.

Permits: National park entry pass. Horses permitted. Bikes not permitted.

Trail description: Refer to segment 1.

Vehicle access: Refer to segment 1, South access for the Cameron Falls trailhead parking area and the North access for the Cameron Lake parking area. The view from 2330m-high Carthew Summit seems to have inspired the park motto of "Where the mountains meet the prairie." The trail gives the opportunity to hike from Waterton to Cameron Lake without having to return on the same route. Even starting from 1665m at Cameron Lake means a 735m climb. Be sure to take plenty of water or a purifier to quench your thirst. Do not let the blue sky fool you; there is usually a stiff wind at altitude in this part of the Rockies and a storm can blow in at any time. Bring some warm clothing just in case the weather turns. Staying overnight at the Alderson Lake campsite is an alternative if you obtain a backcountry permit at the visitor information centre in Waterton.

3. Lineham Ridge on Tamarack Trail, Waterton Lakes National Park

Distance: 17.6km return.

Permits: Horses permitted. Bikes not permitted.

Trail description: Refer to segment 2.

Vehicle access: Refer to segment 2, South access for the Rowe Lakes trailhead.

This steep trail gives day hikers the opportunity to bag the second-highest point of the GDT on Lineham Ridge. This is a long climb, nearly a vertical kilometre, and there are no campsites on this stretch of the Tamarack trail. The view of the park is worth all the effort, though. The trail reaches a minor 2565m summit on Mount Lineham's western ridgeline, only 700m from the Great Divide. Start early and bring lots of water, along with some warm layers in case of poor weather.

4. Willoughby Ridge Crest, Castle Provincial Park

Distance: 15.1km one way.

Permits: Horses and bikes permitted.

Trail description: Refer to segment 5.

Vehicle access: Refer to segment 5, South and North access descriptions. This route is a real treasure in an area that has a lot of industrial activity. Grass covers much of this crest route. The views of the Flathead Range and the Divide to the west are astounding. From the bald summit near the northern end of the crest, a full panorama allows you to see much of the Divide and the Crowsnest Pass.

5. Deadman Pass, Bow/Crow Forest District

Distance: 13km return.

Permits: Horses and bikes permitted.

Trail description: Refer to segment 7

Vehicle access: Refer to segment 7, Other access

This multiple-use trail accommodates OHV traffic during the summer. The track leads up to the Great Divide at a relatively low point below timberline. The total elevation gain is only 50m. The trail lies on the northern extremity of the Allison-Chinook cross-country ski area and receives much use during the winter.

6. West Elk Pass, Peter Lougheed Provincial Park

Distance: 12.2km return.

Permits: Horses not permitted. Bikes permitted.

Trail description: Refer to segment 13.

Vehicle access: Refer to segment 13, North access for the Elk Pass trailhead.

This easy trail climbs alongside Fox Creek to the Great Divide. West Elk Pass is below timberline. There are good views of the surrounding valley near the pass. The trail receives much use during the ski season as part of the Kananaskis Lakes cross-country ski area. Hike up to Fox Lake and perhaps Frozen Lake while you are there. Trail junctions are signed.

7. Sunshine Village Loop Trail, Banff National Park

Distance: 18.3km (or 6.3km with bus access to Sunshine Village).

Permits: National park entry pass. Horses and bikes not permitted.

Trail description: Refer to segment 18.

Vehicle access: Refer to segment 18, South access for the Sunshine Village parking area and bus information. Sunshine offers a gondola service during the summer.

This spectacular loop trail takes advantage of the GDT and a short alternate route, crossing the Great Divide twice in the alpine. Climb 400m, over a 6km walk from the parking area to Sunshine Village at 2200m, where the loop trail begins. Ascend to waypoint c15 and then follow the main route to c16 and back down to where you started. A good time to hike this route is during mid- to late summer, in time to miss the snow but to catch the alpine flowers.

8. Signal Mountain Fire Road, Jasper National Park

Distance: 17km return.

Permits: National park entry pass. Hiking and mountain biking only.

Trail description: Refer to segment 28.

Vehicle access: Refer to segment 28, North access for the Signal Mountain trailhead at the northern end of the Skyline trail.

The trail is a gravel road with some steep sections and climbs over 800m to the Skyline trail. (You can continue up the road to the Signal Mountain peak.) Woven among the switchbacks of the road is a steep trail that seems to be a favourite with local mountain bikers. Watch out for windfall and tight corners, though. The views from the upper reaches of the road afford a good vista of the valley. An overnight option is to stay at the Signal campsite with a backcountry permit available at the Jasper Information Centre.

Overnight hikes

1. Fording River Pass, Kananaskis Country

Distance: 32km return.

Permits: Bikes and horses permitted.

Trail description: Refer to segment 12.

Vehicle access: Refer to segment 12, Other access for the Baril Creek trailhead. If you are approaching from BC, refer to the North access for the Aldridge Creek trailhead.

An immense alpine meadow covers Fording River Pass. There is a beautiful lake in the area and unlimited access to the surrounding peaks such as Baril, Armstrong, Bolton and Cornwell. You will find a stiff 800m climb to the point where the GDT crosses over the pass. The trail itself is a disintegrating access road. In 11km the GDT crosses the road and mostly stays above it up to the pass. The Fording River campsite is 1km over the pass on the GDT. The hike up to the pass on the Aldridge Creek trail in BC is 37km return.

2. Elk Pass and Elk Lakes Loop, Elk Lakes and Peter Lougheed provincial parks

Distance: 23km loop.

Permits: Horses and bikes not permitted. An adjacent trail does allow bikes.

Trail description: Refer to segment 13.

Permits: There is a $5 fee per night at the Lower Elk Lake campsite.

Vehicle access: Refer to segment 13, North access for the Elk Pass trailhead. You can access Elk Lakes Provincial Park from BC and do a 13km variation of this hike.

This is an overnight version of the Elk Pass day hike. Follow the trail to Elk Pass on the border of Elk Lakes Provincial Park. Turn left and take the trail down Elkan Creek to the trailhead parking area. Turn right and go 1km to the Lower Elk Lake campsite, 11km from the start. Follow excellent trail to Upper Elk Lake and then take the Fox Lake trail back to Elk Pass, returning on the same Elk Pass trail in Peter Lougheed Provincial Park. Mountain bikers could ride the nearby Kananaskis Power Line road 5km to the Elk Lakes Provincial Park parking area and then walk 1km to get to the Lower Elk Lake campsite for a return trip on the same route.

3. North Kananaskis Pass, Peter Lougheed Provincial Park

Distance: 33km return with a 38km loop variation.

Permits: Horses and bikes not permitted.

Trail description: Refer to segment 14.

Vehicle access: Refer to segment 14, South access for the North Interlakes trailhead.

North Kananaskis Pass is a fantastic area to spend a day exploring the lakes and Turbine Canyon, a deeply eroded slot. A 600m ascent is well worth the effort to travel to this part of the GDT. You can do a loop by continuing over the pass into the Height of the Rockies Provincial Park and return over South Kananaskis Pass, following the Three Isle Lake trail back to the parking area. This loop is about 38km and has a bit of cross-country travel between the lower Le Roy and Beatty creeks.

4. Hawk Creek Trail to Ball Pass campsite, Kootenay and Banff national parks

Distance: 25.4km return.

Permits: National park entry pass and backcountry permit. Horses permitted. Bikes not permitted.

Trail description: Refer to segment 18.

Vehicle access: Refer to segment 18, North access for the Floe Lake and Hawk Creek trailhead.

Like the ascent to Floe Lake on the other side of the highway, the climb to Ball Pass is often steep. You climb an excruciating 900m from the parking area and then descend 300m to the campsite over the pass. In comparison to the Floe Lake trail, this one receives less use and provides almost continuous views. This valley was burned in 2003 but the trail is in fair condition.

5. Floe Lake Trail, Kootenay National Park

Distance: 21.8km return

Permits: National parks entry pass and backcountry permit. Horses permitted. Bikes not permitted.

Trail description: Refer to segment 19

Vehicle access: Refer to segment 19, South access for the Floe Lake and Hawk Creek trailhead.

If it were not for the 700m ascent to Floe Lake this route could feasibly be a day hike. The area the trail accesses is the start of the renowned Rockwall trail, known for hanging glaciers, waterfalls, alpine meadows and a continuous headwall. It is best to do this hike in the latter half of summer, when most of the snow has melted and fed the budding flowers. The trail to Floe Lake is in fair shape and offers good views. Reserve the Floe Lake campsite, one of the nicest in the Rockies.

6. Skyline Trail to Little Shovel Pass, Jasper National Park

Distance: 20.6km return.

Permits: National parks entry pass and a backcountry permit. Dogs, horses, bikes not permitted.

Trail description: Refer to segment 28.

Vehicle access: Refer to segment 28, South access for the Skyline trailhead. You gain 550m from the Maligne Lake parking area to Little Shovel Pass. This excellent trail brings you up to the alpine for some wonderful views. Unfortunately, this is just the beginning of the Skyline trail's alpine traverse. If you have the time and manage to get the permits, you should consider a weekend hike of the whole trail (see the next section). Reserve either of the Evelyn Creek or Little Shovel Pass campsites well in advance.

Weekend hikes

1. Tamarack Trail and Snowshoe Trail, Waterton Lakes National Park

Distance: 36.3km one way.

Permits: National park entry pass and backcountry permits. Horses permitted. Bikes not permitted.

Trail description: Refer to segment 2.

Vehicle access: Refer to segment 2, South and North accesses for the Rowe Lakes and Red Rock Canyon trailheads.

The Tamarack trail is a well-maintained path that leads through a variety of terrain, owing to the elevation changes en route. From the Rowe Lakes trailhead on the Akamina Parkway it is nearly a 1000m ascent to the 2565m-high summit on Lineham Ridge. The trail parallels the Great Divide within a kilometre of its crest for over 20km. At the Snowshoe campsite the trail turns away from the Divide and follows Bauerman Creek down to the Red Rock Canyon. For those intimidated by the initial ascent from the Akamina Parkway, leaving from the Red Rock Canyon offers a gentler climb. The campsites en route are Lone Lake, Twin Lake and Snowshoe.

2. North Kananaskis Pass to Burstall Pass, Peter Lougheed Provincial Park, Height of the Rockies Provincial Park and Banff National Park

Distance: 47.9km one way.

Permits: National park entry pass and backcountry permit if staying overnight in Banff National Park. Campsite reservation in Peter Lougheed Provincial Park. Horses not permitted. Bikes permitted only a short way up the Burstall Pass trail.

Trail description: Refer to segments 14 and 15.

Vehicle access: Refer to segment 14, South access and segment 15, Other access for the North Interlakes and Burstall Pass trailheads.

This strenuous slice of the GDT traverses the high country of three separate parks and crosses the Great Divide twice. In total, you do a cumulative elevation gain of 1700m northbound and 1500m southbound. Compounding the difficulty of this route is the fact that the trail between both of these passes is only in fair condition and even obscure at times. If you are looking for a secluded hike in the central Rockies, though, this is the one.

3. North Saskatchewan River to Sunset Pass, Banff National Park

Distance: 47.5km one way.

Permits: National park entry pass. NP backcountry permit only if you plan to stay at the Norman Creek campsite. Horses permitted. Bikes not permitted.

Trail description: Refer to segment 24.

Vehicle access: Refer to segment 24, South and North accesses for the Owen Creek, Sunset Pass and Nigel Pass trailheads.

This rigorous hike over four high passes includes the highest point reached on the GDT, at 2590m. The most difficult hiking is along upper Owen Creek, where you have to pick your own route up the steep creekbed. The rewards are worth all the effort: Owen Creek canyon, Michele Lakes alpine meadows, Pinto Lake and Sunset Pass. I recommend using the steep gully route up to Sunset Pass from Pinto Lake as described in North access for segment 24.

4. Nigel Pass over Jonas Shoulder to Poboktan Creek, Jasper National Park

Distance: 57.9km one way.

Permits: National park entry pass and backcountry permits. Horses and bikes not permitted.

Trail description: Refer to segment 26.

Vehicle access: Refer to segment 26, South and North accesses for the Nigel Pass and Poboktan Creek trailheads.

Although 2450m Jonas Shoulder, the highpoint of this route, is far above the trailheads on the Icefields Parkway, the elevation changes are absorbed into the overall distance of the trail. Excellent, well-maintained trail passes a number of backcountry campsites, making this a very accessible leg of the GDT. The distance might convince you to make this a long-weekend hike, though. Nearly 30km of this trail traverses alpine terrain and offers spectacular views.

5. Skyline Trail, Jasper National Park

Distance: 47km one way.

Permits: National park entry pass and backcountry permits. Hikers only.

Trail description: Refer to segment 28.

Vehicle access: Refer to segment 28, South and North accesses.

Most people save themselves the hefty ascent from the northern end of the trail and start from the Maligne Lake parking lot. The trail has gained its popular status partly through accessibility and partly because of its 25km spent above timberline, swimming in panoramic views. Keep in mind that there is little water available for 8km between Curator Lake and Centre Lakes over the 2480m Notch unless you melt snow. Come prepared for high exposure to sun and wind during clear weather. This is not an early season hike; wait for the snow to melt and the flowers to bloom.

APPENDIX 2: *Alternate routes list and recommendations*

This is a list of the available alternate routes to help you plan your hike on the GDT. You can find the route description in each of the sections where these alternates occur. Li Brannfors originally conceived of this list after his hike in 2012. I have adapted it for this book but kept some of the hiker comments that have been added over time.

Alternate route	Goat Haunt in Section A, segment 1. Hikers only. Dogs not permitted in Glacier National Park.
Departs/rejoins main route at	km 0.
Distance	Longer – this adds 7.4km but saves having to repeat the 6.4km walk south on the Lakeshore trail to get to monument 276, the southern terminus of the GDT.
Pros	Save your legs and take the boat instead. Sit back and enjoy the cruise.
Cons	Besides the cost of the trip, you must deal with a class "B" border entry at the ranger station and have your passport and other identification with you. Also, you can't bring your dog.
Recommendations	River Taig, author of the GDT app, recommends this alternate start to the route for the boat cruise, adding that some hikers have negotiated a drop-off at the monument itself. There is a small dock at the border.

Alternate route	Mount Rowe alternate route, aka Akamina Ridge, in Section A, segment 2. No horses or bikes.
Departs/rejoins main route at	Departs at km 26.0 on the Akamina Parkway (road) and continues to km 54.4 on Sage Pass.
Distance	Shorter – 19.3km instead of 28.4km on the main route.
Pros	The views are outrageous and you follow the Continental Divide the whole way. You don't need camping permits – a bonus if you can't get your backcountry campsites reserved on the Tamarack trail in Waterton Lakes National Park. There's no reservation required for the Akamina Creek campsite, near the southern end of this route.
Cons	Don't hike this route to save time. Although shorter, it is difficult and cross-country. The 724m climb from Akamina Pass to Mount Rowe is the single hardest ascent of the GDT. It follows a cutline, not a trail, and is overgrown with much deadfall. There is also a lot of bear activity in this area. There is no water on this route until Sage Pass unless you find snow to melt.

Recommendations	"Wonderful 360 degree views. After a steep initial ascent, the ridgeline walking is mostly open and straightforward except for the long, wooded saddle south of Festubert Mtn." —Li Brannfors, 2012
	"Excellent hike. Good ridge walking with panoramic views. One off our best days on the GDT. Would do it again." —Larry Tyler, 2015
	"I took this alternate route in 2013 and again in 2016 – while I do recommend the cross-country ridge – I must strongly caution that the climb to the ridge is very arduous..." —River Taig (GDT app, Atlas Guides), 2016

Alternate route	Barnaby Ridge alternate route, in Section A, segment 3. No horses or bikes. Be prepared to carry your dog over difficult spots.
Departs/rejoins main route at	Departs at km 73.3 on La Coulotte Peak and rejoins at km 98.1 on Hwy 774.
Distance	Shorter – 22.4km instead of 24.8km.
Pros	Stunning views from a high ridge crest and awesome campsite at Southfork Lakes.
Cons	Difficult hiking with a couple of short, harrowing sections of scrambling. You will have to backtrack on Hwy. 774 if you plan to resupply at Castle Ski Resort.
Recommendations	"Walking out Barnaby Ridge looked less difficult to me than continuing along the roller-coaster ridge crest of La Coulotte Ridge, so I took it. Probably easier at first than the standard route, but harder overall. If you have the energy and the weather is good, the views are worth it." —Li Brannfors, 2012
	"The wide and expansive ridges are vast and offer breathtaking views that in my opinion epitomize the GDT experience." —River Taig, (GDT app, Atlas Guides), 2016

Alternate route	Blairmore alternate route. Horses and bikes permitted.
Departs/rejoins main route at	Departs at km 129.7 and rejoins the main route at km 145.1.
Distance	Same – 15.5km instead of 15.4km.
Pros	Compared to Coleman, there are more amenities in Blairmore. The campground has showers and a laundry.
Cons	Road walking. The road into Blairmore can be busy.
Recommendations	"If I had the authority to, I'd make this the standard route. If staying at A Safe Haven B&B in Coleman, the trail angel hosts will gladly drive you back into Blairmore for shopping," —Li Brannfors, 2012

Alternate route	Coral Pass alternate route, Section B, segment 13. No horses or bikes. Dogs may need to be carried over steep terrain.

Departs/rejoins main route at	Departs at km 316.4 from the Elk Lakes road and joins main route at km 338.9.
Distance	Longer – 30.5km instead of 18.9km. Plan on a full day at least for this alternate.
Pros	Avoids road walking and instead takes advantage of a worth-while trail over a high pass with many views and fields of fossils.
Cons	Time-consuming and difficult route-finding on the north side of Coral Pass. The Elk River might be running too high to safely ford, but this isn't as much of an issue if you are NOBO, because you can see the water level right from the start. Scrambling can be dangerous if this route is wet.
Recommenda-tions	"The first ⅓ of this route can be muddy on the road and not too eventful. The crossing our year was fine, but was a low water year. The middle ⅓ was a highlight of our whole trip! The final ⅓ was a challenge and very time-consuming to find a way down in overgrowth off sometimes cliffed-out, crum-bly dead ends. Lots of backtracking and trial and error until we found ways down (old flagging helped!) Be sure to allot at least a full day for this alternate. All worth it and we had a great time." —Erin "Wired" Saver, 2015

Alternate route	Sunshine Village alternate route, aka Trapper's Saloon alter-nate – Section C, segment 17. Hikers and dogs.
Departs/rejoins main route at	Departs at km 442.6 and joins at km 445.9.
Distance	About the same – 3km instead of 3.3km.
Pros	You will want to take this alternate if you plan to resupply through Sunshine Village or want to leave the trail by catch-ing a shuttle bus to Banff. There are restaurants and a pub, as well as a hotel that is open during the summer.
Cons	The trail loses elevation to go down to the village. The area can be busy and may detract from your wilderness experi-ence if you don't need to stop here.
Recommenda-tions	"Yes, decent food at Trapper Cafe. Also can pick up a resup-ply package here at the cafe via White Mountain Adventure, cutting the Kananaskis to Field section in half." —Larry Tyler, 2015

Alternate route	Six Passes alternate route. Hikers only.
Departs/rejoins main route at	Departs at km 762.5 and rejoins at km 794.1 or 798.9.
Distance	Longer – 36.9km instead of 31.6km.
Pros	Avoids the brushy and muddy Maligne River trail and stays in the high alpine. Several highpoints offer incredible vistas.
Cons	A lot of elevation gain and loss plus cross-country travel and route-finding. One easy scramble en route.
Recommenda-tions	If you can get a random camping permit from the Jasper trail office, do it!

Alternate route	Saturday Night Lake loop trail alternate route, aka Dorothy Lakes or Caledonia Lake alternate route – Section F, segment 29. Hikers and dogs.
Departs/rejoins main route at	Leaves the main route at km 851.1, rejoins at km 862.2.
Distance	Longer – 14.6km instead of 12.6km.
Pros	This trail provides access to the Minnow Lake campsite #40, 9.2km outside Jasper on the Saturday Night Lake loop.
Cons	To make the connection with the Dorothy Lake trail and the bridge over the Miette River, the route requires a bit of nasty cross-country navigation and bushwhacking.
Recommendations	Third-hand accounts say this route is not worth it due to the bushwhacking involved.

Alternate route	Tote road alternate route – Section F, segment 29. Hikers and dogs.
Departs/rejoins main route at	Leaves the main route at km 862.2 (leaves off the Saturday Night Lake loop alternate), rejoins at km 872.4.
Distance	Slightly longer.
Pros	Follow a historic road that was used in constructing the railway a century ago. Links up with the Saturday Night Lake alternate to avoid the road walk on the busy highway.
Cons	This isn't an official trail and can be brushy with many blowdowns.
Recommendations	I would rather walk this route than the highway.

Alternate route	Elysium Pass alternate route – Section F, segment 29. Hikers and dogs. Horses can travel half the route as depicted but can likely make it the whole way with a slight route change.
Departs/rejoins main route at	Leaves the main route at km 862.2 (connects with the Saturday Night Lake loop alternate); rejoins at waypoint f7, at km 903.0.
Distance	Longer – 50km instead of 40.8km, measured from the Meadowland Creek trailhead on Hwy. 16.
Pros	Links up with the Saturday Night alternate to avoid the road walk on the busy highway. Follows a spectacular high alpine route.
Cons	Besides the very good trail up to Elysium Pass, the rest of this route is cross-country with navigation challenges. It's only for those who like such route-finding in trackless alpine. Also 6km of bushwhacking!
Recommendations	I've hiked two variations of this route now and love it. It is extremely rewarding and worthwhile.

Alternate route	Jackpine alternate route – Section G, segment 32. Hikers and dogs. Horses and bikes permitted but impractical.
Departs/rejoins main route at	Leaves at km 999.6 and rejoins at km 1020.8 and at km 1029.1.

Distance	Longer – 41.6km instead of 30.7km.
Pros	Awesome high traverse right on the Great Divide.
Cons	Lots of elevation gain and loss with bushwhacking going across Loren Pass and a dangerous scramble on the way down the ridge to Little Shale Hill. There is only a faint trail in parts.
Recommenda-tions	"We took ⅔ of a day to add on the first part of the Jackpine High Route from Jackpine Pass to Jackpine Mtn and it was well worth the effort. As Lynx mentions, head down the faint trail to Jackpine River from there. We had difficulty finding the trail at points, but it was straightforward to just head down." —Erin "Wired" Saver, 2015 "If the weather is expected to be good and you are an experienced cross-country scrambler (not just a hiker), then I can't recommend the alternate route highly enough." —River Taig (GDT app, Atlas Guides), 2016

Alternate route	Mount Talbot alternate – Section G, segment 33. Hikers and dogs. Horses and bikes permitted but impractical.
Departs/rejoins main route at	Leaves at km 1038.3 and rejoins at km 1047.8.
Distance	Longer – 14.2km instead of 9.5km.
Pros	This alternate offers another high section of trail over the Divide. There are cairns marking the way onto and off the route as of 2015.
Cons	More elevation gain and loss; also longer.
Recommenda-tions	This trail was originally explored and documented by a GDTA member and is in the GDT app. I can see it becoming main route in the future.

Alternate route	Grande Cache – Section G, segment 34. Horses, dogs and bikes.
Departs/rejoins main route at	Departs the main route at km 1070.0 and km 1074.5; however, you will likely want to finish at Kakwa Lake at km 1094.1 and then backtrack to this point if you would like to finish in Grande Cache.
Distance	72.8km on horse trail and road.
Pros	Easier access to amenities and transportation options than using Walker Creek Road.
Cons	A valley bottom trail. Long, but so is Walker Creek Road.
Recommenda-tions	This alternate opens up the northernmost section to those who can't access Kakwa Lake.

Alternate route	Surprise Pass high alternate route, aka Wallbridge Glaciers alternate – Section G, segment 34. Hikers and dogs. Horses and bikes permitted but impractical.
Departs/rejoins main route at	Departs at km 1082.6 and rejoins at km 1093.4.
Distance	About the same – 10.5km instead of 10.8km.

Pros	Avoids the muddy section near Cecilia Lake and offers better views.
Cons	More elevation gain and loss and difficult cross-country travel and route-finding.
Recommendations	"Coming down the last km or two had its sketchy parts with some steep scree and then thick brush I wouldn't want to do wet, but it was short lived and I think it depends on which way you choose to scramble down. Looking back, there were various options... Highly recommended vs the marshy, muddy lower option. More time-consuming, but straightforward and a short, sweet alternate. What the GDT is all about!" —Erin "Wired" Saver, 2015

Alternate route	Providence Pass high alternate route, aka Mount Ruth alternate – Section G, segment 34. Hikers, horses and dogs.
Departs/rejoins main route at	Departs at km 1093.4 and rejoins at km 1103.7.
Distance	Shorter – 9.1km instead of 10.3km.
Pros	The signed trail over Kakwa Pass seems to have deteriorated. There is almost no trail to follow between Broadview and Wapumun lakes. This alternate is dryer and offers more views.
Cons	None. Will likely become main route if trails in this area continue to be unmaintained.
Recommendations	"Once we embraced the grassy, somewhat brushy, uneven, sidehill hiking, it was good. Not a must do, but probably better than being down low if weather is clear. Views were great to do more of the final stretch up high." —Erin "Wired" Saver, 2015

Alternate route	Walker Creek Road – Section G, segment 34. Horses, dogs and bikes permitted.
Departs/rejoins main route at	Leaves the end of the trail at the Bastille Creek bridge trailhead parking area at km 1133.2.
Distance	73.5km to the Yellowhead Highway, where you can arrange in advance for pickup by vehicle or train. See 'Access and transportation' at page 26.
Pros	There is no chance of hitchhiking on the Grande Cache alternate route save for the last 10km.
Cons	A long walk on a dirt road that can be very wet in places due to beaver dams that flood the road. However, the province of BC has indicated they will continue maintaining this road.
Recommendations	"It's 29km to get to Bastille Creek where a high clearance 4WD car could come in to get you (if you know someone) or you might luck out with someone driving out... we did, but it's really a 50/50 shot, it seems, that someone would be driving that road at all that day... or for days to come. Walking the old dirt road was quick miles, but could be slower going if there was a lot of rain/mud." —Erin "Wired" Saver, 2015

APPENDIX 3: *Sample itineraries*

Sample 12-day horse trip on the original GDT, with gear list: Wendy Bush, 2009

Bar U Ranch → Pekisko Creek → Original GDT → Fording River Pass → Aldridge Creek → Forsyth Creek → Connor Lake (in Height of the Rockies PP) → White River → Sylvan Pass → Joffre Creek → Palliser River → Palliser Pass → Spray River → Bryant Creek → Allenby Pass → Brewster Creek → Banff

"We didn't take any rest days, Connor Lakes was a bust and Joffre Creek is on the trail blacklist."

GEAR:

Maps?
2 riding saddles
3 pack saddles
2 sets of boxes
1 set soft packs
3 lash ropes
3 pack tarps
1 rain tarp 12×16
2 gel seats
2 bridles, 5 halters
6 sets hobbles; 3 muzzles; two bells
Shoeing kit: shoes, nails, knife, nippers, clincher
High line; 5 swivels
Horse first aid kit
Feed: 4 × 25 lb sacks 12% protein pellets (1 scoop = 4lbs); lined grain bags; small square salt block
Human first aid kit
Sat phone
Whisky for medicinal purposes
Water filtration
Leatherman on all belts
Sewing kit: hole punch, heavy needles, thread, spare latigo, leather strips, 5-minute epoxy
Writing tools: book, pencil, pen, paint

Small Thermos

Matches, lighter, fire-starter

100 lb scale

Tents, pegs, extra 3mm rope

Chainsaw, chainsaw tools, chain oil, mixed gas

Axe, folding saw

Stove, propane bottles, plates, cutlery, pots

Sleeping bags, silk sheet

Clothes: rain gear, riding outfit, one change clothes, long underwear, silk
scarf

Hats: baseball and cowboy

Water bottles metal; plastic water bottles for food rehydration

12 days' human food, dog food

Sample 21-day trail-running itinerary with a support crew (old distances): Dustin Lynx

Main route = 1191.4km (59.6km/day over 20 days).

July 9, travel day to Waterton Lakes, km = 10.1

Car camp at the townsite campground in Waterton and run the lakeshore trail to the border and back, 20.2km total travel.

July 10, Lakeshore campground to a19 campsite past Font Mountain,
km = 65.9

Meet car at a9, km 20.8, and pick up overnight backpack, eat a meal.
The camp is at nearly 2100m. Prepare for a cold camp and slow going
at elevation.

July 11, a19 to Lynx Creek campground, km = 122.5

Meet car at Castle Ski Resort, km 99.8, for dinner and drop packs for
last 22km to campground. Use GPS – this is a very tricky area with lots
of OHV trails.

July 12, Lynx Creek campground to Alexander Creek campsite, km = 180.5

Leave packs in car and meet in Coleman for lunch, km = 153.7.

Pick up 2-night packs at Allison Creek campground at km 167.7 and
continue over Deadman Pass to Alexander Creek.

July 13, Alexander Cr Cg to Hidden Creek campsite (b19), km = 234.4

July 14, Hidden Cr Cg (b19) to James Lake campsite (b30), km = 294.1

Jul 15, James Lake CG to (56.7 to end of section) to Interlakes car campground, km = 354.8

There is an opportunity to meet a car on Elk Lakes Road but it is a
long, long drive to Kananaskis Lakes from there unless you have two

sets of friends to meet you at each place.

Pick up two days of food. Will meet car again on Hwy 93 South.

July 16, Interlakes car camp to Big Springs campsite, km = 412.8

July 17, Big Springs Camp to Egypt Lake campsite (or shelter), km = 472

July 18, Egypt Lake to Helmet Falls campsite, km = 534.7

62.7km for today but you meet the car at the Hwy 23km into the day. Have a meal and pick up supplies for a night.

July 19, Helmet Falls campsite to Amiskwi River ford (d3), km = 600.7

Meet car at Natural Bridge parking area, 37.5km into day and have a meal. Pick up supplies for two nights (possible car ride to Truffle Pigs to load up on an early dinner?).

This is a big day, 66km, but it's mostly flat besides Goodsir Pass first thing in the morning.

July 20, Amiskwi R ford (d3) to Howse River (d13), km = 667.1

Another long, 66.4km day to Howse River but there are only two low passes and the route-finding is pretty straightforward.

July 21, Howse River to the Crossing for a rest day, km = 669.7

This is 22.6km to the N. Sask bridge by the Crossing. 1km more to the actual resort on the road. The resort has a good pub with a make-your-own-burger buffet, laundry, phone, etc.

If you get in by noon, plan to leave by noon the next day.

July 22, From the Crossing to Pinto Lake campsite, km = 702.2

This is a 32.5km day. Just follow the DTH out of the Crossing. There is a road at the back of the Crossing that goes east, take that one. Take 2 nights food.

This is a hard day: fresh burn up Owen Creek, route-finding and 3 of the highest passes on GDT!!!

July 23, Pinto Lake campsite to Jonas Cutoff campsite, km = 763.6

July 24, Jonas Cutoff CG to Maligne Lake, km = 826

62.4km day to trailhead parking area at Maligne Lake. Leave packs with car. Eat and head out early to meet in Jasper later on.

July 25, Maligne Lake to Jasper, km = 882.4

56.4km to T-junction of Old Fort Point Road and Hwy 16, meet car here or walk into Jasper another 1–2km depending on where you are staying, or 3km to south in Whistlers campground.

July 26, Jasper to just past Miette/Centre Pass (f7), km = 942.7

60.3km day. Meet car at Miette River trailhead near Decoigne warden station, 22.9km into day. Pick up packs with 4 nights (5 days) food and eat an early meal.

July 27, Miette/Centre Pass point f7 to Wolverine campsite, km = 1007.7

Ford?

July 28, Wolverine CG to lower Jackpine River waypoint f24, km = 1067.1

July 29, Point f24 to Casket Pass campsite, km = 1117.4

July 30, Casket Pass CG to Kakwa Lake trailhead on the Walker Creek road, km = 1173.1

Meet the vehicle this evening at the trailhead, eat meal here.

July 31, drive home.

NOTES

1. If you have an extra day for a rest, stay in Jasper on July 26 and head out on the morning of the 28th. This would give you the steam you need for the last section. This would bump your drive home to August 1, but you could leave very early in the morning if you need to.

2. The longest food carry on this trip is 4.5 days from Hwy 16 to Kakwa Lake trailhead.

3. There are 13 days where you can use some friends with a car (support team!). They can carry the food you need and extra equipment and make camp in advance when needed. They can also carry a better first aid kit, extra shoes, beer, etc.

4. The itinerary assumes that you will have a couple of hours on July 9 after travelling to Waterton campground to run down to the border and back. This buys some valuable time for the itinerary.

5. The last two days of hiking are less than 60km/day which gives you a little leeway in the last section to make it to the car on July 30, It's all random camping in this section, so see how it goes.

Author's note: Looking over this itinerary now, I see several issues, not least of which is the Smoky River ford on July 27, which only works in the early morning.

River Taig's sample itinerary (for next time!)

"I will say that it's easiest to get accommodations in Waterton, Coleman, Canmore, Field, the Crossing, Jasper, and McBride mid-week. By starting on a Tuesday morning from Waterton you can arrive in Coleman next Monday afternoon (that should give you plenty of time) to play on both of the big alternate routes – 7 days. Leaving on Tuesday morning from Coleman, most hikers could get to Kananaskis reasonably by the following Monday afternoon – again 7 days (it might be tough to squeeze in Coral Pass, but it could be done if you are fit. Taking a Tuesday off in Canmore would be nice. So then Section C starts on Wednesday morning and probably ends on the next Wednesday afternoon in Field – 8 days. You might want a day off in Field if you can afford it. Leaving on Friday morning from Field you could get to the Crossing pretty easily on Monday afternoon or

Tuesday morning ... perhaps getting a room at the resort or hitching to David Thompson Resort (2 night min. stay). Regardless of what you do at the end of Section D, though, you are pretty much gonna hit Jasper in the middle of the week about 7 days later. For sections F and G (Section G begins at the Mount Robson exit point to the Berg Lake trail), I prefer to not resupply at Mount Robson, but rather keep going and take advantage of Cara Peters's for-hire service to bring a package up the Holmes River road. Hopefully you read the Facebook post in the GDT hikers group entitled "Vehicle Resupply (for hire) for Final Section of GDT," but if you didn't, you can still find it there. Once again, it should take about a week to get from Jasper to the point where you can head down the Blueberry trail to the Holmes River road. (Author's note: this resupply option doesn't exist as of 2017.) The final stretch is also about a week, and again I plan to get Cara to come up and grab me from the Bastille Creek trailhead (mid-week again).

"One nice thing you can do if you need extra calories at the end of Section E and want to put your heavy pack down for a few days is this: when you arrive at Maligne Lake (just before the Skyline trail starts), hitchhike down to Whistlers campground in Jasper just before the start of the Skyline and reserve four nights! – binge eat like crazy in town that evening and enjoy your first night's stay at Whistlers. The next morning, take a bus or hitch up to Maligne early and knock out the entire Skyline trail in one long, tough day (but you would be doing this without a full backpack which is back at camp – bring a headlamp just in case). This has the advantage of not having to worry about permits on the Skyline trail, which are tough to get... after 45 km in a single day, hitchhike back to Jasper, binge eat some more, and head to camp at Whistlers for night #2. The next day, hitch back to the end of the Skyline (again without your pack) and walk an easy trail back to Jasper (I think it's 15 km or something) ...binge eat in town and enjoy night #3 at Whistlers. The next day, do the road walk along Highway 16 to the Decoigne guard station (or Rogier's alternate) (about 20 km) and then hitchhike back to Whistlers and Jasper for night #4. The next morning, pack up your gear and hitch to Decoigne guard station."

Jordan Tamborine's 2017 40-day sample itinerary

Day	Campground/Destination	Day km	Resupply? Notes
1	Alderson Lake	20	
2	Akamina campground	16.8	
3	Sage Pass	29.7	
4	West Castle Rd	27.8	
5	Lynx Creek	34.7	
6	Coleman	31.2	Resupply
7	0 day	0	
8	Alexander Creek	26.8	
9	Dutch Creek	40.7	
10	Cache Creek	23.3	
11	Lost Creek	28.6	
12	Fording River Pass	27.1	
13	Riverside	32.5	
14	Forks	30.2	Stop for 3-day
15			resupply at
16			trading post
17	Birdwood	32.2	
18	Lake Magog	29.9	
19	Sunshine Village, Banff	23.5	
20	0 day in Banff	0	Resupply
21	Ball Pass Junction	24	
22	Numa Creek	34.5	
23	McArthur Creek	32.2	
24	Field	23.5	Resupply in Field
25	Amiskwi Pass	41.6	
26	Lambe Creek	35.6	
27	The Crossing Resort	37	
28	0 day	0	Resupply
29	Pinto Lake North	32.7	
30	Boulder Creek	35.8	
31	Waterfalls	35.5	
32	Mary Schaffer	33.5	
33	Little Shovel	27.2	
34	Signal Mountain	33.6	
35	Jasper	16.6	
36	0 day	0	Resupply
37	Miette River	41.2	
38	Colonel Pass	31.2	
39	Calumet	36.6	
40	Mt. Robson Visitor Centre	29	

Li Brannfor's 2012 sample itinerary

Location	Date	Days Between	Km/ Day	Km Between	Total km
Start (USA border – Waterton-Glacier)	Jul. 30				0.0
		2.9	35	100.2	
(0) Castle Mtn Ski Lodge & Hostel, AB			(~22mi)		100.2
(888) 627-5121		1.6	35	56.5	
(0) Coleman/Blairmore, AB	Aug. 3				156.7
(800) 290-0860	nero	3.5	40	140.4	
(11) Highwood House, AB	Aug. 7		(~25mi)		297.1
(403) 558-2151		1.9	40	76.7	
(7) Peter Lougheed Provincial Park VC, AB	Aug. 9				373.8
(403) 591-6322	nero	2.2	40	89.5	
(0) Mt. Assiniboine Lodge, AB					463.3
(403) 678-2883		0.7	40	27.7	
(0/24) Sunshine Village/Banff, AB	Aug. 12				491.0
(403) 762-6500		3.0	40	119.2	
(4/??) Field, BC/Lake Louise, AB	Aug. 15				610.2
(800) 267-1177	nero	3.0	40	120.2	
(2) The Crossing, AB	Aug. 18				730.4
(403) 761-7000		4.0	40	158.3	
(1) Maligne Lake Lodge, AB					888.7
		1.4	40	55.2	
(0) Jasper, AB	Aug. 24				943.9
(780) 852-3041	nero	3.6	40	142.9	
(27) Mt Robson Provincial Park VC, AB	Aug. 28				1086.8
(250) 566-4325	nero	8.7	35	303.7	
End (Kakwa Provincial Park, BC	Sep. 6	36.4	38.2		1390.5
Totals	o full rest	39	35.7	864 miles	
	5 half-rest	~5.5 weeks			

Arrival Day	PO or UPS Hours & Address	Store	Showers	Laundry	Meals	Lodging	Gas	Buy
Mon		Y	Y	Y	Y	Y	M+S	
	M-F 8:30-5, S 11:30-1:30	N	Y	Y	Y	Y		
	Suite 201 – 800 Railway Ave							
Fri	A Safe Haven B&B	Y	Y	Y	Y	Y	M	Y
	8126 Hwy 3, Coleman, AB					B&B	B&B	
Tues		Y	?	?	N	N		
		small						
Thurs	7 days, 9-5	Y	Y	N	Y	N	?	
	Canmore, AB T1W 1P1		@CG			@BCTP		
	Box 8128	N	N	N	Y	Y		
	Canmore, AB T1W 2T8							
Sun	PO Box 1510	Y	N	N	Y	N		
	Banff, AB TOL OCO	all amenities available at Banff						
Wed	M-F 9:30-4:00	Y	Y	Y	Y	Y		
	Field, BC VOA 1GO		@hostel	@hotel		unlikely		
Sat	Mail Bag 333	Y	?	?	Y	Y		
	Lake Louise, AB TOL 1EO					unlikely		
		?	?	?	Y	Y		
						unlikely		
Fri	M-F 9-5	Y	Y	Y	Y	Y	M+S	Y
	502 Patricia St, TOE 1EO	all amenities available at Jasper						
Mon	Viewpoint Rd, off Hwy 16	?	?	N	?	N		
	Mount Robson, BC VOE 2ZO		@CG?					
Thurs								

Contacts

Permits, passes and reservations – at a glance

Reserve any front country campground in the national parks at reservation .pc.gc.ca or call 1-877-737-3783. Except for Waterton, you can also reserve any backcountry site in the national parks at reservation.pc.gc.ca. You might still need to contact an info centre if you need a random camping site, for instance. These are the direct numbers and emails. I've also included the two provincial parks that require backcountry reservations.

Waterton Lakes: 403-859-5133 or waterton.info@pc.gc.ca

Banff: 403-762-1556 or banff.vrc@pc.gc.ca

Jasper: online at is.gd/M8kS6M or 780-852-6177 or jnp.backcountry@pc.gc.ca

Kootenay: 250-347-9505 (seasonal) or kootenay.info@pc.gc.ca

Yoho: 250-343-6783 (seasonal) or yoho.info@pc.gc.ca

Peter Lougheed Provincial Park: 403-678-3136 or albertaparks.ca

Mount Robson Provincial Park: 250-566-4038 or discovercamping.ca

Parks and forest service offices

BANFF VISITOR CENTRE

224 Banff Avenue
403-762-1550 • fax: 403-762-1551
banff.vrc@pc.gc.ca
Hours: 8am to 8pm daily
Backcountry reservations:
403-762-1556
Car campground reservations:
1-877-RESERVE (1-877-737-3783)
reservation.pc.gc.ca

KOOTENAY NATIONAL PARK

Box 220
Radium Hot Springs, BC V0A 1M0
250-347-9615 • fax: 250-347-9980
kootenay.info@pc.gc.ca

LAKE LOUISE VISITOR CENTRE

Village of Lake Louise, next to Samson Mall
403-522-3833 • fax: 403-522-1212
ll.info@pc.gc.ca
Hours: 8:30am to 7pm daily
Backcountry reservations:
403-522-1264

MCBRIDE COMMUNITY FOREST CORPORATION

200 Robson Centre
855 South West Frontage Road, Box 519
McBride, BC V0J 2E0
250-569-0262
mcbridecommunityforest.com

MOUNT ROBSON VISITOR CENTRE

BC Parks, Mount Robson, Box 579
Valemount, BC VOE 2Z0
250-566-4038
MountRobson@shaw.ca
Hours: 8am to 7pm daily
Open daily 8am-5pm

PARKS CANADA INFORMATION, ICEFIELD CENTRE

(open mid-May to early September)
103 km south of Jasper on Icefields
Parkway
780-852-6288 • fax: 780-852-6287
jasper.icefields@pc.gc.ca

PARKS CANADA TRAIL OFFICE

Jasper Townsite Information
Centre
500 Connaught Dr., Box 10
Jasper, AB TOE 1E0
780-852-6177 • fax: 780-852-6152
jnp.backcountry@pc.gc.ca
Hours: 8am to 8pm daily
Backcountry reservations:
reservation.pc.gc.ca/Jasper

PETER LOUGHEED PARK DISCOVERY & INFORMATION CENTRE

Peter Lougheed Provincial Park
403-678-0760
Hours: 9:30am to 4:30pm, and to
5:30pm on weekends

ROCKY MOUNTAIN FOREST DISTRICT (BC)

1902 Theatre Road
Cranbrook, BC V1C 7G1
1-877-855-3222
www.for.gov.bc.ca/drm

WATERTON LAKES NATIONAL PARK

Information Centre
Waterton Park, AB TOK 2M0
403-859-5133,fax: 403-859-2650
waterton.info@pc.gc.ca
Canada Customs, 403-653-3535

WILLMORE WILDERNESS PARK

780-865-8395 or 780-865-5600
(Switzer Park Visitor Centre)
albertaparks.ca/willmore

WILLMORE WILDERNESS FOUNDATION

4600 Pine Plaza, Box 93
Grande Cache, AB TOE 0Y0
1-780-827-2696
willmorewilderness.com

YOHO NATIONAL PARK VISITOR CENTRE

Box 99
Field, BC V0A 1G0
250-343-6783 • fax: 250-343-6330
yoho.info@pc.gc.ca
Hours: 8:30am to 7 pm daily

Accommodations

A SAFE HAVEN B&B (RECOMMENDED, TRAIL ANGELS)

PO Box 1209
Coleman, Crowsnest Pass, AB T0K
0M0
403-563-5030 or 1-800-290-0860
mountainmoments@asafehaven.ca
asafehaven.ca

ALPINE STABLES

Waterton Lakes National Park,
Marquis Road, Waterton Park, AB
T0K 2M0
403-859-2462
alpinestables.com

AMISKWI LODGE (BACKCOUNTRY, SEGMENT D)

1013 Rundleview Drive
Canmore, AB T1W 2P5
403-678-1800
info@amiskwi.com
amiskwi.com

BANFF INTERNATIONAL HOSTEL

449 Banff Avenue
Banff, AB T1L 1A6
1-855-5-HOSTEL (546-7835),
403-985-7744
info@banffinternationalhostel.com
banffinternationalhostel.com

BANFF ALPINE CENTRE, HOSTELING INTERNATIONAL

801 Hidden Ridge Way, Box 1358
Banff, AB T1L 1B3
1-866-762-4122
hihostels.ca/en/destinations/
alberta/hi-banff

BANFF HOSTEL – SAMESUN YOUTH HOSTEL

433 Banff Avenue
Banff, AB T1L 1B4
Tel: 1-877-972-6378
samesun.com/backpackers
-hostels/banff

BC FOREST RECREATION SITE INFORMATION

sitesandtrailsbc.ca

BOULTON CREEK CAMPGROUND

In Peter Lougheed Provincial Park
km 10 of the Kananaskis Lakes
Trail
877-537-2757
reserve.albertaparks.ca/
campground/9-BoultonCreek

CANADIAN ALPINE CENTRE AND INTERNATIONAL HOSTEL

Box 115, Lake Louise, AB T0L 1E0
403-522-2200

CASTLE MOUNTAIN HI YOUTH HOSTEL

Banff National Park,
Highways 1A & 93 South
Banff, AB T1L 1B3
1-866-762-4122, 403-762-2367
hihostels.ca/en/destinations/
alberta/hi-castle-mountain

CASTLE SKI LODGE & HOSTEL

PO Box 566
Pincher Creek, AB T0K 1W0
403-627-5121 or 1-888-627-5121
info@castlerental.ca
staycastle.ca
Dogs are welcome but there may
be an extra fee.

COUNTRY ENCOUNTERS HOSPITALITY (COLEMAN)

7701 17th Avenue, Box 655
Coleman, AB T0K 0M0
403-563-5299
thepass@shaw.ca
countryencounters.com

(DOGS) HINTON & DISTRICT SPCA

209 Kelley Road
Hinton, AB T7V 1H2
780-865-2800
hintonspca.blogspot.ca

GLACIER VIEW INN

On the Icefields Parkway at the
Columbia Icefield Glacier Discovery
Centre
with a daily shuttlebus on Brewster
Express to Jasper, Banff and Calgary
Altitude Restaurant is open daily
from 7am to 10am and 6pm to 9pm
1-888-770-6914
banffjaspercollection.com/hotels/
glacier-view-inn

NORTH FACE PIZZA (OKAY, THIS IS A RESTAURANT BUT IT MAY BECOME A SECOND HOME IN JASPER)

618 Connaught Drive
Jasper, AB T0E 1E0
780-852-5830
Open 11am to 2am every day

Transportation

ALPINE HELICOPTERS LTD.

91 Bow Valley Trail
Canmore, AB T1W 1N8
403-678-4802

KOOTENAY PARK LODGE

9500 Highway 93 South
Vermilion Crossing, BC V0A 1M0
250-434-9648
info@kootenayparklodge.com
kootenayparklodge.com

STELLA'S INN AND RESTAURANT

731 1st Avenue, Box 3272
Beaver Mines, AB T0K 1W0
403-627-9798 or 403-627-2588
1-888-627-2585

LOST LEMON CAMPGROUND

11001 19th Avenue
Box 1590
Blairmore, AB T0K 0E0
403-562-2932
lostlemon.com

LYNX CREEK CAMPGROUND

RT Contracting, Box 1810
Pincher Creek, AB T0K 1W0
403-627-2920

SUNSHINE VILLAGE SKI & SNOWBOARD RESORT

1 Sunshine Access Road
Banff, AB T1L 1J5
1-877-542-2633, 403-705-4000
reservations@skibanff.com
sunshinemountainlodge.com/
summer-at-sunshine

BANFF AIRPORTER

Servicing Calgary airport,
Canmore and Banff
1-888-449-2901
banffairporter.com

BREWSTER EXPRESS

Servicing Calgary, Canmore, Banff, Lake Louise, Saskatchewan Crossing, Icefield Discovery Centre and Jasper.

1-877-625-4372

banffjaspercollection.com/brewster-express

GREYHOUND

1-800-661-TRIP (8747)

greyhound.ca

HOSTELING INTERNATIONAL

Inter-hostel shuttle

403-762-4122

SUNDOG TOUR COMPANY

1-888-786-3641

Servicing Jasper to Edmonton and Lake Louise to Calgary

sundogtours.com

TAMARACK OUTDOOR OUTFITTERS

aka Waterton Outdoor Adventures (shuttle service)

214 Mount View Road

Waterton Park, AB T0K 2M0

403-859-2378

hikewaterton.com

WATERTON SHORELINE CRUISE COMPANY

403-859-2362

watertoncruise.com

YELLOWHEAD HELICOPTERS INC.

McBride Airport

250-566-4401, ym@yhl.ca

Head office in Valemount, BC

888-566-4401, yhl@yhl.ca

Resupply stations and mailing addresses

Make sure you check the GDTA website during your planning phase to confirm the resupply contact information and availability. This information can change frequently.

A SAFE HAVEN B&B (RECOMMENDED, TRAIL ANGELS)

PO Box 1209

Coleman, Crowsnest Pass, AB T0K 0M0

403-563-5030 or 1-800-290-0860

mountainmoments@asafehaven.ca

asafehaven.ca

BANFF POST OFFICE – GENERAL DELIVERY

204 Buffalo Street

Banff, AB T1L 1A0

403-762-2586

Open M–F 9am–5pm and Sat. 11am–3:30pm

BLAIRMORE POST OFFICE – GENERAL DELIVERY

12537 20th Avenue

Blairmore, AB T0K 0E0

403-562-2977

Open M–F 9am–5pm

CASTLE SKI LODGE & HOSTEL

PO Box 566

Pincher Creek, AB T0K 1W0

403-627-5121 or 1-888-627-5121

info@castlerental.ca

staycastle.ca

Dogs are welcome but there may be an extra fee.

COLEMAN REMEDY'SRX POSTAL SERVICES

8335 – 20th Avenue, Box 550
Coleman, AB T0K 0M0
403-563-3242
M–F 9am–6pm and Sat. 10am–4pm

FIELD POST OFFICE – GENERAL DELIVERY

312 Stephen Avenue
Field, BC V0A 1G0
1-800-267-1177
M–F 9:30am–1:30pm

FIREWEED HOSTEL

313 Stephen Avenue, Box 37
Field, BC V0A 1G0
250-343 6999, 1-877-343-6999
fireweedhostel.com

JASPER DOWNTOWN HOSTEL

PO Box 268,
400 Patricia Street
Jasper, AB T0E 1E0
780-852-2000
info@jasperdowntownhostel.ca
jasperdowntownhostel.ca

JASPER POST OFFICE – GENERAL DELIVERY

502 Patricia Street
Jasper, AB T0E 1E0
780-852-3041
M–F, 9am–5pm

MOUNT ASSINIBOINE LODGE

Box 8128
Canmore, AB T1W 2T8
403-678-2883, fax: 403-678-4877
info@assiniboinelodge.com
assiniboinelodge.com

MOUNT ROBSON VISITOR CENTRE

BC Parks, Mount Robson, Box 579
Valemount, BC V0E 2Z0
250-566-4038, fax: 250-566-8215
Open daily 8am–5pm

SUNSHINE VILLAGE C/O WHITE MOUNTAIN ADVENTURES

131 Eagle Crescent, Box 4259
Banff, AB T1L 1A6
1-800-408-0005, 403-760-4403
info@whitemountainadventures.com

THE CROSSING RESORT

Mail Bag 333
Lake Louise, AB T0L 1E0
1-800-387-8103 or 403-761-7000;
fax 403-761-7006
info@thecrossingresort.com
thecrossingresort.com

PETER LOUGHEED PARK DISCOVERY & INFORMATION CENTRE

Peter Lougheed VIC
c/o Alberta Parks
Suite 201 – 800 Railway Avenue
Canmore, AB T1W 1P1
403-678-0760
Open daily 9:30am–4:30pm,
until 5:30 on weekends

WATERTON LAKES POST OFFICE – GENERAL DELIVERY

209 Fountain Avenue
Waterton, AB T0K 2M0
1-800-267-1177
Open M–F 8:30am–4:30pm

Map key

Gem Trek

Map name	Covers these waypoints
Waterton Lakes National Park #16	a1–a18
Highwood & Cataract Creek #9	b27–b31
Kananaskis Lakes #7	b38–c6
Banff & Mount Assiniboine #5	c3–c22
Canmore & Kananaskis Village #6	c7–c8
Banff Egypt Lake #17	c14–c23
Kootenay National Park #10	c15–c37
Lake Louise & Yoho #4	c37–d1
Bow Lake & Saskatchewan Crossing #3	d6–e6
Jasper & Maligne Lake #1	e22–e34
Best of Jasper #12	e31–e34

National Topographic System

Map name	Covers these waypoints
Waterton Lakes 82 H/4	a1–a5
Sage Creek 82 G/1	a7–a28
Beaver Mines 82 G/8	a29–a35
Blairmore 82 G/9	a37–a43
Crowsnest 82 G/10	a44–b6
Tornado Mountain 82 G/15	b7–b20
Fording River 82 J/2	b21–b27
Mount Head 82 J/7	b28–b34
Mount Abruzzi 82 J/6	b35
Kananaskis Lakes 82 J/6	b36–c5
Spray Lakes Reservoir 82 J/14	c6–c7
Mount Assiniboine 82 J/13	c8–c12
Banff 82 O/4	c13–c22
Mount Goodsir 82 N/1	c23–c36
Lake Louise 82 N/8	c37
Golden 82 N/7	c38–d2
Blaeberry River 82 N/10	d3–d9
Mistaya Lake 82 N/15	d10–d15
Cline River 82 C/2	e1–e11
Sunwapta Peak 82 C/6	e13–e22
Southesk Lake 82 C/11	e22
Athabasca Falls 82 C/12	e22–e27
Medicine Lake 82 C/13	e28–e31
Jasper 82 D/16	e34–f2
Lucerne 82 D/15	f3–f4
Snaring River 83 E/1	(Elysium alternate only)
Resplendent Creek 82 E/2	f5–f15

Map name	Covers these waypoints
Mount Robson 83 E/3	f15–f16
Twintree Lake 83 E/6	g1–g6
Chalco Mountain 83 E/5	g6–g8
Pauline Creek 83 E/12	g9–g17
Dry Canyon 83 E/13	g21
Mount Sir Alexander 93 H/16	g22–g27
Jarvis Lakes 93 I/1	g28

Waypoints list

Remember that you can download a complete track for your GPS device from the GDTA website that includes all of the waypoints listed here.

a1	GDT southern terminus	48.9986695, –113.9060127
a2	Lakeshore trailhead	49.0469430, –113.917097
a3	Carthew–Alderson trail junction	49.0509530, –113.917025
a4	Alderson Lake campsite	49.0329960, –113.973581
a5	Lower Carthew Lake	49.0299536, –113.9921314
a6	Carthew summit	49.0206628, –114.0017116
a7	Summit Lake–Boundary Creek trail junction	49.0079908, –114.0250745
a8	Carthew–Alderson trailhead	49.0197316, –114.0450544
a9	Rowe Lakes trailhead	49.0575793, –114.0113908
a10	Footbridge in Rowe Meadow	49.0555050, –114.066834
a11	Lineham Ridge summit	49.0665684, –114.07928
a12	Blakiston Creek tributary ford	49.0773369, –114.1120465
a13	Saddle north of Festubert Mountain	49.0837910, –114.123536
a14	Lone Lake outflow	49.0881570, –114.130391
a15	Saddle west of Mount Bauerman	49.1295821, –114.1502009
a16	Sage Pass trail junction	49.1369772, –114.1525035
a17	Sage Pass	49.1393500, –114.1594994
a18	Ridge crest above Lost Lake	49.1470870, –114.154869
a19	Font Creek campsite	49.1737705, –114.2023128
a20	Northeast ridge crest of Font Mountain	49.1803310, –114.200358
a21	Unnamed pass by Mount Matkin	49.1828860, –114.217185
a22	Unnamed treed pass	49.1803302, –114.2527234
a23	Forested ridge crest	49.1803390, –114.263797
a24	Scarpe Pass	49.1780705, –114.281474
a25	La Coulotte Ridge crest	49.1799510, –114.288891
a26	La Coulotte Peak	49.2000070, –114.318242
a27	Unnamed pass	49.1968237, –114.3565905
a28	Creek ford	49.2254990, –114.353003
a29	ATV bridge	49.2708540, –114.355847
a30	West Castle River bridge	49.3169139, –114.410436
a31	Suicide Creek bridge	49.3646290, –114.400211
a32	High point in a clearing	49.3672859, –114.4204696
a33	Intersection in a meadow	49.3845443, –114.4217066
a34	Intersection	49.3969130, –114.402926
a35	Mount Haig road junction	49.4351552, –114.411015
a36	ATV trail junction	49.4647672, –114.4382391

a37	Ridge crest summit	49.4762770, −114.4459770
a38	Flat clearing	49.5102820, −114.4704990
a39	Minor summit	49.5273948, −114.4794285
a40	Willoughby Ridge summit	49.5365930, −114.4838930
a41	Four-way intersection	49.5502887, −114.4854833
a42	Creek gully	49.5459416, −114.4905322
a43	Lynx Creek road	49.5470152, −114.4972397
a44	ATV trail junction	49.5408330, −114.5035350
a45	Trail junction	49.5663719, −114.5255788
a46	York Creek bridge	49.6029045, −114.5014843
a48	Coleman post office	49.6364580, −114.4933800

b1	66th Street intersection	49.6355904, −114.5232133
b2	Overhead powerline	49.6559124, −114.5354539
b3	Atlas road	49.6659082, −114.5859782
b4	Intersection	49.6909465, −114.6045101
b5	Deadman Pass	49.7045358, −114.6660215
b6	Alexander Creek bridge	49.7162868, −114.7089012
b7	ATV trail junction	49.7708040, −114.7208810
b8	Final ford of Alexander Creek	49.8256626, −114.7098715
b9	Creek crossing and campsite	49.8454450, −114.7197420
b10	The Crown	49.8559466, −114.7199387
b11	ATV trail junction	49.8714680, −114.727927
b12	South Line Creek road	49.9138445, −114.7597778
b13	North Fork Pass	49.9226486, −114.6903156
b14	Dutch Creek road	49.9264590, −114.669293
b15	Dutch Creek campsite	49.9452946, −114.6771274
b16	Tornado Pass	49.9678964, −114.6721057
b17	Tornado saddle	49.9583909, −114.6530984
b18	South Hidden Creek campsite	49.9625321, −114.6025022
b19	Hidden Creek bridge	49.9800166, −114.5785354
b20	Trail junction	49.9872070, −114.59343
b21	Cache Creek bridge	50.0418870, −114.61411
b22	Beehive Creek	50.0577189, −114.64974
b23	Lyall Creek bridge	50.0893340, −114.673431
b24	Oldman River bridge	50.1128490, −114.708515
b25	Broad meadow	50.1457080, −114.713553
b26	Saddle west of peak 2270	50.1773900, −114.684806
b27	Junction with seismic line	50.2161360, −114.681265
b28	Cataract Creek bridge	50.2517140, −114.725102
b29	Etherington Creek bridge	50.2917040, −114.706191
b30	Baril Creek trail junction	50.3307342, −114.7343409
b31	Fording River Pass	50.319100, −114.787100
b32	Kananaskis Powerline road	50.3320400, −114.900897
b33	Elk River road	50.3991100, −114.918205
b34	Cadorna Creek trailhead (Coral Pass alternate)	50.4464740, −114.949185
b35	Abruzzi Lake trail junction (Coral Pass alternate)	50.4517340, −115.029098

b36	Cadorna Lake campsite (Coral Pass alternate)	50.5023010, −115.112744
b37	Coral Pass (Coral Pass alternate)	50.4989740, −115.142733
b38	Upper Elk Lake trail junction	50.555000, −115.090300
b39	West Elk Pass/Elkan Creek junction	50.581997, −115.081385
b40	Elk Pass trailhead	50.6170650, −115.112676

c1	North Interlakes trailhead	50.6336840, −115.142841
c2	Maude–Lawson Lakes trail junction	50.6356300, −115.233533
c3	North Kananaskis Pass	50.6908638, −115.2985298
c4	Palliser River ford	50.6653118, −115.3434315
c5	Palliser Pass	50.7077550, −115.387193
c6	Birdwood Creek bridge	50.7877160, −115.427166
c7	Watridge Lake trail junction	50.8586300, −115.4456730
c8	Big Springs	50.8761522, −115.4780270
c8a	Wonder Pass trail junction	50.8950659, −115.513524
c9	Wonder Pass	50.8923100, −115.593599
c10	Assiniboine Lodge	50.9101010, −115.619952
c11	Og Lake campsite	50.9515960, −115.634676
c12	Simpson River trail junction	50.9769960, −115.673187
c13	Citadel Pass	51.0201619, −115.710512
c14	Quartz Hill saddle	51.0410030, −115.754185
c15	Sunshine Loop trail junction	51.0679539, −115.779495
c16	Simpson Pass trail junction	51.0847670, −115.7944000
c17	Simpson Pass	51.0801462, −115.8288833
c18	Healy Pass	51.0974920, −115.8648930
c19	Egypt Lake shelter	51.1083486, −115.8979049
c20	Whistling Pass	51.1073310, −115.9255860
c21	Ball Pass junction campsite	51.1355170, −115.9691040
c22	Ball Pass	51.1262710, −115.9895700
c23	Floe Lake–Hawk Creek trailhead	51.0815325, −116.0536022
c24	Floe Creek bridge	51.0842864, −116.0739944
c25	Reclaimed campsite	51.0550370, −116.120932
c26	Floe Lake campsite	51.0543370, −116.136058
c27	Numa Pass	51.0730850, −116.143475
c28	Meadow at waterfall	51.0888812, −116.1647254
c29	Numa Creek campsite	51.1096193, −116.1828875
c30	Tumbling Pass	51.1251480, −116.230841
c31	Tumbling Creek campsite	51.1400361, −116.2354136
c32	Rockwall Pass	51.1559940, −116.259728
c33	Bridge	51.1723690, −116.272501
c34	Limestone Peak saddle	51.1868680, −116.285283
c35	Helmet Falls campsite	51.1960359, −116.304934
c36	Goodsir Pass	51.2186080, −116.326499
c37	Ottertail River bridge	51.2706060, −116.381647
c38	Ottertail trailhead	51.3357384, −116.5504585
c39	Field, BC	51.3951820, −116.489714

d0	Natural bridge	51.3826811, −116.5308373
d1	Amiskwi picnic area	51.3809177, −116.5481796

d2	Otto Creek bridge	51.4710601, –116.668093
d3	First ford of Amiskwi River	51.5200973, –116.6712288
d4	Tributary ford	51.5583610, –116.665018
d5	Third crossing of Amiskwi River	51.5810786, –116.6625526
d6	Amiskwi Pass	51.6098200, –116.671939
d7	Ensign Creek road	51.6187279, –116.6806600
d8	Blaeberry River bridge	51.6575210, –116.7349200
d9	David Thompson trailhead	51.7157649, –116.7111800
d10	Lambe Creek	51.7674160, –116.734335
d11	Howse Pass	51.7998537, –116.7565388
d12	Conway Creek campsite	51.8199079, –116.7758403
d13	Howse River flood plain	51.8758310, –116.8012500
d14	Glacier Lake trail junction	51.9176119, –116.8067822
d15	Sask Crossing trail junction	51.9508900, –116.765053
d16	Howse Pass trailhead	51.9414690, –116.717285
d17	Saskatchewan River bridge	51.9704978, –116.7204695

e1	Owen Creek trailhead	52.0008280, –116.671943
e2	Owen Creek confluence	52.0178666, –116.7211281
e3	Owen Pass	52.0572040, –116.745725
e4	Michele Lakes Pass highest point	52.0796639, –116.766176
e5	Pinto Pass	52.1020780, –116.803799
e6	Sunset Pass trail junction	52.1333839, –116.864673
e7	White Goat trail register	52.1391840, –116.860801
e8	Cataract Creek ford	52.1466400, –116.846245
e9	Cataract Creek trail junction	52.1520920, –116.843653
e10	Pictograph boulder	52.1570060, –116.866991
e11	Cataract Pass trail junction	52.2117069, –116.983679
e12	Cataract Pass	52.2208540, –117.0298800
e13	Nigel Pass trail junction	52.2419802, –117.088357
e14	Brazeau River bridge	52.2597570, –117.103254
e15	Four Point campsite	52.2803359, –117.07666
e16	Jonas Pass	52.3365859, –117.171682
e17	Jonas Shoulder	52.3746410, –117.198822
e18	Poboktan Pass trail junction	52.3970310, –117.208381
e19	Bridged tributary	52.4471180, –117.302236
e20	Maligne Pass trailhead	52.4683550, –117.366164
e21	Avalanche campsite	52.4885030, –117.409533
e22	Maligne Pass	52.5097129, –117.455292
e23	Maligne River ford	52.6348080, –117.588143
e24	Trapper Creek campsite	52.6891918, –117.6237707
e25	Maligne Pass trailhead	52.7258810, –117.645261
e26	Evelyn Creek campsite	52.7348852, –117.7031314
e27	Little Shovel Pass	52.7366510, –117.763718
e28	Big Shovel Pass	52.7792290, –117.830461
e29	The Notch	52.7976840, –117.878326
e30	Creek ford near Centre Lakes	52.8271769, –117.9174300
e31	Signal Mountain road junction	52.8724930, –117.978808
e32	Signal Mountain trailhead	52.9142169, –118.001336
e33	Soggy Dog Lake	52.9168250, –118.023915

| e34 | Old Fort Point trailhead | 52.8711180, −118.0621520 |

f1	Miette River trailhead	52.8829807, −118.3901906
f2	Miette River trail junction	52.8924642, −118.4573732
f3	Tributary bridge	52.9325450, −118.544679
f5	Miette–Centre Pass trail junction	53.0150852, −118.6249729
f6	Miette–Centre Pass	53.0137180, −118.654453
f7	Creek ford	53.0219260, −118.684899
f8	Grant Pass	53.0472560, −118.754691
f9	Colonel Pass campsite	53.0694340, −118.762938
f10	Colonel Creek ford	53.0700240, −118.8068947
f11	Colonel Creek trail junction	53.074100, −118.851400
f12	Second ford of Moose River	53.1271750, −118.890832
f13	Steppe Creek ford	53.1670566, −118.9284486
f14	Final ford of Moose River	53.1854390, −118.943764
f15	Moose Pass	53.2299830, −119.018379
f16	Smoky River ford	53.2105293, −119.1170336

g1	Wolverine campsite	53.2572300, −119.197246
g2	Chown Creek bridge	53.3391220, −119.266774
g3	Bess Pass	53.3297330, −119.352015
g4	Mount Bess shoulder	53.3267300, −119.3870200
g5	Jackpine Pass junction	53.3561690, −119.4285580
g6	Blueberry Lake campsite	53.3539250, −119.5445500
g7	Jackpine alternate route junction	53.3712860, −119.5784800
g8	Jackpine Mountain trail junction	53.4004823, −119.5727468
g9	Tributary confluence	53.4941251, −119.7136754
g10	Meadowland Creek ford	53.5214325, −119.7061002
g11	Ridgecrest of Little Shale Hill	53.5477250, −119.735148
g12	Pauline Creek ford	53.5613990, −119.741927
g13	Big Shale Hill	53.5913880, −119.749019
g14	Shale Pass	53.6109100, −119.7400454
g15	Morkill Pass campsite	53.6854120, −119.778696
g16	Mount Morkill sw col	53.6906860, −119.849285
g17	Featherstonhaugh Pass	53.7121369, −119.862505
g18	Mount Featherstonhaugh ridge	53.7298740, −119.891643
g19	Casket Creek campsite	53.7855210, −119.928066
g20	Casket Mountain shoulder	53.8122512, −119.9218649
g21	Sheep Creek campsite	53.8297219, −119.9411029
g22	Tributary ford	53.8423781, −119.976542
g23	Surprise Pass	53.8811489, −120.0192093
g24	Cecilia Lake trail junction	53.9368802, −120.0460777
g25	Providence Pass	53.9490913, −120.0713866
g26	Broadview Lake campsite	53.9541999, −120.1044026
g27	Kakwa Pass	53.9603027, −120.1372071
g28	Kakwa Lake	53.9974942, −120.172381
g29	Bastille Creek trailhead	53.8462780, −120.4195790

Emergency contacts

In case of emergency, call 9-1-1

Tell them which park you are calling from. In some cases you will need to know the following specific emergency contacts and procedures beyond calling 911.

Parks Canada emergency contact numbers (sections B–G):

Waterton Lakes National Park: 9-1-1 and state that you are calling from 'Waterton Lakes National Park'

Banff, Kootenay, Yoho: 1-403-762-4506

Jasper: 1-780-852-3100 or 1-877-852-3100

For non-emergencies in the national parks you can contact the warden service anytime at 1-888-WARDENS (1-888-927-3367). Use this line to report poachers, campground disturbances, polluting, instances of people harassing or feeding wildlife, and removal of cultural artifacts.

Using an inReach device to call Parks Canada Visitor Safety for HELP

Push the SOS button and then exchange texts with the inReach Emergency Call Center (ECC) to clarify the location and nature of your emergency.

The ECC will notify Parks Canada and pass this information on to the Parks Canada dispatch centre.

The Parks Canada dispatch centre may send you the phone number of the Parks Canada Visitor Safety leader through the inReach ECC.

If you receive the number for Parks Canada Visitor Safety, send the leader a text from your inReach device to initiate two-way texting directly with Visitor Safety.

PLEASE NOTE THE FOLLOWING LIMITATIONS WITH AN INREACH DEVICE:

Currently Parks Canada emergency dispatch centres are not set up to receive texts directly. Only voice calls from a cell phone, satellite phone or VHF radio will go directly to the Parks Canada dispatch centre.

Remember that all two-way texting conversations using an inReach device must be initiated from the user's device. Parks Canada Visitor Safety cannot initiate a text if they have not received a text from the InReach device first.

Parks Canada Visitor Safety may also send an email to the inReach user to open communication lines if texting is not working.

Keeping your emergency contacts up to date and informed about your activities helps speed up emergency responses, and helps emergency responders bring appropriate resources to the incident.

Including information on how to reach the Parks Canada dispatch centre with your emergency contact information can help speed up responses within the National Parks.

If in or near Kananaskis Country (sections B and C):

Tell the 911 dispatcher you have an emergency in Kananaskis Country. The dispatcher will then transfer you to the Kananaskis Country Emergency Services Centre.

With a satellite phone, dialling 9-1-1 may transfer you to an emergency centre unfamiliar with Kananaskis Country. If you're using a satellite phone, call the local emergency number instead (403-591-7767).

Kananaskis Country Emergency Services Centre dispatch will ask questions to better understand the exact location of the emergency; the nature of the accident and seriousness of any injuries; your name and callback number; and when the accident occurred.

Signalling a helicopter

On occasion, a helicopter may be used for backcountry rescue.

Rescue staff in the helicopter are not able to communicate with people on the ground, so it is imperative that you use standard visual signals to reduce confusion.

Although dispatchers will coach you on how to make these signals, it is preferable to know them before you head into the backcountry.

To reduce confusion when a helicopter approaches, the person on the ground with a satellite phone or cell phone should remain on the line with dispatch.

Body Language when signalling an approaching helicopter from the ground:

NEED HELP?

 YES
Make a "Y" with your arms to signal: YES – I need help

 NO
Make an "N" with your arms to signal: NO – Help is not needed

When signalling, stay still, and remain in your signalling position

ABOUT THE AUTHOR

Dustin Lynx hiked the 4300km Pacific Crest Trail, from Mexico to Canada, in 1994. Shortly afterward, while browsing antiquarian bookstores in Vancouver and longing to be back on the trail, he came across *High Summer: Backpacking the Canadian Rockies*, by Chris Townsend. That book, more than any other, changed his life. Thanks to Townsend's book, Dustin discovered the Great Divide Trail and moved to the University of Calgary so he could hike it in 1996 between the final two years of his arts degree. He currently lives in Canmore, Alberta, and operates an information technology consultancy and an award-winning publishing company called Imaginary Mountain Surveyors. Besides the third edition of this guidebook, Dustin has written for several magazines, including *Explore*, and contributed to *Imagine this Valley: Essays and Stories Celebrating the Bow Valley* (RMB | Rocky Mountain Books, 2016).